Design America

BEST-SELLING HOME Plans

The plans in our Design America Series have been created by many of the nation's top architects and designers. No matter what your taste, you're sure to find several homes you would be thrilled to call your own.

Design America Best-Selling Home Plans is a collection of plans that have consistently been our best sellers.

Plan #565-0298 on page 66

These plans cover a wide range of architectural styles in a popular range of sizes. A broad assortment is presented to match a wide variety of lifestyles and budgets. Each design page features floor plans, a front view of the house, interior square footage of the home, number of bedrooms, baths, garage size and foundation types. All floor plans show room and exterior dimensions.

Technical Specifications - Every effort has been made to ensure that these plans and specifications meet

Plan #565-0135 on page 84

most nationally recognized building codes (BOCA, Southern Building Code Congress and others). Drawing modifications and/or the assistance of a local architect or professional designer are sometimes necessary to comply with local codes or to accommodate specific building site conditions.

Blueprint Ordering - Fast and Easy - Your ordering is made simple by following the instructions on page 9. See page 8 for more information on which types of blueprint packages are available and how many plan sets to order.

Your Home, Your Way - The blueprints you receive are a master plan for building your new home. They start you on your way to what may well be the most rewarding experience of your life.

CONTENTS

Design America Best-Selling Home Plans is published by Home Design Alternatives, Inc. (HDA, Inc.) 4390 Green Ash Drive, St. Louis, MO 63045. All rights reserved. Reproduction in whole or in part without written permission of the publisher is prohibited. Printed in U.S.A © 2002. Artist drawings shown in this publication may vary slightly from the actual working blueprints.

House shown on front cover is Plan #565-0298 and is featured on page 66.

MW01089684

Our Blueprint Packages Offer...

Quality plans for building your future, with extras that provide unsurpassed value, ensure good construction and long-term enjoyment.

A quality home - one that looks good, functions well, and provides years of enjoyment - is a product of many things - design, materials, craftsmanship. But it's also the result of outstanding blueprints - the actual plans and specifications that tell the builder exactly how to build your home.

And with our BLUEPRINT PACKAGES you get the absolute best. A complete set of blueprints is available for every design in this book. These "working drawings," are highly detailed, resulting in two key benefits:

- *Better understanding by the contractor of how to build your home, and...*
- *More accurate construction estimates.*

When you purchase one of our designs, you'll receive all of the BLUEPRINT components shown here - elevations, foundation plan, floor plans, sections and details. Other helpful building aids are also available to help make your dream home a reality.

COVER SHEET

This sheet is the artist's rendering of the exterior of the home. It will give you an idea of how your home will look when completed and landscaped.

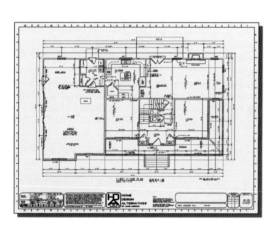

FOUNDATION PLAN

The foundation plan shows the layout of the basement, walk-out basement, crawl space, slab or pier foundation. All necessary notations and dimensions are included. See plan page for the foundation types included. If the home plan you choose does not have your desired foundation type, our Customer Service Representatives can advise you on how to customize your foundation to suit your specific needs or site conditions.

FLOOR PLANS

These plans show the placement of walls, doors, closets, plumbing fixtures, electrical outlets, columns, and beams for each level of the home.

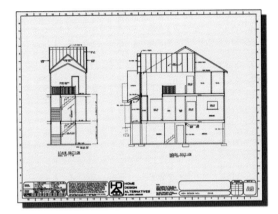

EXTERIOR ELEVATIONS

These drawings illustrate the front, rear and both sides of the house, with all details of exterior materials and the required dimensions.

INTERIOR ELEVATIONS

Interior elevations provide views of special interior elements such as fireplaces, kitchen cabinets, built-in units and other special features of the home.

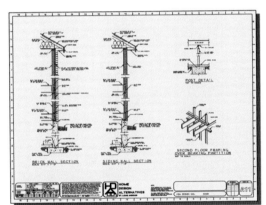

DETAILS

Details show how to construct certain components of your home, such as the roof system, stairs, deck, etc.

SECTIONS

Sections show detail views of the home or portions of the home as if it were sliced from the roof to the foundation. This sheet shows important areas such as load-bearing walls, stairs, joists, trusses and other structural elements, which are critical for proper construction.

Other Helpful Building Aids...

Your Blueprint Package will contain the necessary construction information to build your home. We also offer the following products and services to save you time and money in the building process.

Rush Delivery - Most orders are processed within 24 hours of receipt. Please allow 7 working days for delivery. If you need to place a rush order, please call us by 11:00 a.m. CST and ask for overnight or second day service.

Technical Assistance - If you have questions, call our technical support line at 1-314-770-2228 between 8:00 a.m. and 5:00 p.m. CST. Whether it involves design modifications or field assistance, our designers are extremely familiar with all of our designs and will be happy to help you. We want your home to be everything you expect it to be.

Material List - Material lists are available for many of our plans. Each list gives you the quantity, dimensions and description of the building materials necessary to construct your home. You'll get faster and more accurate bids from your contractor and material suppliers, and you'll save money by paying for only the materials you need. Refer to the Home Plan Index for availability.

Home Plans Index

Plan Number	Square Feet	Price Code	Page	Material List Available	Plan Number	Square Feet	Price Code	Page	Material List Available	Plan Number	Square Feet	Price Code	Page	Material List Available
565-0112	1,668	C	47	✓	565-0300	3,072	E	118	✓	565-0406	3,169	E	322	✓
565-0118	1,816	C	113	✓	565-0301	2,024	C	140	✓	565-0408	2,498	D	233	✓
565-0119	1,833	C	146	✓	565-0302	1,854	D	90	✓	565-0410	1,742	B	206	✓
565-0126	1,983	C	57	✓	565-0303	2,024	C	268	✓	565-0411	2,696	F	336	✓
565-0127	1,996	D	249	✓	565-0304	2,255	D	236	✓	565-0414	2,563	D	264	✓
565-0128	2,565	D	295	✓	565-0305	2,605	E	227	✓	565-0415	1,492	A	255	✓
565-0129	2,032	C	204	✓	565-0306	2,360	D	263	✓	565-0416	1,985	C	210	✓
565-0130	2,356	D	304	✓	565-0307	3,153	E	341	✓	565-0417	2,828	E	29	✓
565-0131	2,336	D	258	✓	565-0308	2,563	D	252	✓	565-0418	3,850	F	69	✓
565-0132	2,195	C	270	✓	565-0309	2,106	C	277	✓	565-0419	1,882	C	34	✓
565-0133	2,214	D	218	✓	565-0311	2,041	C	246	✓	565-0420	1,941	C	112	✓
565-0134	2,216	D	137	✓	565-0313	3,503	F	240	✓	565-0426	2,444	D	150	✓
565-0135	2,529	E	84	✓	565-0314	3,443	F	273	✓	565-0427	3,411	F	158	✓
565-0136	2,583	D	53	✓	565-0315	2,481	D	235	✓	565-0428	3,808	F	221	✓
565-0137	2,282	E	106	✓	565-0316	1,824	C	245	✓	565-0429	3,149	E	327	✓
565-0138	2,286	E	45	✓	565-0317	2,274	D	200	✓	565-0430	2,869	E	243	✓
565-0139	2,773	F	74	✓	565-0318	2,147	C	190	✓	565-0431	2,824	E	244	✓
565-0141	2,826	E	88	✓	565-0319	3,796	F	37	✓	565-0432	2,826	F	343	✓
565-0143	2,449	E	95	✓	565-0320	2,228	D	23	✓	565-0433	2,673	E	247	✓
565-0146	3,116	F	60	✓	565-0321	3,160	E	167	✓	565-0434	2,357	D	321	✓
565-0147	2,820	E	70	✓	565-0322	2,135	D	139	✓	565-0435	2,993	E	294	✓
565-0149	3,017	E	291	✓	565-0323	2,744	E	310	✓	565-0436	2,801	E	198	✓
565-0153	2,912	E	265	✓	565-0324	2,871	E	288	✓	565-0437	2,333	D	119	✓
565-0154	2,498	D	212	✓	565-0326	2,539	D	279	✓	565-0438	2,558	D	75	✓
565-0156	3,050	E	281	✓	565-0327	2,081	C	351	✓	565-0439	2,665	E	30	✓
565-0158	3,200	F	334	✓	565-0331	2,730	E	232	✓	565-0440	2,365	D	138	✓
565-0159	3,368	F	330	✓	565-0333	2,723	E	326	✓	565-0445	3,427	F	175	✓
565-0160	4,120	G	187	✓	565-0334	2,813	E	133	✓	565-0449	2,505	D	15	✓
565-0167	2,282	D	99	✓	565-0335	1,865	D	97	✓	565-0450	1,708	B	25	✓
565-0168	2,940	E	109	✓	565-0337	3,164	E	28	✓	565-0477	1,140	AA	52	✓
565-0169	2,401	D	68	✓	565-0338	2,397	E	54	✓	565-0478	1,092	AA	83	✓
565-0170	2,618	E	32	✓	565-0341	3,290	F	148	✓	565-0479	1,294	A	114	✓
565-0171	2,058	C	130	✓	565-0344	2,887	F	116	✓	565-0480	1,618	B	176	✓
565-0173	1,220	A	93	✓	565-0348	2,003	D	58	✓	565-0481	2,012	C	164	✓
565-0175	1,908	C	63	✓	565-0349	2,204	D	170	✓	565-0482	1,619	B	219	✓
565-0177	2,562	D	59	✓	565-0351	3,315	F	65	✓	565-0483	1,330	A	284	✓
565-0178	2,846	E	123	✓	565-0352	3,144	F	21	✓	565-0484	1,403	A	331	✓
565-0182	2,353	D	197	✓	565-0354	2,597	D	195	✓	565-0485	1,195	AA	311	✓
565-0183	2,847	E	254	✓	565-0355	3,814	F	172	✓	565-0486	1,239	A	283	✓
565-0184	2,411	D	308	✓	565-0356	2,806	E	12	✓	565-0487	1,189	AA	278	✓
565-0187	3,035	E	239	✓	565-0360	2,327	D	124	✓	565-0488	2,059	C	92	✓
565-0190	1,600	C	222	✓	565-0361	2,613	E	296	✓	565-0493	976	AA	136	✓
565-0204	2,128	C	318	✓	565-0363	2,128	C	328	✓	565-0494	1,085	AA	126	✓
565-0205	2,665	E	348	✓	565-0364	2,531	D	229	✓	565-0496	977	AA	79	✓
565-0208	2,445	E	35	✓	565-0365	2,336	D	286	✓	565-0503	1,000	AA	31	✓
565-0210	2,361	D	111	✓	565-0366	2,624	E	292	✓	565-0505	1,104	AA	117	✓
565-0213	2,059	C	103	✓	565-0367	2,523	D	290	✓	565-0506	1,375	A	120	✓
565-0219	3,234	F	11	✓	565-0368	2,452	D	31	✓	565-0512	1,827	C	76	✓
565-0220	3,391	F	107	✓	565-0369	2,716	E	17	✓	565-0518	1,705	B	166	✓
565-0222	2,358	D	316	✓	565-0370	1,721	C	207	✓	565-0521	2,050	C	196	✓
565-0223	2,328	D	345	✓	565-0371	2,733	E	50	✓	565-0522	1,818	C	276	✓
565-0234	2,066	C	72	✓	565-0373	2,838	E	78	✓	565-0526	2,262	D	350	✓
565-0224	2,461	D	313	✓	565-0374	2,213	D	153	✓	565-0528	2,511	D	293	✓
565-0227	1,674	B	285	✓	565-0375	1,954	C	128	✓	565-0540	2,352	C	214	✓
565-0228	1,996	C	51	✓	565-0376	3,019	E	192	✓	565-0541	2,080	C	269	✓
565-0229	1,676	B	77	✓	565-0377	2,459	D	163	✓	565-0542	1,832	C	224	✓
565-0230	2,073	D	26	✓	565-0378	2,180	C	156	✓	565-0599	2,511	D	275	✓
565-0231	2,213	E	38	✓	565-0379	1,711	B	110	✓	565-0600	3,025	E	238	✓
565-0232	2,932	F	86	✓	565-0380	2,321	D	183	✓	565-0652	1,524	B	314	✓
565-0234	2,066	C	72	✓	565-0381	2,045	C	274	✓	565-0655	624	AAA	36	✓
565-0236	3,357	F	155	✓	565-0382	1,546	B	266	✓	565-0656	1,700	B	194	✓
565-0244	1,994	D	73	✓	565-0383	1,813	C	208	✓	565-0662	1,516	B	154	✓
565-0245	2,260	D	149	✓	565-0384	2,013	C	324	✓	565-0664	1,776	B	98	✓
565-0246	1,539	B	104	✓	565-0385	1,814	C	250	✓	565-0667	1,560	B	67	✓
565-0249	1,501	B	101	✓	565-0386	2,186	C	298	✓	565-0670	1,170	AA	43	✓
565-0250	2,520	D	178	✓	565-0387	1,958	C	89	✓	565-0672	2,043	C	55	✓
565-0284	1,672	C	315	✓	565-0388	1,695	B	144	✓	565-0677	3,006	E	96	✓
565-0285	2,648	E	215	✓	565-0389	1,777	B	56	✓	565-0690	1,400	A	64	✓
565-0286	1,856	C	302	✓	565-0393	1,684	B	39	✓	565-0691	2,730	E	191	✓
565-0287	2,178	E	231	✓	565-0397	2,883	E	169	✓	565-0701	2,308	D	52	✓
565-0288	2,731	E	307	✓	565-0399	2,397	D	134	✓	565-0702	1,558	B	107	✓
565-0290	1,700	B	225	✓	565-0400	1,923	C	339	✓	565-0703	2,412	D	134	✓
565-0291	1,600	B	108	✓	565-0401	2,715	E	259	✓	565-0705	2,758	E	131	✓
565-0298	3,216	F	66	✓	565-0403	3,316	F	332	✓	565-0706	1,791	B	33	✓
565-0299	3,013	E	46	✓	565-0405	3,494	F	306	✓	565-0707	2,723	E	80	✓

Home Plans Index

Plan Number	Square Feet	Price Code	Page	Material List Available	Plan Number	Square Feet	Price Code	Page	Material List Available	Plan Number	Square Feet	Price Code	Page	Material List Available
565-0708	2,615	E	152	✓	565-CHP-2443-A-67	2,450	D	346		565-HDS-2454	2,458	D	89	
565-0709	2,521	D	127	✓	565-DBI-1748-19	1,911	C	302		565-HDS-2551	2,551	D	62	
565-0710	2,334	D	338	✓	565-DBI-2206-24	2,498	D	224		565-HDS-2636	2,636	E	307	
565-0711	1,575	B	285	✓	565-DBI-2311	2,486	D	299		565-HDS-2962	2,962	E	352	
565-0712	2,029	C	213	✓	565-DBI-2316	2,345	D	297		565-JA-53394	1,763	B	76	
565-0713	3,199	E	267	✓	565-DBI-2408	2,270	D	242		565-JA-54294	1,370	A	293	
565-0714	2,808	E	203	✓	565-DBI-2461	1,850	C	39		565-JA-61395	1,456	A	104	
565-0715	4,826	G	272	✓	565-DBI-2733	3,904	F	132		565-JA-67596	1,919	C	127	
565-0716	3,169	F	14	✓	565-DBI-4144	3,040	E	100		565-JA-78798	1,806	C	28	
565-0717	1,268	A	274	✓	565-DBI-4948	1,758	B	63		565-JA-79298	2,229	D	112	
565-0718	1,340	A	303	✓	565-DBI-8013	1,392	A	131		565-JA-79798	1,553	B	223	
565-0719	2,483	D	216	✓	565-DDI-94-203	1,398	A	22		565-JFD-10-1456-2	1,456	A	83	
565-0720	3,138	E	94	✓	565-DDI-96-206	1,278	A	223		565-JFD-10-1875-1	1,875	C	95	
565-0721	2,437	D	70	✓	565-DDI-98-106	1,588	B	84		565-JFD-10-2096-2	2,096	C	165	
565-0725	1,977	C	177	✓	565-DDI-100-218	2,995	E	123		565-JFD-20-1992-1	1,992	C	122	
565-0727	1,477	A	184	✓	565-DDI-100-224	2,339	D	216		565-JFD-20-17921	1,792	B	325	
565-0728	2,967	E	91	✓	565-DDI-101-103	2,148	C	205		565-JFD-20-1868-1	1,868	C	27	
565-0729	2,218	D	24	✓	565-DL-17104L1	1,710	D	162		565-JFD-20-1887-1	1,887	C	105	
565-0730	2,408	D	49	✓	565-DL-17353L1	1,735	B	181		565-JFD-20-2050-1	2,050	C	145	
565-0734	929	AA	18	✓	565-DL-19603L2	1,960	C	19		565-JV-1268A	1,268	A	19	
565-0735	3,657	F	160	✓	565-DL-23804L2	2,380	D	61		565-JV-1418-A	1,418	A	37	
565-0738	4,281	G	186	✓	565-DRD-1478	920	AA	235		565-JV-1646-A	1,646	B	136	
565-0739	1,004	AA	313	✓	565-DRD-2837	2,300	D	329		565-JV-1781-B	1,781	B	40	
565-0741	1,578	B	54	✓	565-DRD-2686	1,995	C	115		565-JV-1896-A	1,896	C	48	
565-0743	1,598	B	34	✓	565-DRD-2688	1,922	C	257		565-JV-2115-A	2,115	C	188	
565-0744	2,164	C	77	✓	565-DRD-2801	1,760	B	161		565-JV-2542-A	2,542	D	141	
565-0747	1,977	C	13	✓	565-DRD-2835	1,976	C	199		565-JV-2788-A	2,788	E	40	
565-0748	2,514	D	146	✓	565-DRD-2837	2,300	D	157		565-LBD-18-5A	1,862	C	75	
565-0749	2,727	E	10	✓	565-DRD-2853	2,089	C	135		565-LBD-18-11A	1,890	C	264	
565-0750	2,900	E	87	✓	565-DRD-2884	2,135	C	217		565-LBD-19-23A	1,932	C	245	
565-0769	1,440	A	333	✓	565-DRD-2891	2,310	D	220		565-LBD-25-22A	2,586	D	151	
565-0803	3,366	F	33	✓	565-DRD-2896	1,938	C	289		565-LBD-26-23A	2,678	E	44	
565-0806	1,452	A	48	✓	565-ES-103-1 & 2	1,364	A	97	✓	565-LBD-28-1A	2,838	E	20	
565-0809	1,084	AA	138	✓	565-ES-125-1 & 2	1,605	B	43	✓	565-MG-9305	1,606	B	226	
565-0811	1,161	AA	16	✓	565-FB-676	1,373	A	315		565-MG-9510	2,379	D	237	
565-1072	2,678	E	47	✓	565-FB-766	1,671	B	349		565-MG-96108	2,499	D	320	
565-1101	1,643	B	58	✓	565-FB-845	1,779	D	23		565-MG-96132	2,450	D	42	
565-1112	2,137	C	159	✓	565-FB-851	2,349	D	185		565-MG-96183	2,737	E	262	
565-1114-1 & 2	2,851	E	189	✓	565-FB-902	1,856	C	120		565-MG-97162	3,304	F	248	
565-1117	1,440	A	290	✓	565-FB-930	2,322	D	93		565-N118	527	AAA	101	
565-1128-1 & 2	2,155	C	234	✓	565-FB-933	2,193	C	179		565-N149	1,332	A	67	
565-1134-1 & 2	2,212	D	344	✓	565-FB-963	2,126	C	147		565-NDG-113-1	1,525	A	173	
565-1162-1 & 2	2,528	D	253	✓	565-FB1119	1,915	C	71		565-NDG-137	2,485	D	261	
565-1163-1 & 2	2,087	C	309	✓	565-FB-1224	2,246	D	82		565-NDG-148	1,538	B	222	
565-1197-1 & 2	1,536	B	284	✓	565-FD6970	2,464	D	209		565-NDG-206	1,758	B	44	
565-1199-1 & 2	1,200	A	231	✓	565-FD7099	1,624	B	213		565-NDG-347	1,957	C	300	
565-1208-1 & 2	2,763	E	353	✓	565-FD8077	3,022	E	301		565-NDG-379	1,800	C	188	
565-1209-1 & 2	2,304	D	287	✓	565-FDG-7963-L	1,830	C	184		565-NDG-483	1,880	C	282	
565-1211-1 & 2	2,414	D	260	✓	565-FDG-8378-L	2,591	D	73		565-NDG-508	2,100	C	303	
565-1214-1 & 2	1,852	C	342	✓	565-FDG-8425-L	2,434	D	41		565-NDG-514	2,394	D	319	
565-1216-1 & 2	1,668	B	252	✓	565-FDG-8575-L	2,793	E	317		565-NDG-517	1,989	C	141	
565-1217-1 & 2	2,372	D	340	✓	565-FDG-8701-L	2,578	D	312		565-NDG-521	1,922	C	206	
565-1218-1 & 2	2,751	E	251	✓	565-FDG-8729-L	2,529	D	178		565-NDG-525	1,250	A	21	
565-1243-1 & 2	2,705	E	215	✓	565-FDG-9035	1,760	B	149		565-NDG-526	2,261	D	337	
565-1276-1 & 2	1,533	B	339	✓	565-GH-10839	1,738	B	181		565-NDG-538	2,635	E	280	
565-1289-1 & 2	2,729	E	80		565-GH-20069	2,007	C	121		565-NDG-540	3,419	F	142	
565-1303-1 & 2	2,414	D	174		565-GH-20161	1,307	A	168		565-NDG-541	2,499	D	81	
565-1335	1,858	C	171		565-GH-20164	1,456	A	203		565-NDG-543	1,863	C	228	
565-1425	2,617	E	102		565-GH-20405	3,658	F	256		565-NDG-544	1,965	C	347	
565-1427	2,586	D	180		565-GH-24326	1,505	B	202		565-NDG-546	2,379	D	354	
565-AMD-1135	1,467	A	312		565-GH-24610	1,785	B	230		565-NDG-549	2,189	C	61	
565-AMD-1213	2,197	C	309		565-GH-24720	1,741	B	201		565-P-124	2,760	E	168	✓
565-AMD-2189	1,994	C	260		565-GM-1849	1,849	C	172		565-RDD-1429-9	1,429	A	165	
565-AMD-2294	2,391	D	271		565-GM-1855	1,855	C	335		565-RDD-1791-9	1,791	B	226	
565-AX-93308	1,793	B	352		565-GM-2008	2,008	C	85		565-RDD-1896-9	1,896	C	241	
565-AX-95367	1,595	B	173		565-GM-2009	2,009	C	182		565-RDD-2050-7A	2,050	C	230	
565-AX-96355	1,699	B	211		565-GM-2148	2,148	C	125		565-RJ-A1175	1,192	AA	323	
565-AX-98364	2,585	D	71		565-GSD-1123	1,734	B	319		565-RJ-A1390	1,389	A	189	
565-BF-1314	1,375	A	249		565-GSD-1260	2,788	E	266		565-RJ-A1485	1,436	A	338	
565-BF-1416	1,434	A	311		565-HDS-1167	1,167	AA	117		565-T-109-1 & 2	1,872	C	193	✓
565-BF-1426	1,420	A	64		565-HDS-1758	1,783	B	269		565-T-110	1,973	C	162	✓
565-BF-1901	1,925	C	25		565-HDS-1993	1,993	C	333		565-T-128	2,366	D	143	✓
565-BF-2107	2,123	E	129		565-HDS-2224	2,224	D	346		565-T-131	2,200	D	211	✓
565-CHP-1843A	1,857	C	50		565-HDS-2244	2,362	D	282		565-T-143-1 & 2	2,258	D	305	✓
565-CHP-2333-A-29	2,279	D	126		565-HDS-2278	2,278	D	41		565-T-145	2,007	C	323	✓

What Kind Of Plan Package Do You Need?

Once you find the home plan you've been looking for, here are some suggestions on how to make your Dream Home a reality. To get started, order the type of plans that fit your particular situation.

Your Choices:

The One-set package - This single set of blueprints is offered so you can study or review a home in greater detail. But a single set is never enough for construction and it's a copyright violation to reproduce blueprints.

The Minimum 5-set package - If you're ready to start the construction process, this 5-set package is the minimum number of blueprint sets you will need. It will require keeping close track of each set so they can be used by multiple subcontractors and tradespeople.

The Standard 8-set package - For best results in terms of cost, schedule and quality of construction, we recommend you order eight (or more) sets of blueprints. Besides one set for yourself, additional sets of blueprints will be required by your mortgage lender, local building department, general contractor and all subcontractors working on foundation, electrical, plumbing, heating/air conditioning, carpentry work, etc.

Reproducible Masters - If you wish to make some minor design changes, you'll want to order reproducible masters. These drawings contain the same information as the blueprints but are printed on erasable and reproducible paper. This will allow your builder or a local design professional to make the necessary drawing changes without the major expense of redrawing the plans. This package also allows you to print as many copies of the modified plans as you need.

Mirror Reverse Sets - Plans can be printed in mirror reverse. These plans are useful when the house would fit your site better if all the rooms were on the opposite side than shown. They are simply a mirror image of the original drawings causing the lettering and dimensions to read backwards. Therefore, when ordering mirror reverse drawings, you must purchase at least one set of right reading plans.

OTHER GREAT PRODUCTS TO HELP YOU BUILD YOUR DREAM HOME

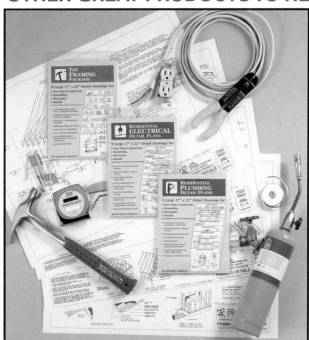

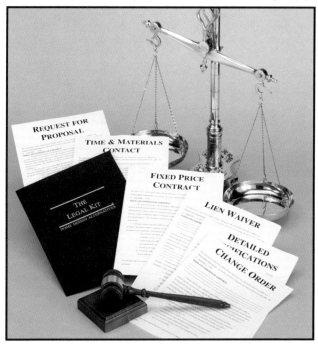

DETAIL PLAN PACKAGES:
FRAMING • ELECTRICAL • PLUMBING

Three separate packages offer details for constructing various foundations; numerous floor, wall and roof framing techniques; simple to complex residential wiring; sump and water softener hookups; plumbing connection methods; installation of septic systems, and more. Each package includes three-dimensional illustrations and a glossary of terms. Purchase one or all three. **Note: These drawings do not pertain to a specific home plan.**
Cost: $20.00 each or all three for $40.00

THE LEGAL KIT

Avoid many legal pitfalls and build your home with confidence using the forms and contracts featured in this kit. Included are request for proposal documents, various fixed price and cost plus contracts, instructions on how and when to use each form, warranty statements and more. Save time and money before you break ground on your new home or start a remodeling project. All forms are reproducible. The kit is ideal for homeowners and contractors.
Cost: $35.00

ORDER FORM

IMPORTANT INFORMATION TO KNOW
BEFORE YOU ORDER YOUR HOME PLANS

❏ **Exchange Policies** - Since blueprints are printed in response to your order, we cannot honor requests for refunds. However, if for some reason you find that the plan you have purchased does not meet your requirements, you may exchange that plan for another plan in our collection. At the time of the exchange, you will be charged a processing fee of 25% of your original plan package price, plus the difference in price between the plan packages (if applicable) and the cost to ship the new plans to you. ***Please note:*** *Reproducible drawings can only be exchanged if the package is unopened, and exchanges are allowed only within 90 days of purchase.*

❏ **Building Codes & Requirements** - Our plans conform to most national building codes. However, they may not comply completely with your local building regulations. Some counties and municipalities have their own building codes, regulations and requirements. The assistance of a local builder, architect or other building professional may be necessary to modify the drawings to comply with your area's specific requirements. We recommend you consult with your local building officials prior to beginning construction.

❏ **Material List** - Remember to order your material list. You'll get faster and more accurate bids while saving money.

Plan prices guaranteed through December 31, 2002.

BLUEPRINT PRICE SCHEDULE — BEST VALUE

Price Code	One-Set	SAVE $75.00 Five-Sets	SAVE $150.00 Eight-Sets	Material List*	Reproducible Masters
AAA	$195	$260	$290	$50	$390
AA	245	310	340	55	440
A	295	360	390	60	490
B	345	410	440	60	540
C	395	460	490	65	590
D	445	510	540	65	640
E	495	560	590	70	690
F	545	610	640	70	740
G	650	715	745	75	845
H	755	820	850	80	950

OTHER OPTIONS...

Additional Plan Sets*	$ 35.00
Print In Mirror Reverse* . .	add $ 5.00 per set
Legal Kit	$ 35.00

Detail Plan Packages: (Buy 2, get 3rd FREE)
Framing, Electrical & Plumbing $20.00 ea.
Rush Charges . . . . Next Day Air $38.00
Second Day Air $25.00

Available only within 90 days after purchase of plan package or reproducible masters of same plan.

ORDER FORM

Please send me Plan Number 565 - _____

Price Code _____
(See Home Plans Index)

❏ Reproducible Masters $ _____
❏ Eight-Set Plan Package $ _____
❏ Five-Set Plan Package $ _____
❏ One-Set Plan Package (no mirror reverse) $ _____
❏ ____(Qty.) Additional Plan Sets ($35.00 each) $ _____
❏ Print ____(Qty.) sets in Mirror Reverse (add $5.00/set) $ _____
❏ Material List (see index for availability) $ _____
❏ Legal Kit (see page 8) $ _____
Detail Plan Packages: (see page 8)
   ❏ Framing ❏ Electrical ❏ Plumbing $ _____
   SUBTOTAL $ _____
   SALES TAX (MO residents add 7%) $ _____
❏ Rush Charges $ _____
   SHIPPING & HANDLING $ 12.50
   TOTAL ENCLOSED (US funds only) $ _____

❏ Enclosed is my check or money order payable to HDA, Inc. (Sorry, no COD's)

Please note that plans are not returnable.

Mail to: **HDA, Inc.**
4390 Green Ash Drive
St. Louis, MO 63045-1219

I hereby authorize HDA, Inc. to charge this purchase to my credit card account (check one):

❏ MasterCard ❏ VISA ❏ DISCOVER NOVUS ❏ AMERICAN EXPRESS Cards

My card number is _____

The expiration date is _____

Signature _____

Name _____
(Please print or type)

Street Address _____
(Please **do not** use P.O. Box)

City, State, Zip _____

My daytime phone number (_____) - _____ - _____

I am a ❏ Builder/Contractor ❏ Homeowner ❏ Renter

I ❏ have ❏ have not selected my general contractor.

Thank you for your order!

9

PLAN DATA

Total Living Area: 2,727
Bedrooms: 4
Baths: 2 1/2
Garage: 2-car
Foundation Type:
   Walk-out basement
Features:
   -Vaulted master
    bedroom
   - Screened-in porch

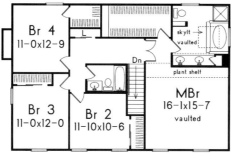

**Second Floor
1,204 sq. ft.**

Br 4
11-0x12-9

skylt
vaulted

plant shelf

Dn

MBr
16-1x15-7
vaulted

Br 3
11-0x12-0

Br 2
11-10x10-6

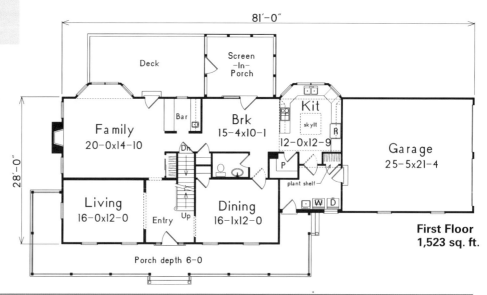

81'-0"

Deck

Screen
-In-
Porch

28'-0"

Family
20-0x14-10

Bar

Brk
15-4x10-1

Kit
skylt
12-0x12-9

R

Garage
25-5x21-4

Dn

P

plant shelf

Living
16-0x12-0

Entry

Up

Dining
16-1x12-0

W D

**First Floor
1,523 sq. ft.**

Porch depth 6-0

Second Floor 961 sq. ft.

Br 2
12-11x12-7

open to below

Br 3
12-0x13-3

Dn

open to below

Br 4
12-1x12-4

PLAN DATA

Total Living Area: 3,234
Bedrooms: 4
Baths: 3 1/2
Garage: 2-car
Foundation Types:
  Basement standard
  Slab
  Crawl space
Features:
  Built-in breakfast
  booth

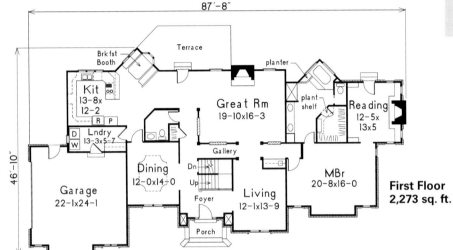

87'-8"

46'-10"

Brkfst Booth

Terrace

planter

Kit
13-8x
12-2

Great Rm
19-10x16-3

plant shelf

Reading
12-5x
13x5

R P

D W

Lndry
13-3x5-7

Gallery

MBr
20-8x16-0

Garage
22-1x24-1

Dining
12-0x14-0

Dn
Up

Living
12-1x13-9

Foyer

Porch

First Floor 2,273 sq. ft.

**Second Floor
785 sq. ft.**

**First Floor
1,473 sq. ft.**

**Lower Level
548 sq. ft.**

PLAN DATA

Total Living Area:	2,806
Bedrooms:	4
Baths:	2 1/2
Garage:	2-car
Foundation Type:	
Walk-out basement	

Rear View

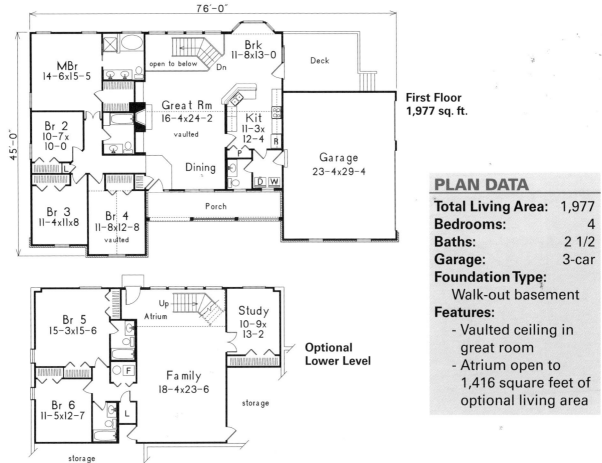

76'-0"

45'-0"

MBr
14-6x15-5

open to below   Dn

Brk
11-8x13-0

Deck

Great Rm
16-4x24-2
vaulted

Kit
11-3x
12-4

Br 2
10-7x
10-0

Dining

First Floor
1,977 sq. ft.

Garage
23-4x29-4

Br 3
11-4x11x8

Br 4
11-8x12-8
vaulted

Porch

Br 5
15-3x15-6

Up
Atrium

Study
10-9x
13-2

Optional
Lower Level

Family
18-4x23-6

Br 6
11-5x12-7

storage

storage

PLAN DATA

Total Living Area: 1,977
Bedrooms: 4
Baths: 2 1/2
Garage: 3-car
Foundation Type:
    Walk-out basement
Features:
    - Vaulted ceiling in
      great room
    - Atrium open to
      1,416 square feet of
      optional living area

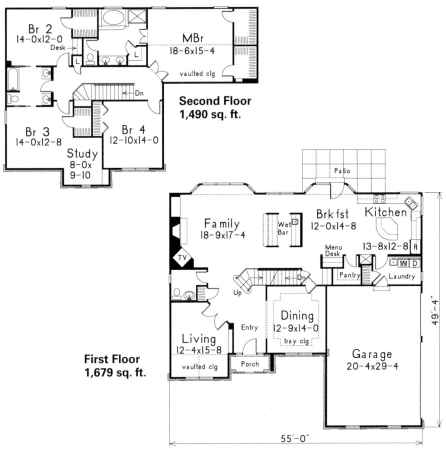

Second Floor
1,490 sq. ft.

Br 2
14-0x12-0

Desk

MBr
18-6x15-4

vaulted clg

Br 3
14-0x12-8

Br 4
12-10x14-0

Study
8-0x
9-10

Dn

PLAN DATA

Total Living Area:	3,169
Bedrooms:	4
Baths:	2 1/2
Garage:	3-car
Foundation Type:	
Basement	

First Floor
1,679 sq. ft.

Patio

Family
18-9x17-4

Wet
Bar

TV

Brkfst
12-0x14-8

Kitchen

13-8x12-8

Menu
Desk

Pantry

Laundry
W D

Up

Dn

Dining
12-9x14-0
tray clg

Living
12-4x15-8

Entry

Porch

vaulted clg

Garage
20-4x29-4

49'-4"

55'-0"

**Second Floor
1,069 sq. ft.**

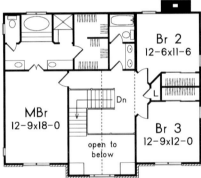

Br 2
12-6x11-6

MBr
12-9x18-0

Dn

L

Br 3
12-9x12-0

open to
below

PLAN DATA

Total Living Area:	2,505
Bedrooms:	3
Baths:	2 1/2
Garage:	2-car
Foundation Types:	
Basement standard	
Crawl space	

70'-0"

Patio

40'-0"

Storage
13-6x10-6

D
W

Kitchen

15-0x
14-8

P

R

Brk
9-0x
14-8

Family
20-6x14-8

sloped clg

Garage
23-4x25-0

Dining
12-9x14-2

Up

Dn

Living
12-9x14-2

Foyer

Porch depth 6-0

**First Floor
1,436 sq. ft.**

PLAN DATA

Total Living Area:	1,161
Bedrooms:	3
Baths:	2
Foundation Type:	
Basement	

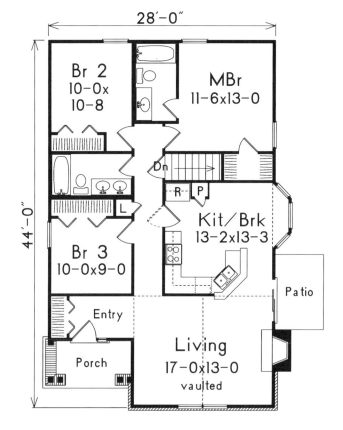

PLAN DATA

Total Living Area: 2,716
Bedrooms: 4
Baths: 4 1/2
Garage: 2-car
Foundation Type:
Basement
Features:
9' ceilings throughout
first floor

Second Floor
962 sq. ft.

First Floor
1,754 sq. ft.

PLAN DATA

Total Living Area:	929
Bedrooms:	2
Baths:	1
Garage:	3-car
Foundation Type:	
Slab	

Second Floor
819 sq. ft.

Deck

Dn

Living
16-0x18-4

Br 2
10-1x11-0

Dining

L

Kit
9-0x
11-0

MBr
14-0x11-1

R

vaulted clg

Patio

Util

Sto

Up

W
D

Entry

Garage
23-4x29-4

35'-0"

Covered porch depth 5-0

First Floor
110 sq. ft.

31'-0"

PLAN DATA

Total Living Area: 1,268
Bedrooms: 3
Baths: 2
Garage: 2-car
Foundation Type:
   Basement
Features:
   - 10' ceilings throughout living/ dining area
   - Drive-under garage

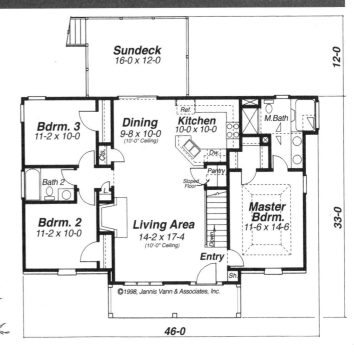

Sundeck
16-0 x 12-0

12-0

Bdrm. 3
11-2 x 10-0

Dining
9-8 x 10-0
(10'-0" Ceiling)

Kitchen
10-0 x 10-0

Ref.

M.Bath

Dw.

Pantry

Bath 2

Sloped Floor

Bdrm. 2
11-2 x 10-0

Living Area
14-2 x 17-4
(10'-0" Ceiling)

Down

Master Bdrm.
11-6 x 14-6

Entry

Sh.

33-0

©1998, Jannis Vann & Associates, Inc.

46-0

Width: 50'-0"
Depth: 60'-8"

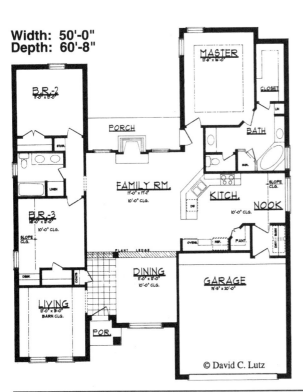

B.R.-2

MASTER

CLOSET

PORCH

BATH

FAMILY RM.
10'-0" CLG.

KITCH.
10'-0" CLG.

NOOK

B.R.-3
10'-0" CLG.

SLOPE CLG.

DINING
10'-0" CLG.

GARAGE
19'-8" x 20'-0"

LIVING
BARN CLG.

POR.

© David C. Lutz

PLAN DATA

Total Living Area: 1,960
Bedrooms: 3
Baths: 2
Garage: 2-car
Foundation Type:
   Slab

Second Floor
872 sq. ft.

BEDROOM 3
12-6 X 12-6

BATH 3

BEDROOM 2
12-6 X 11-6

LIN

BALCONY

BALCONY

OPEN TO GREAT
ROOM BELOW

OPEN TO
FOYER BELOW

ATTIC

BEDROOM 4
11-4 X 13-6

WIDTH 79–10

PLAN DATA

Total Living Area: 2,838
Bedrooms: 4
Baths: 3
Garage: 2-car
Foundation Types:
　Slab
　Basement
　Crawl space
Please specify when ordering

MASTER
BATH
9 FT CLG

HIS

HERS

STUDY/
BEDROOM
12-6 X 11-6
9 FT CLG

LIN

BATH
2

MASTER BEDROOM
16-0 X 13-6
9 FT CLG

COVERED
PORCH

BOOKCASE

GREAT ROOM
17-0 X 18-6
2 STORY CLG

FP

PATIO

First Floor
1,966 sq. ft.

FOYER
2 STORY CLG

PORCH

DINING ROOM
11-4 X 13-0
9 FT CLG

PAN

KITCHEN
12-0 X 13-0

FRZ

9 FT CLG

STORAGE

GARAGE

UTIL
5-8 X 6-0

BRKFST RM
11-4 X 10-0
CATHEDRAL CLG

DEPTH 63–10

COPYRIGHT LARRY E. BELK

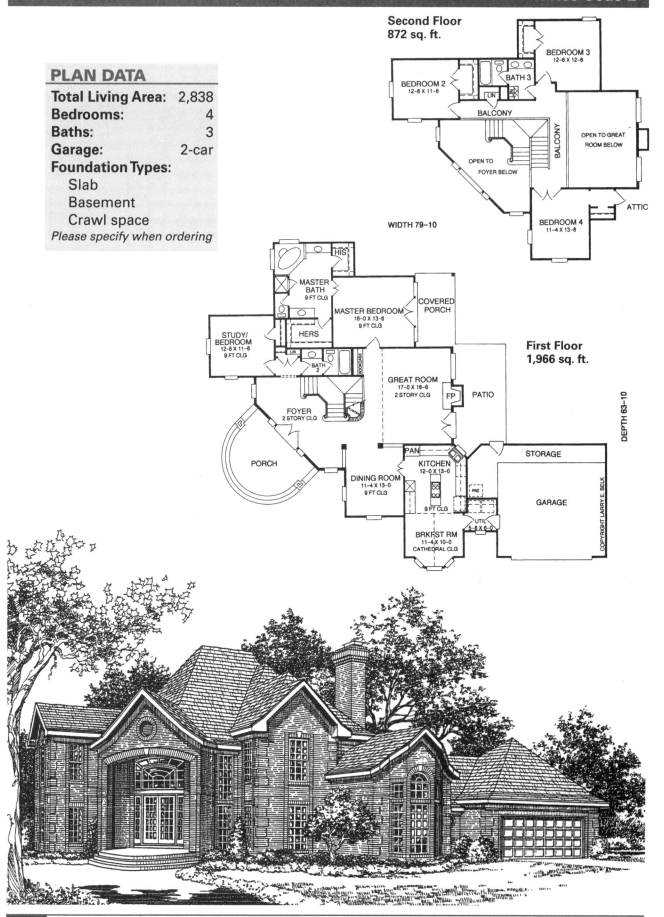

PLAN DATA

Total Living Area: 3,144
Bedrooms: 4
Baths: 4 1/2
Garage: 3-car
Foundation Type:
Basement
Features:
9' ceilings on first floor

First Floor
1,724 sq. ft.

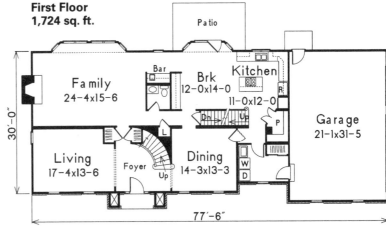

Second Floor
1,420 sq. ft.

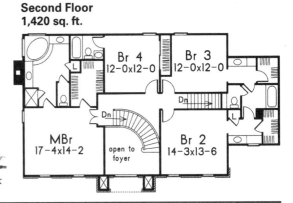

PLAN #565-NDG-525

Price Code A

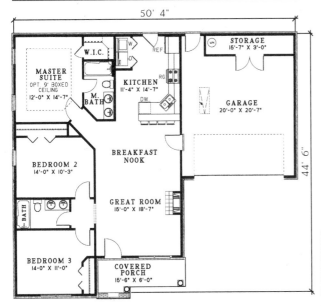

PLAN DATA

Total Living Area: 1,250
Bedrooms: 3
Baths: 2
Garage: 2-car
Foundation Types:
Slab
Crawl space
Please specify when ordering

Width: 26'-0"
Depth: 44'-0"

Second Floor
775 sq. ft.

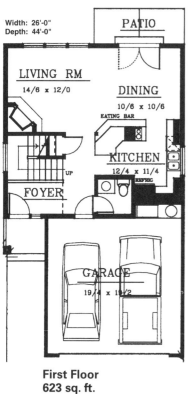

LIVING RM
14/6 x 12/0

PATIO

DINING
10/6 x 10/6

EATING BAR

KITCHEN
12/4 x 11/4

REFRIG

FOYER

UP

GARAGE
19/4 x 19/2

First Floor
623 sq. ft.

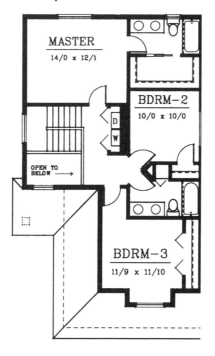

MASTER
14/0 x 12/1

BDRM-2
10/0 x 10/0

D
W

OPEN TO
BELOW

BDRM-3
11/9 x 11/10

PLAN DATA

Total Living Area:	1,398
Bedrooms:	3
Baths:	2 1/2
Garage:	2-car
Foundation Type:	
Crawl space	

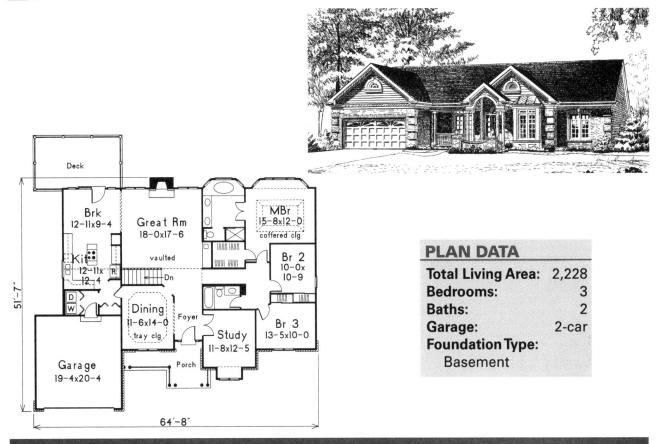

PLAN DATA

Total Living Area: 2,228
Bedrooms: 3
Baths: 2
Garage: 2-car
Foundation Type:
Basement

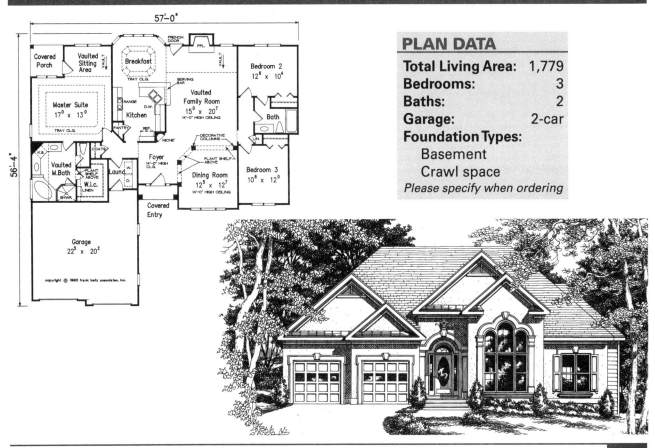

PLAN DATA

Total Living Area: 1,779
Bedrooms: 3
Baths: 2
Garage: 2-car
Foundation Types:
Basement
Crawl space
Please specify when ordering

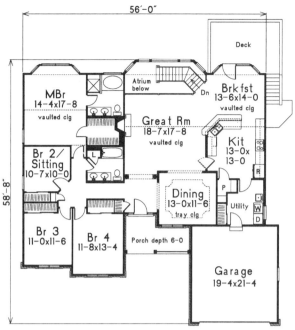

56'-0"

58'-8"

Deck

MBr
14-4x17-8
vaulted clg

Atrium
below

Brkfst
13-6x14-0
vaulted clg

Dn

Great Rm
18-7x17-8
vaulted clg

Kit
13-0x
13-0

Br 2/
Sitting
10-7x10-0

L

P

R

Dining
13-0x11-6
tray clg

Utility
W
D

Br 3
11-0x11-6

Br 4
11-8x13-4

Porch depth 6-0

Garage
19-4x21-4

**First Floor
2,218 sq. ft.**

PLAN DATA

Total Living Area: 2,218
Bedrooms: 4
Baths: 2
Garage: 2-car
Foundation Type:
  Walk-out basement
Features:
  - Vaulted ceilings in
    kitchen
  - Atrium opens to
    1,217 square feet of
    optional living area

**Optional
Lower Level**

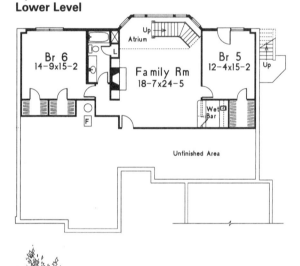

Up
Atrium

Br 6
14-9x15-2

L

Family Rm
18-7x24-5

Br 5
12-4x15-2

Up

Wet
Bar

F

Unfinished Area

Rear View

PLAN #565-0450

PLAN DATA

Total Living Area: 1,708
Bedrooms: 3
Baths: 2
Garage: 2-car
Foundation Types:
   Basement standard
   Crawl space

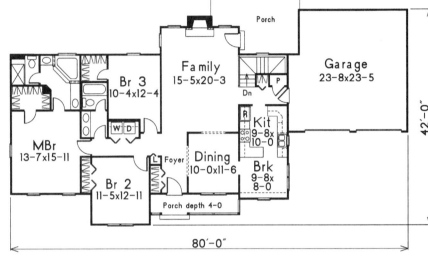

Porch

Family
15-5x20-3

Garage
23-8x23-5

Br 3
10-4x12-4

Dn   P

R   Kit
9-8x
10-0

MBr
13-7x15-11

W D

Foyer   Dining
10-0x11-6

Brk
9-8x
8-0

Br 2
11-5x12-11

Porch depth 4-0

42'-0"

80'-0"

PLAN #565-BF-1901

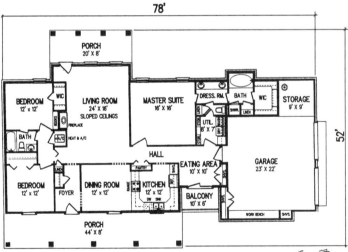

78'

PORCH
20' X 8'

BEDROOM
12' X 12'

WIC

LIVING ROOM
24' X 16'
SLOPED CEILINGS
FIREPLACE

MASTER SUITE
16' X 16'

DRESS. RM.   BATH   WIC

STORAGE
9' X 9'

BATH

HVS   HEAT & A/C

UTIL.
8' X 7'

HALL

BEDROOM
12' X 12'

FOYER

DINING ROOM
12' X 12'

PANTRY

KITCHEN
12' X 12'

EATING AREA
10' X 10'

GARAGE
23' X 22'

52'

BALCONY
10' X 6'

WORK BENCH

PORCH
44' X 8'

PLAN DATA

Total Living Area: 1,925
Bedrooms: 3
Baths: 2
Garage: 2-car
Foundation Types:
   Slab
   Crawl space
Please specify when ordering
Features:
   2" x 6" exterior walls

PLAN DATA

Total Living Area: 2,073
Bedrooms: 4
Baths: 2 1/2
Garage: 2-car
Foundation Type:
   Basement
Features:
   Vaulted ceilings in
   family room and
   master bedroom

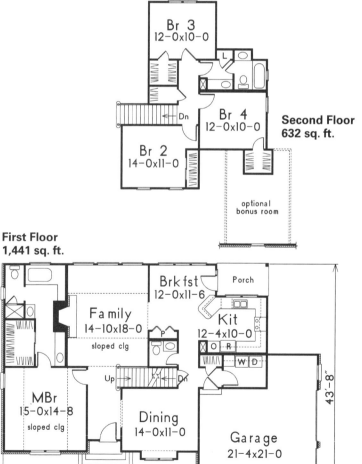

Br 3
12-0x10-0

Br 4
12-0x10-0

Second Floor
632 sq. ft.

Br 2
14-0x11-0

Dn

optional
bonus room

First Floor
1,441 sq. ft.

Brkfst
12-0x11-6

Porch

Family
14-10x18-0
sloped clg

Kit
12-4x10-0

P

O   R

W   D

Up   Dn

MBr
15-0x14-8
sloped clg

Dining
14-0x11-0

Garage
21-4x21-0

43'-8"

58'-0"

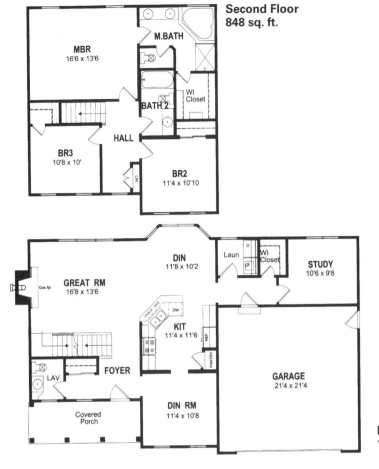

**Second Floor
848 sq. ft.**

MBR
16'6 x 13'6

M.BATH

BATH 2

WI Closet

HALL

BR3
10'8 x 10'

BR2
11'4 x 10'10

PLAN DATA

Total Living Area:	1,868
Bedrooms:	3
Baths:	2 1/2
Garage:	2-car
Foundation Type:	
Basement	

DIN
11'8 x 10'2

Laun

WI Closet

STUDY
10'6 x 9'8

GREAT RM
16'8 x 13'6

Gas fpl

KIT
11'4 x 11'6

PANTRY

GARAGE
21'4 x 21'4

LAV

FOYER

DIN RM
11'4 x 10'8

Covered Porch

**First Floor
1,020 sq. ft.**

**Width: 52'-8"
Depth: 34'-0"**

M. MAXON

PLAN DATA

Total Living Area: 3,164
Bedrooms: 4
Baths: 4
Garage: 3-car
Foundation Type:
Slab
Features:
Varied ceiling heights
throughout

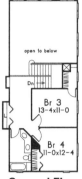

Second Floor
540 sq. ft.

First Floor
2,624 sq. ft.

PLAN DATA

Total Living Area: 1,806
Bedrooms: 3
Baths: 2
Garage: 2-car
Foundation Type:
Basement
Features:
Vaulted ceiling in
great room

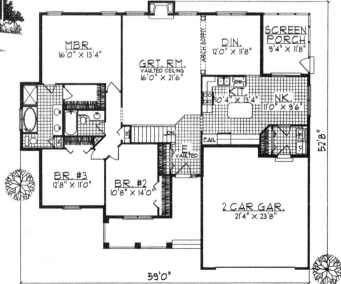

PLAN DATA

Total Living Area: 2,828
Bedrooms: 5
Baths: 3 1/2
Garage: 2-car
Foundation Types:
   Basement standard
   Slab
   Crawl space
Features:
   Vaulted ceilings in
   master bedroom and
   family room

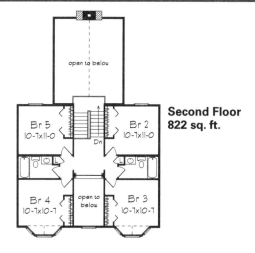

**Second Floor
822 sq. ft.**

Br 5
10-7x11-0

Br 2
10-7x11-0

open to below

Dn

Br 4
10-7x10-7

open to below

Br 3
10-7x10-7

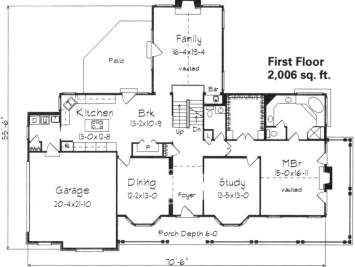

**First Floor
2,006 sq. ft.**

Family
16-4x19-4
vaulted

Patio

Bar

Kitchen
13-0x12-8

Brk
13-2x10-9

Up   Dn

MBr
15-0x16-11
vaulted

Garage
20-4x21-10

Dining
12-2x13-0

Foyer

Study
13-5x13-0

55'-6"

Porch Depth 6-0

70'-6"

PLAN DATA

Total Living Area: 2,665
Bedrooms: 4
Baths: 3
Garage: 2-car
Foundation Types:
  Slab standard
  Crawl space
Features:
  9' ceilings on first floor

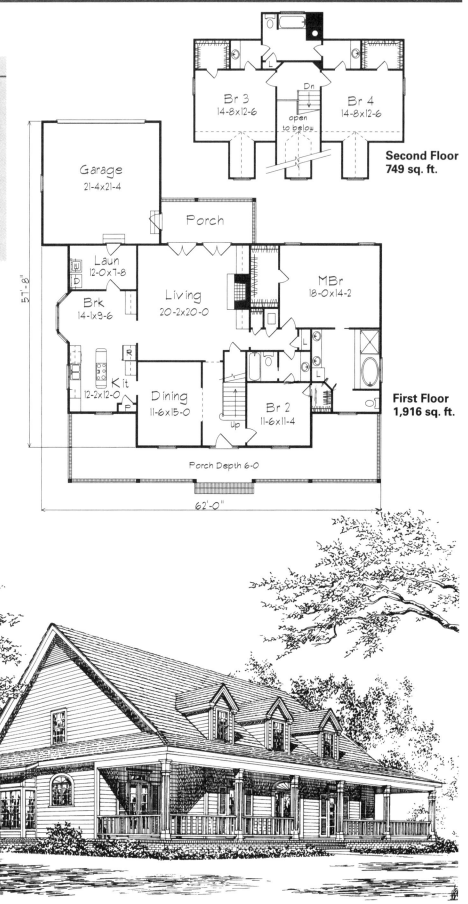

Second Floor
749 sq. ft.

Br 3
14-8x12-6

Br 4
14-8x12-6

Dn
open to below

Garage
21-4x21-4

Porch

Laun
12-0x7-8

Brk
14-1x9-6

Living
20-2x20-0

MBr
18-0x14-2

Kit
12-2x12-0

Dining
11-6x15-0

Br 2
11-6x11-4

Up

First Floor
1,916 sq. ft.

Porch Depth 6-0

51'-8"

62'-0"

PLAN #565-0368

PLAN DATA

Total Living Area: 2,452
Bedrooms: 4
Baths: 2 1/2
Garage: 3-car
Foundation Type:
 Basement
Features:
 Vaulted ceilings in
 great room and
 master bedroom

PLAN #565-0503

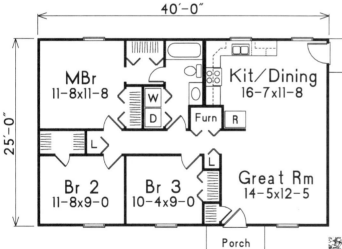

PLAN DATA

Total Living Area: 1,000
Bedrooms: 3
Baths: 1
Foundation Types:
 Crawl space standard
 Basement
 Slab

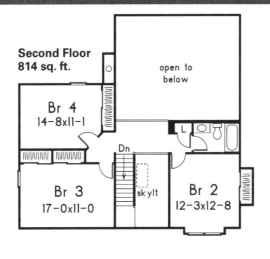

Second Floor
814 sq. ft.

open to below

Br 4
14-8x11-1

Dn

L

Br 3
17-0x11-0

sk ylt

Br 2
12-3x12-8

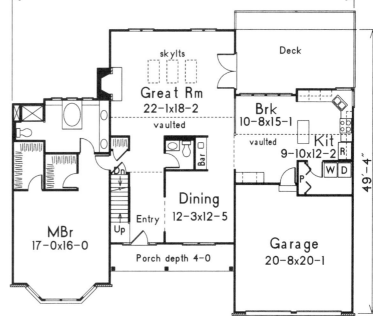

First Floor
1,804 sq. ft.

61'-0"

sk ylts

Deck

Great Rm
22-1x18-2
vaulted

Brk
10-8x15-1
vaulted

Kit
9-10x12-2

Bar

Dn

MBr
17-0x16-0

Up

Entry

Dining
12-3x12-5

Porch depth 4-0

Garage
20-8x20-1

49'-4"

W | D

P

R

PLAN DATA

Total Living Area:	2,618
Bedrooms:	4
Baths:	2 1/2
Garage:	2-car
Foundation Type:	
Basement	

PLAN #565-0706

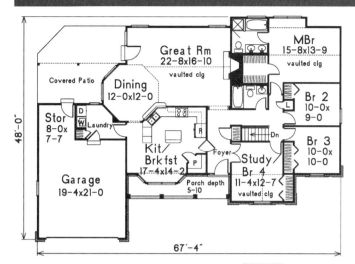

PLAN DATA

Total Living Area: 1,791
Bedrooms: 4
Baths: 2
Garage: 2-car
Foundation Type:
    Basement
Features:
    Extra storage in garage

PLAN #565-0803

Width 70' - 10"
Depth 79' - 0"

PLAN DATA

Total Living Area: 3,366
Bedrooms: 4
Baths: 3 1/2
Garage: 2-car
Foundation Types:
    Crawl space
    Slab
Please specify when ordering

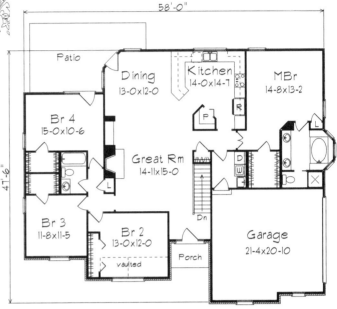

PLAN DATA

Total Living Area: 1,882
Bedrooms: 4
Baths: 2
Garage: 2-car
Foundation Type:
  Basement

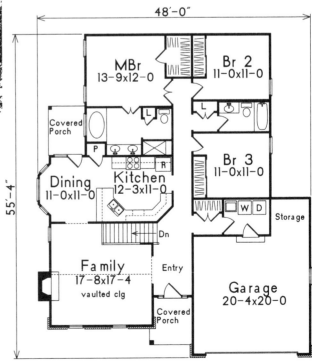

PLAN DATA

Total Living Area: 1,598
Bedrooms: 3
Baths: 2
Garage: 2-car
Foundation Type:
  Basement

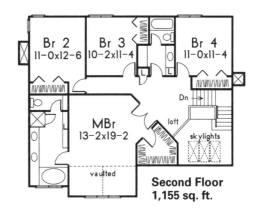

**Second Floor
1,155 sq. ft.**

PLAN DATA

Total Living Area: 2,445
Bedrooms: 4
Baths: 2 1/2
Garage: 3-car
Foundation Type:
   Basement
Features:
   Vaulted ceilings in
   living room, foyer and
   master bedroom

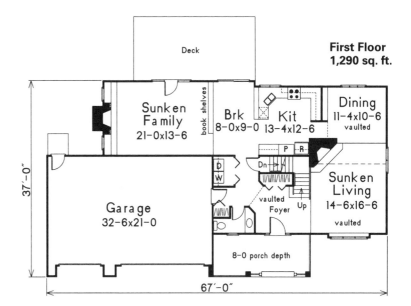

**First Floor
1,290 sq. ft.**

PLAN DATA

Total Living Area: 624
Bedrooms: 1
Baths: 1
Garage: 2-car
Foundation Type:
  Slab
Features:
  Vaulted ceiling in
  entry

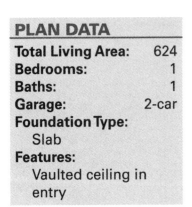

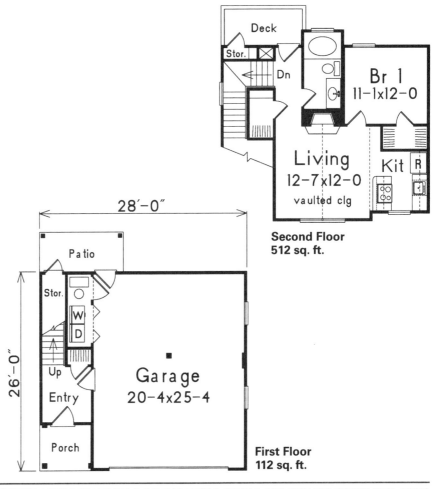

Deck

Stor.

Dn

Br 1
11-1x12-0

Living
12-7x12-0
vaulted clg

Kit
R

Second Floor
512 sq. ft.

28'-0"

26'-0"

Patio

Stor.

W
D

Up

Entry

Garage
20-4x25-4

Porch

First Floor
112 sq. ft.

PLAN #565-0319

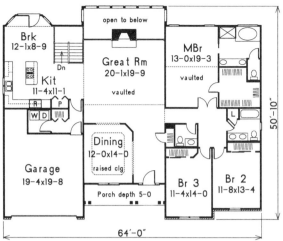

First Floor
2,436 sq. ft.

- Brk 12-1x8-9
- open to below
- Great Rm 20-1x19-9 vaulted
- MBr 13-0x19-3 vaulted
- Kit 11-4x11-1
- Dn
- R P
- W D
- Dining 12-0x14-0 raised clg
- Garage 19-4x19-8
- Br 3 11-4x14-0
- Br 2 11-8x13-4
- Porch depth 5-0
- 50'-10"
- 64'-0"

PLAN DATA

Total Living Area:	3,796
Bedrooms:	4
Baths:	3 1/2
Garage:	2-car
Foundation Type:	Basement

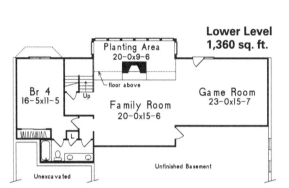

Lower Level
1,360 sq. ft.

- Planting Area 20-0x9-6
- floor above
- Br 4 16-5x11-5
- Up
- Family Room 20-0x15-6
- Game Room 23-0x15-7
- L
- Unfinished Basement
- Unexcavated

PLAN #565-JV-1418-A

PLAN DATA

Total Living Area:	1,418
Bedrooms:	3
Baths:	2
Garage:	2-car
Foundation Types:	Basement Crawl space Slab

Please specify when ordering

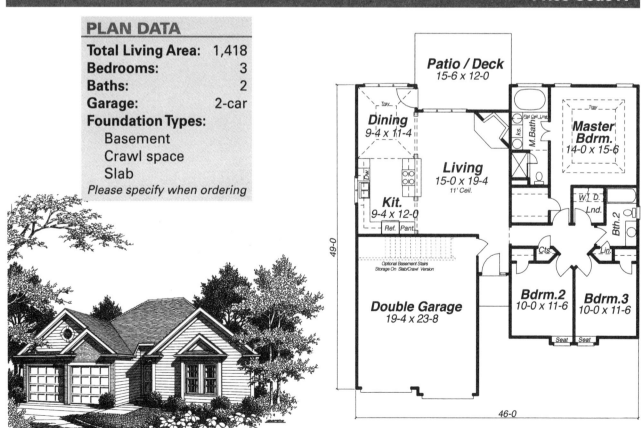

- Patio / Deck 15-6 x 12-0
- Dining 9-4 x 11-4
- Living 15-0 x 19-4 11' Ceil.
- M.Bath
- Master Bdrm. 14-0 x 15-6
- Kit. 9-4 x 12-0
- Ref. Pant
- W.I.D. Lnd.
- Bth.2
- Optional Basement Stairs Storage On Slab/Crawl Version
- Double Garage 19-4 x 23-8
- Bdrm.2 10-0 x 11-6
- Bdrm.3 10-0 x 11-6
- Seat   Seat
- 49-0
- 46-0

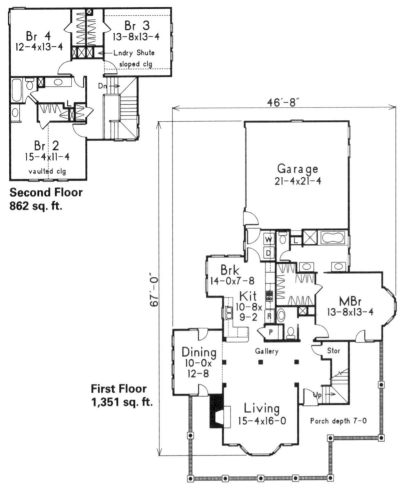

Second Floor
862 sq. ft.

Br 4
12-4x13-4

Br 3
13-8x13-4

Lndry Shute
sloped clg

Dn

Br 2
15-4x11-4
vaulted clg

46'-8"

67'-0"

Garage
21-4x21-4

Brk
14-0x7-8

Kit
10-8x
9-2

MBr
13-8x13-4

Dining
10-0x
12-8

Gallery

Stor

Living
15-4x16-0

Porch depth 7-0

First Floor
1,351 sq. ft.

PLAN DATA

Total Living Area:	2,213
Bedrooms:	4
Baths:	2 1/2
Garage:	2-car
Foundation Type:	
Slab	
Features:	
9' ceilings	

PLAN #565-0393

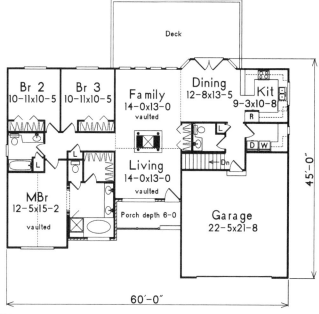

PLAN DATA

Total Living Area:	1,684
Bedrooms:	3
Baths:	2 1/2
Garage:	2-car
Foundation Type:	
Basement	

PLAN #565-DBI-2461

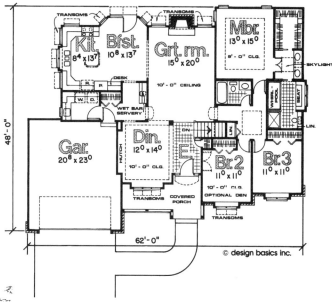

PLAN DATA

Total Living Area:	1,850
Bedrooms:	3
Baths:	2
Garage:	2-car
Foundation Type:	
Basement	

PLAN DATA

Total Living Area: 2,788
Bedrooms: 3
Baths: 2 1/2
Garage: 2-car
Foundation Type:
  Basement

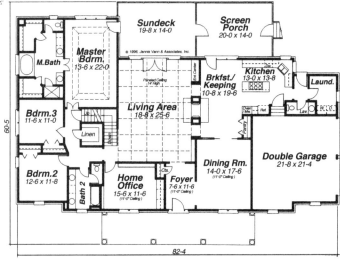

PLAN #565-JV-1781-B

Price Code B

PLAN DATA

Total Living Area: 1,781
Bedrooms: 3
Baths: 2
Garage: 2-car
Foundation Types:
  Slab
  Crawl space
Please specify when ordering

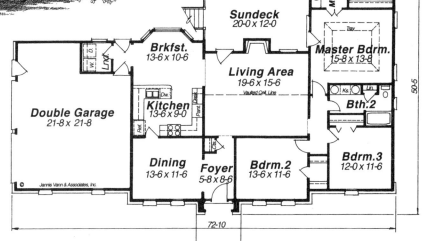

PLAN DATA

Total Living Area: 2,278
Bedrooms: 3
Baths: 2
Garage: 2-car
Foundation Type:
  Slab

Width: 58'-0"
Depth: 71'-8"

PLAN DATA

Total Living Area: 2,434
Bedrooms: 4
Baths: 3 1/2
Garage: 3-car
Foundation Type:
  Slab

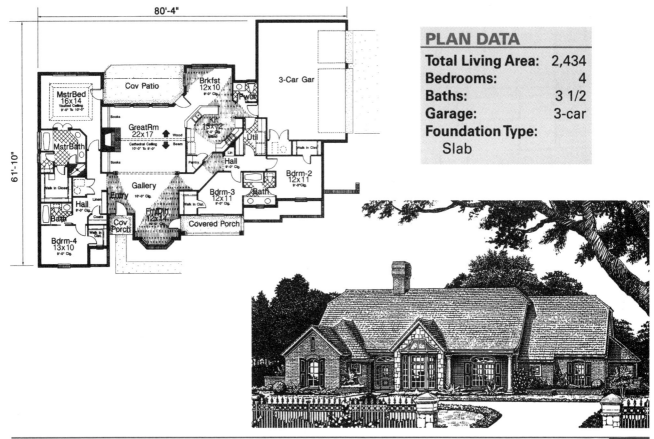

HOLZHAUER

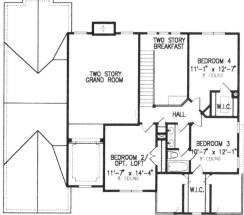

Second Floor
709 sq. ft.

PLAN DATA

Total Living Area:	2,450
Bedrooms:	4
Baths:	2 1/2
Garage:	2-car
Foundation Type:	
Basement	

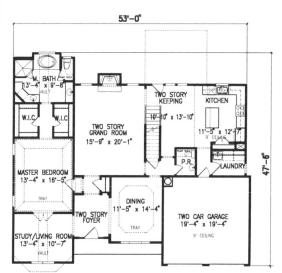

First Floor
1,751 sq. ft.

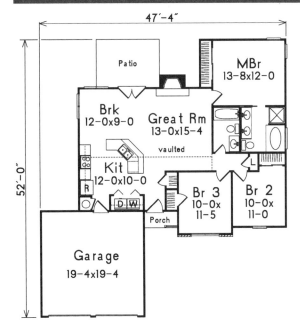

47'-4"

52'-0"

Patio

MBr
13-8x12-0

Brk
12-0x9-0

Great Rm
13-0x15-4
vaulted

Kit
12-0x10-0

Br 3
10-0x
11-5

Br 2
10-0x
11-0

Porch

Garage
19-4x19-4

PLAN DATA

Total Living Area: 1,170
Bedrooms: 3
Baths: 2
Garage: 2-car
Foundation Type:
  Slab

PLAN DATA

Total Living Area: 1,605
Bedrooms: 3
Baths: 2
Garage: 2-car
Foundation Types:
  Plan #565-ES-125-1
  Basement
  Plan #565-ES-125-2
  Crawl space & slab

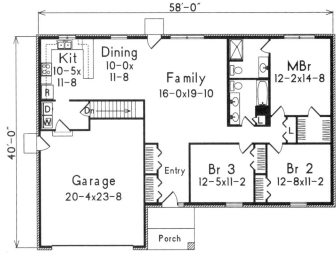

58'-0"

40'-0"

Kit
10-5x
11-8

Dining
10-0x
11-8

Family
16-0x19-10

MBr
12-2x14-8

Garage
20-4x23-8

Entry

Br 3
12-5x11-2

Br 2
12-8x11-2

Porch

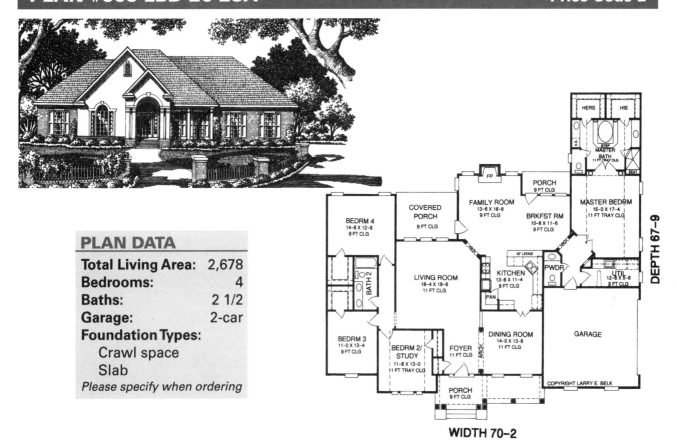

PLAN DATA

Total Living Area: 2,678
Bedrooms: 4
Baths: 2 1/2
Garage: 2-car
Foundation Types:
  Crawl space
  Slab
Please specify when ordering

BEDRM 4
14-8 X 12-8
9 FT CLG

COVERED PORCH
9 FT CLG

FAMILY ROOM
13-6 X 16-6
9 FT CLG

BRKFST RM
10-8 X 11-6
9 FT CLG

MASTER BEDRM
15-0 X 17-4
11 FT TRAY CLG

HERS   HIS

STEP
MASTER
BATH
11 FT CLG

SEAT

FP

PORCH
9 FT CLG

LIVING ROOM
18-4 X 18-6
11 FT CLG

KITCHEN
13-6 X 11-4
9 FT CLG

42" LEDGE

PWDR

PAN

UTIL
12-5 X 5-8
9 FT CLG

BATH 2

BEDRM 3
11-0 X 13-4
9 FT CLG

BEDRM 2/
STUDY
11-6 X 13-0
11 FT TRAY CLG

FOYER
11 FT CLG

DINING ROOM
14-0 X 13-6
11 FT CLG

GARAGE

ARCH

COPYRIGHT LARRY E. BELK

PORCH
9 FT CLG

DEPTH 67–9

WIDTH 70–2

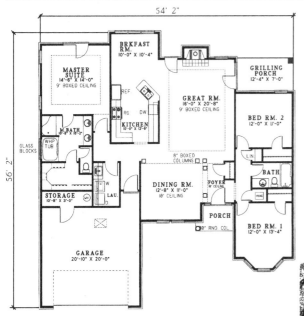

54' 2"

56' 2"

MASTER
SUITE
14'-6" X 14'-0"
9' BOXED CEILING

BRKFAST
RM.
10'-0" X 10'-4"

GRILLING
PORCH
12'-4" X 7'-0"

REF

RG   DW

M.BATH

WHP
TUB

GLASS
BLOCKS

GREAT RM.
18'-0" X 20'-8"
9' BOXED CEILING

KITCHEN
10'-0" X 12'-6"

BED RM. 2
12'-0" X 11'-0"

LIN

8' BOXED
COLUMNS

BATH

STORAGE
10'-8" X 3'-0"

LAU

W

DINING RM.
12'-8" X 11'-0"
10' CEILING

FOYER
10' CEILING

HVAC

PORCH

GARAGE
20'-10" X 20'-0"

8" RND. COL.

BED RM. 1
12'-0" X 13'-4"

PLAN DATA

Total Living Area: 1,758
Bedrooms: 3
Baths: 2
Garage: 2-car
Foundation Types:
  Walk-out basement
  Basement
  Crawl space
  Slab
Please specify when ordering
Features:
  2" X 6" exterior walls

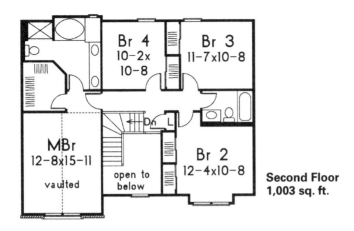

Br 4
10-2x
10-8

Br 3
11-7x10-8

MBr
12-8x15-11
vaulted

open to
below

Br 2
12-4x10-8

Second Floor
1,003 sq. ft.

PLAN DATA

Total Living Area: 2,286
Bedrooms: 4
Baths: 2 1/2
Garage: 2-car
Foundation Types:
  Basement standard
  Crawl space
  Slab

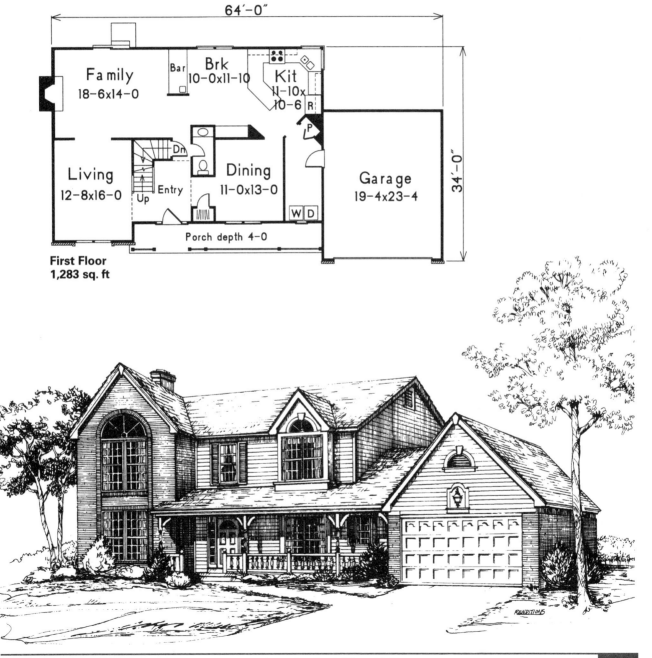

64'-0"

Family
18-6x14-0

Bar

Brk
10-0x11-10

Kit
11-10x
10-6

R

Living
12-8x16-0

Dn

Up

Entry

Dining
11-0x13-0

W D

Garage
19-4x23-4

34'-0"

Porch depth 4-0

First Floor
1,283 sq. ft

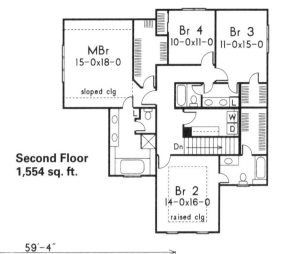

**Second Floor
1,554 sq. ft.**

PLAN DATA

Total Living Area:	3,013
Bedrooms:	4
Baths:	3 1/2
Garage:	2-car
Foundation Type:	
Basement	

**First Floor
1,459 sq. ft.**

PLAN #565-1072

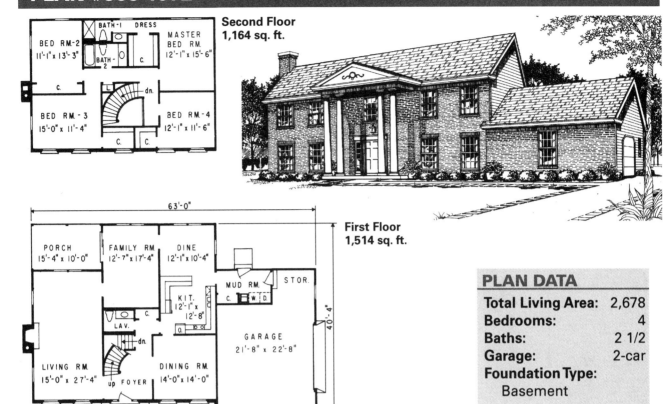

Second Floor
1,164 sq. ft.

BED RM.-2
11'-1" x 13'-3"

BATH-1 DRESS

MASTER
BED RM.
12'-1" x 15'-6"

BATH-2

BED RM.-3
15'-0" x 11'-4"

BED RM.-4
12'-1" x 11'-6"

First Floor
1,514 sq. ft.

63'-0"

PORCH
15'-4" x 10'-0"

FAMILY RM.
12'-7" x 17'-4"

DINE
12'-1" x 10'-4"

MUD RM.

STOR.

KIT.
12'-1" x 12'-8"

LAV.

GARAGE
21'-8" x 22'-8"

40'-4"

LIVING RM.
15'-0" x 27'-4"

DINING RM.
14'-0" x 14'-0"

up FOYER

dn.

PORTICO

PLAN DATA

Total Living Area:	2,678
Bedrooms:	4
Baths:	2 1/2
Garage:	2-car
Foundation Type:	
Basement	

PLAN #565-0112

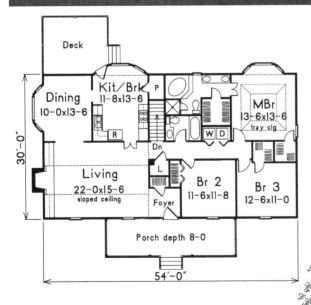

Deck

Dining
10-0x13-6

Kit/Brk
11-8x13-6

P

MBr
13-6x13-6
tray clg

W D

Living
22-0x15-6
sloped ceiling

Dn

L

Br 2
11-6x11-8

Br 3
12-6x11-0

Foyer

Porch depth 8-0

30'-0"

54'-0"

PLAN DATA

Total Living Area:	1,668
Bedrooms:	3
Baths:	2
Garage:	2-car
Foundation Type:	
Basement	
Features:	
Drive-under garage	

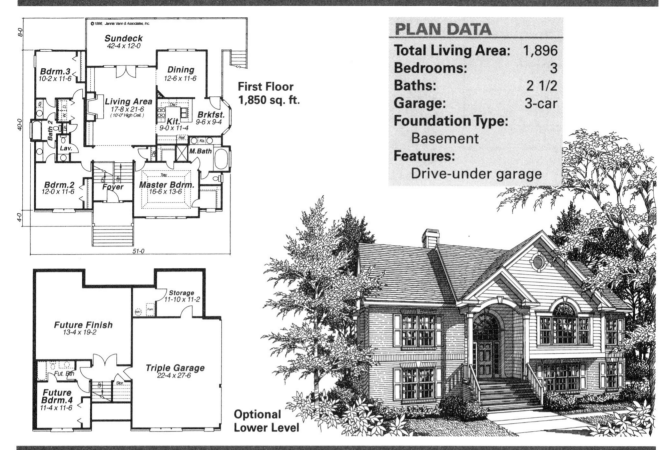

Bdrm.3
10-2 x 11-6

Sundeck
42-4 x 12-0

Dining
12-6 x 11-6

First Floor
1,850 sq. ft.

Living Area
17-8 x 21-6
(10'-0" High Ceil.)

Brkfst.
9-6 x 9-4

Kit.
9-0 x 11-4

Bath 2

Lav.

Bdrm.2
12-0 x 11-6

Foyer

Master Bdrm.
16-6 x 13-6

M.Bath

51-0

© 1996, Jannie Vann & Associates, Inc.

PLAN DATA

Total Living Area: 1,896
Bedrooms: 3
Baths: 2 1/2
Garage: 3-car
Foundation Type:
  Basement
Features:
  Drive-under garage

Storage
11-10 x 11-2

Future Finish
13-4 x 19-2

Triple Garage
22-4 x 27-6

Fut. Bth

Future Bdrm.4
11-4 x 11-6

Optional Lower Level

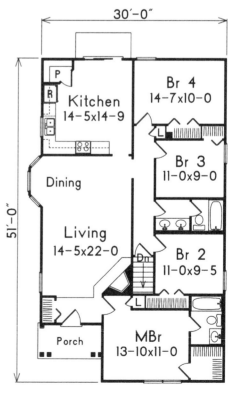

30'-0"

51'-0"

Kitchen
14-5x14-9

Br 4
14-7x10-0

Dining

Br 3
11-0x9-0

Living
14-5x22-0

Br 2
11-0x9-5

Porch

MBr
13-10x11-0

PLAN DATA

Total Living Area: 1,452
Bedrooms: 4
Baths: 2
Foundation Type:
  Basement

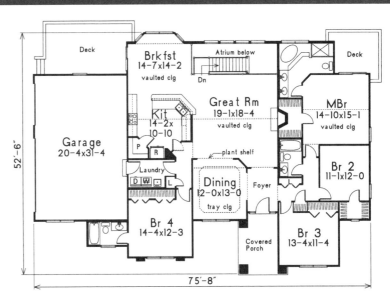

First Floor
2,408 sq. ft.

PLAN DATA

Total Living Area: 2,408
Bedrooms: 4
Baths: 2
Garage: 2-car
Foundation Type:
 Basement
Features:
 Atrium opens to
 1,100 square feet of
 optional living area

Optional
Lower Level

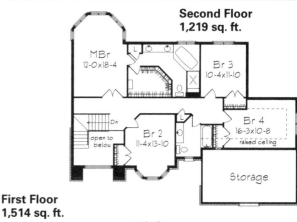

Second Floor
1,219 sq. ft.

MBr
12-0x18-4

Br 3
10-4x11-10

Br 2
11-4x13-10

open to below

Br 4
16-3x10-8
raised ceiling

Storage

PLAN DATA

Total Living Area: 2,733
Bedrooms: 4
Baths: 2 1/2
Garage: 2-car
Foundation Type:
   Basement
Features:
   9' ceilings throughout
   first floor

First Floor
1,514 sq. ft.

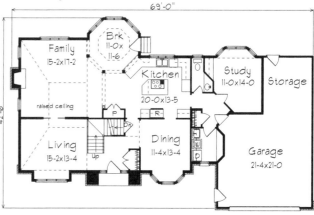

69'-0"

42'-6"

Family
15-2x17-2

Brk
11-0x11-6

Kitchen
20-0x13-5

Study
11-0x14-0

Storage

raised ceiling

Living
15-2x13-4

up

Dining
11-4x13-4

Garage
21-4x21-0

PLAN DATA

Total Living Area: 1,857
Bedrooms: 4
Baths: 3
Foundation Type:
   Slab

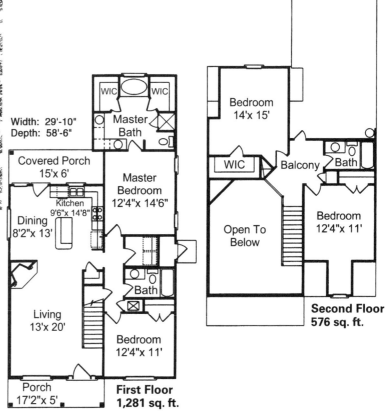

Width: 29'-10"
Depth: 58'-6"

WIC   WIC

Master
Bath

Bedroom
14'x 15'

Covered Porch
15'x 6'

Kitchen
9'6"x 14'8"

Master
Bedroom
12'4"x 14'6"

WIC   Balcony   Bath

Dining
8'2"x 13'

Open To
Below

Bedroom
12'4"x 11'

Bath

Living
13'x 20'

Bedroom
12'4"x 11'

Second Floor
576 sq. ft.

Porch
17'2"x 5'

First Floor
1,281 sq. ft.

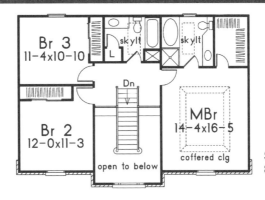

Second Floor
859 sq. ft.

PLAN DATA

Total Living Area: 1,996
Bedrooms: 3
Baths: 2 1/2
Garage: 2-car
Foundation Types:
   Basement standard
   Slab
   Crawl space
Features:
   9' ceilings throughout
   first floor

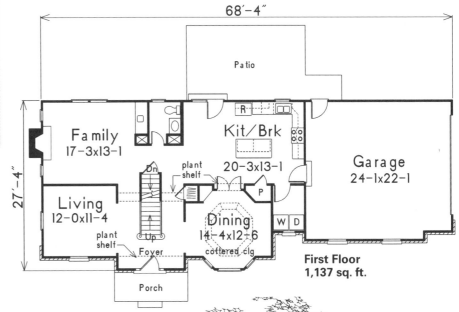

First Floor
1,137 sq. ft.

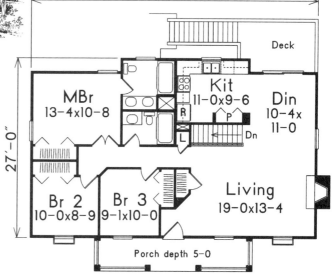

44'-0"

Deck

27'-0"

MBr
13-4x10-8

Kit
11-0x9-6

Din
10-4x
11-0

Br 2
10-0x8-9

Br 3
9-1x10-0

Living
19-0x13-4

Porch depth 5-0

PLAN DATA

Total Living Area:	1,140
Bedrooms:	3
Baths:	2
Garage:	2-car
Foundation Type:	
Basement	
Features:	
Drive-under garage	

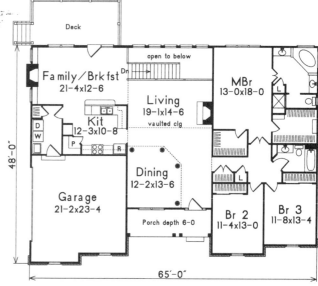

Deck

open to below

Family/Brkfst
21-4x12-6

Living
19-1x14-6
vaulted clg

MBr
13-0x18-0

Kit
12-3x10-8

48'-0"

Dining
12-2x13-6

Garage
21-2x23-4

Porch depth 6-0

Br 2
11-4x13-0

Br 3
11-8x13-4

65'-0"

PLAN DATA

Total Living Area:	2,308
Bedrooms:	3
Baths:	2
Garage:	2-car
Foundation Type:	
Walk-out basement	

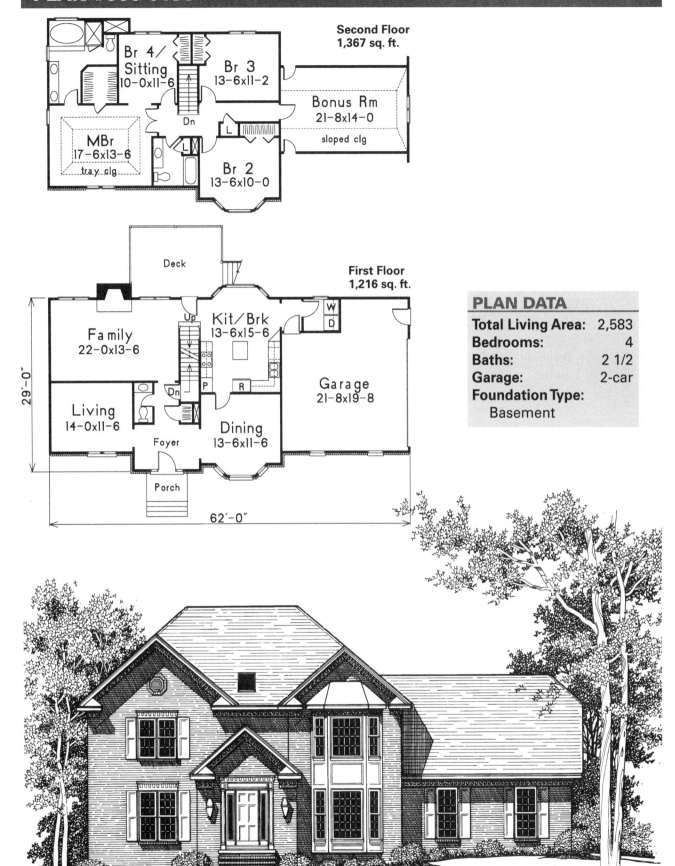

Second Floor
1,367 sq. ft.

Br 4/ Sitting
10-0x11-6

Br 3
13-6x11-2

Bonus Rm
21-8x14-0
sloped clg

MBr
17-6x13-6
tray clg

Dn

Br 2
13-6x10-0

First Floor
1,216 sq. ft.

Deck

Family
22-0x13-6

Up

Kit/Brk
13-6x15-6

W
D

Garage
21-8x19-8

Living
14-0x11-6

Dn

Dining
13-6x11-6

Foyer

Porch

29'-0"

62'-0"

PLAN DATA

Total Living Area:	2,583
Bedrooms:	4
Baths:	2 1/2
Garage:	2-car
Foundation Type:	Basement

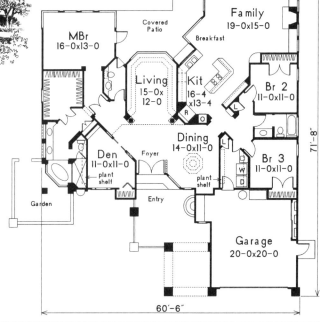

PLAN DATA

Total Living Area: 2,397
Bedrooms: 3
Baths: 2 1/2
Garage: 2-car
Foundation Type:
  Slab

PLAN #565-0741

Price Code B

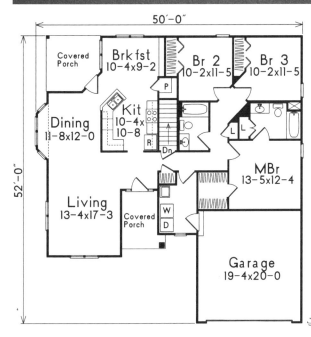

PLAN DATA

Total Living Area: 1,578
Bedrooms: 3
Baths: 2
Garage: 2-car
Foundation Type:
  Basement

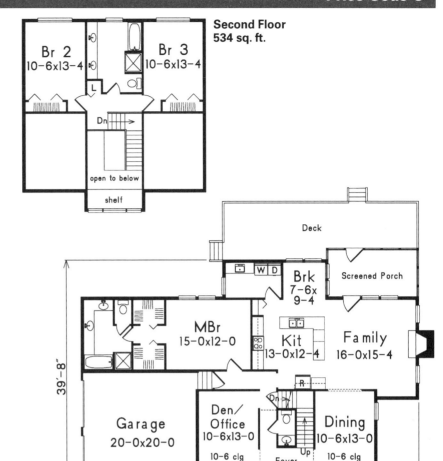

Second Floor
534 sq. ft.

Br 2
10-6x13-4

Br 3
10-6x13-4

L

Dn

open to below

shelf

PLAN DATA

Total Living Area: 2,043
Bedrooms: 3
Baths: 2 1/2
Garage: 2-car
Foundation Types:
 Basement standard
 Slab
Features:
 2" x 6" exterior walls

Deck

Brk
7-6x
9-4

Screened Porch

W D

MBr
15-0x12-0

Kit
13-0x12-4

Family
16-0x15-4

39'-8"

Garage
20-0x20-0

Den/
Office
10-6x13-0

10-6 clg

R

Dn

Foyer

Up

Dining
10-6x13-0

10-6 clg

Porch

60'-0"

First Floor
1,509 sq. ft.

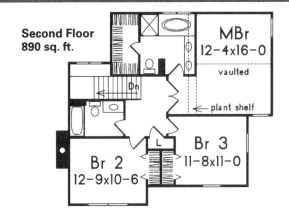

Second Floor 890 sq. ft.

MBr
12-4x16-0

vaulted

← plant shelf

Dn

Br 3
11-8x11-0

Br 2
12-9x10-6

L

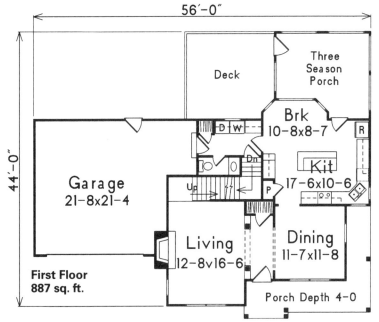

56'-0"

44'-0"

Deck

Three Season Porch

Brk
10-8x8-7

D W

Dn

R

Kit
17-6x10-6

Garage
21-8x21-4

Up

P

First Floor 887 sq. ft.

Living
12-8v16-6

Dining
11-7x11-8

Porch Depth 4-0

PLAN DATA

Total Living Area:	1,777
Bedrooms:	3
Baths:	2 1/2
Garage:	2-car
Foundation Type:	
Basement	

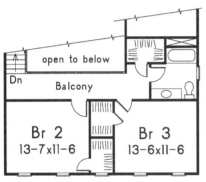

Second Floor
584 sq. ft.

Br 2
13-7x11-6

Br 3
13-6x11-6

open to below

Balcony

Dn

PLAN DATA

Total Living Area: 1,983
Bedrooms: 3
Baths: 2 1/2
Garage: 2-car
Foundation Type:
   Basement
Features:
   Drive-under garage

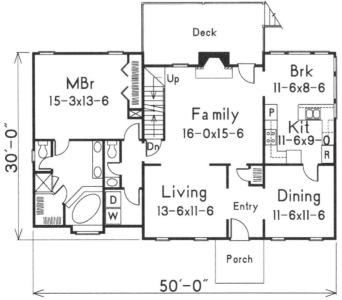

Deck

MBr
15-3x13-6

Up

Brk
11-6x8-6

Family
16-0x15-6

Kit
11-6x9-0

Dn

Living
13-6x11-6

Entry

Dining
11-6x11-6

Porch

30'-0"

50'-0"

First Floor
1,399 sq. ft.

PLAN DATA

Total Living Area: 2,003
Bedrooms: 3
Baths: 2
Garage: 2-car
Foundation Type:
  Basement
Features:
  10' ceiling in living
  room

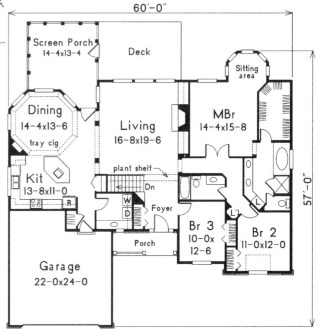

Screen Porch 14-4x13-4
Deck
Dining 14-4x13-6 tray clg
Living 16-8x19-6
MBr 14-4x15-8
Sitting area
Kit 13-8x11-0
plant shelf
Dn
Foyer
Br 3 10-0x 12-6
Br 2 11-0x12-0
Porch
Garage 22-0x24-0

60'-0"
57'-0"

PLAN DATA

Total Living Area: 1,643
Bedrooms: 3
Baths: 2
Garage: 2-car
Foundation Types:
  Basement standard
  Crawl space
  Slab

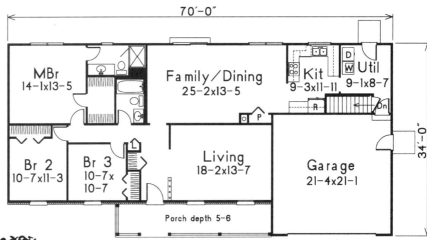

70'-0"
34'-0"

MBr 14-1x13-5
Family/Dining 25-2x13-5
Kit 9-3x11-11
Util 9-1x8-7
Br 2 10-7x11-3
Br 3 10-7x 10-7
Living 18-2x13-7
Garage 21-4x21-1
Dn
Porch depth 5-6

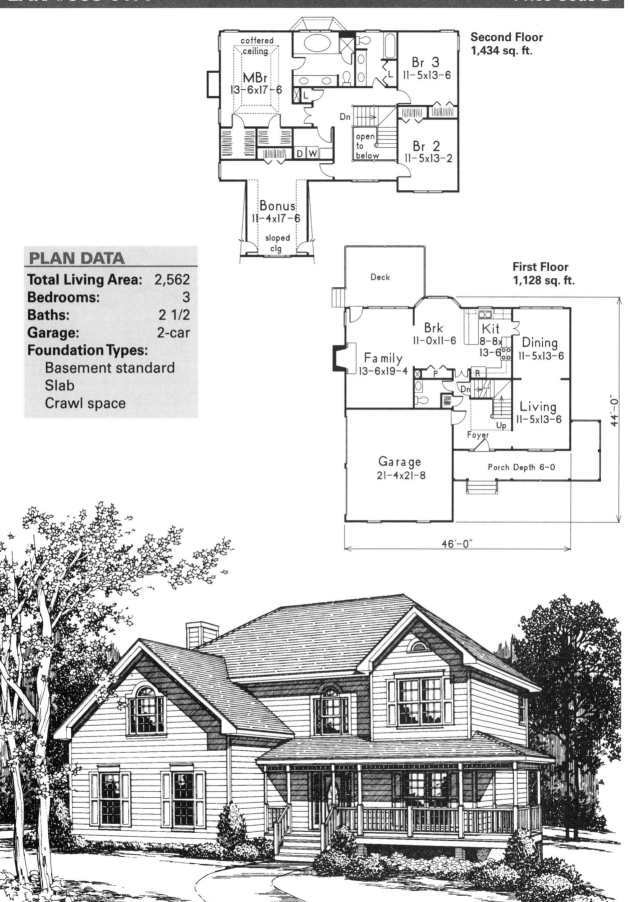

Second Floor
1,434 sq. ft.

coffered ceiling

MBr
13-6x17-6

Br 3
11-5x13-6

L

L

D W

Dn

open to below

Br 2
11-5x13-2

Bonus
11-4x17-6

sloped clg

PLAN DATA

Total Living Area: 2,562
Bedrooms: 3
Baths: 2 1/2
Garage: 2-car
Foundation Types:
  Basement standard
  Slab
  Crawl space

Deck

First Floor
1,128 sq. ft.

Brk
11-0x11-6

Kit
8-8x
13-6

Dining
11-5x13-6

Family
13-6x19-4

P

R

Dn

Living
11-5x13-6

Up

Foyer

Garage
21-4x21-8

Porch Depth 6-0

44'-0"

46'-0"

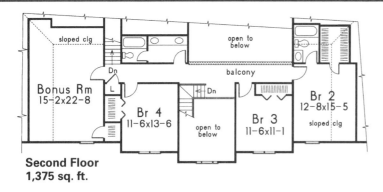

Second Floor
1,375 sq. ft.

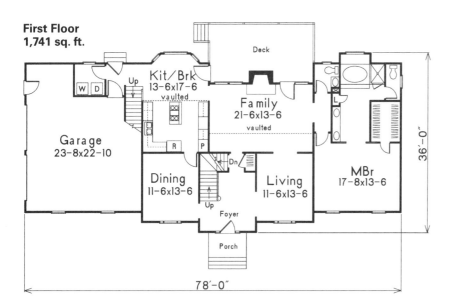

First Floor
1,741 sq. ft.

PLAN DATA

Total Living Area:	3,116
Bedrooms:	4
Baths:	3 1/2
Garage:	2-car
Foundation Type:	
Basement	

PLAN DATA

Total Living Area:	2,189
Bedrooms:	4
Baths:	2
Garage:	2-car

Foundation Types:
  Slab
  Crawl space
Please specify when ordering
Features:
  13' ceiling in foyer

PLAN DATA

Total Living Area:	2,380
Bedrooms:	4
Baths:	3
Garage:	2-car

Foundation Type:
  Slab

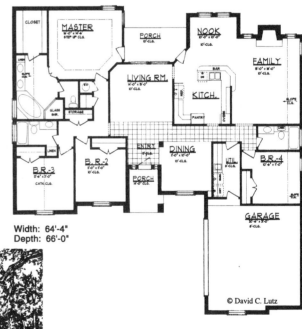

Width: 64'-4"
Depth: 66'-0"

© David C. Lutz

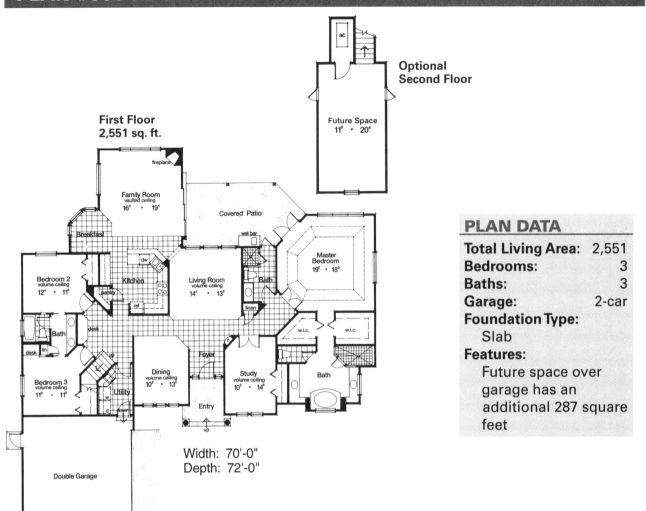

Optional Second Floor

Future Space
11⁰ • 20⁴

First Floor 2,551 sq. ft.

fireplace

Family Room
vaulted ceiling
16⁰ • 19⁴

Covered Patio

wet bar

Master Bedroom
19⁰ • 18⁰

Breakfast

dw

Kitchen

Living Room
volume ceiling
14⁴ • 13⁴

Bath

Bedroom 2
volume ceiling
12⁴ • 11⁰

pantry

ref

linen

Bath

desk

w.i.c.

w.i.c.

desk lin

up

Foyer

Dining
volume ceiling
10⁰ • 13⁰

Study
volume ceiling
10⁰ • 14⁴

Bath

Bedroom 3
volume ceiling
11⁰ • 11⁰

Utility

Entry

up

Double Garage

Width: 70'-0"
Depth: 72'-0"

PLAN DATA

Total Living Area: 2,551
Bedrooms: 3
Baths: 3
Garage: 2-car
Foundation Type:
   Slab
Features:
   Future space over
   garage has an
   additional 287 square
   feet

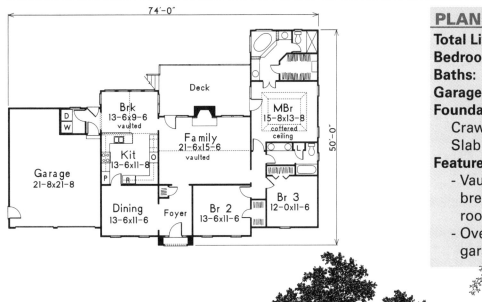

74'-0"

50'-0"

Garage
21-8x21-8

Brk
13-6x9-6
vaulted

Deck

MBr
15-8x13-8
coffered
ceiling

Kit
13-6x11-8

Family
21-6x15-6
vaulted

Dining
13-6x11-6

Foyer

Br 2
13-6x11-6

Br 3
12-0x11-6

PLAN DATA

Total Living Area:	1,908
Bedrooms:	3
Baths:	2
Garage:	2-car

Foundation Types:
Crawl space standard
Slab

Features:
- Vaulted ceilings in breakfast and family rooms
- Oversized two-car garage

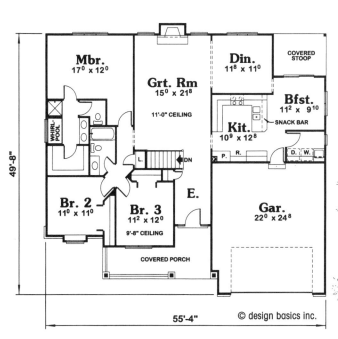

49'-8"

55'-4"

Mbr.
17⁰ x 12⁰

Grt. Rm
15⁰ x 21⁸
11'-0" CEILING

Din.
11⁸ x 11⁰

COVERED STOOP

Bfst.
11² x 9¹⁰

Kit.
10⁹ x 12⁸
SNACK BAR

WHIRL-POOL

L.

DN

P. R.

D. W.

Br. 2
11⁰ x 11⁰

Br. 3
11² x 12⁰
9'-8" CEILING

E.

Gar.
22⁰ x 24⁸

COVERED PORCH

© design basics inc.

PLAN DATA

Total Living Area:	1,758
Bedrooms:	3
Baths:	2
Garage:	2-car

Foundation Type:
Basement

Features:
11' ceiling in great room

PLAN DATA

Total Living Area: 1,400
Bedrooms: 3
Baths: 2
Garage: 2-car
Foundation Types:
Basement standard
Crawl space

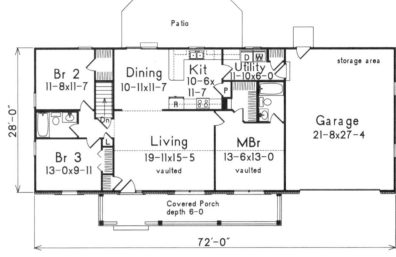

Patio

Br 2
11-8x11-7

Dining
10-11x11-7

Kit
10-6x11-7

Utility
11-10x6-0

D W

storage area

28'-0"

Dn

Br 3
13-0x9-11

Living
19-11x15-5
vaulted

MBr
13-6x13-0
vaulted

Garage
21-8x27-4

Covered Porch
depth 6-0

72'-0"

PLAN DATA

Total Living Area: 1,420
Bedrooms: 3
Baths: 2
Garage: 2-car
Foundation Types:
Crawl space
Slab
Please specify when ordering
Features:
- 2" x 6" exterior walls
- 12' ceiling in living room

6' HIGH WOOD PRIVACY FENCE

BATH

CLO.

MASTER SUITE
15' x 14'

BED RM.
13' x 12'

PORCH
10' x 10'

DINING
12' x 10'

BATH

HALL

LIVING
18' x 16'

KITCHEN
12' x 10'

UTIL
8' x 6'

STOR
12' x 5'

56'

BED RM.
13' x 12'

SLOPE CEILING

PORCH
12' x 6'

HEAT & AC

ATTIC STAIRS

GARAGE
22' x 21'

52'

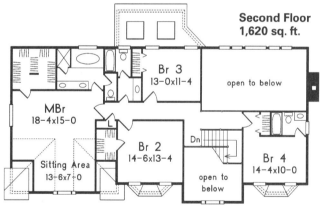

Second Floor
1,620 sq. ft.

Br 3
13-0x11-4

open to below

MBr
18-4x15-0

Br 2
14-6x13-4

Dn

Br 4
14-4x10-0

Sitting Area
13-6x7-0

open to below

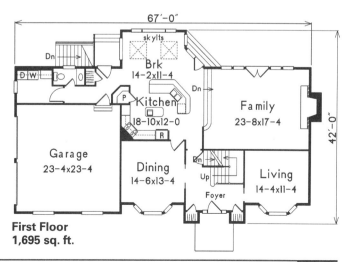

67'-0"

Dn

skylts

Brk
14-2x11-4

Dn

D W

Family
23-8x17-4

Kitchen
18-10x12-0

P

42'-0"

R

Garage
23-4x23-4

Dining
14-6x13-4

Dn

Up

Living
14-4x11-4

Foyer

First Floor
1,695 sq. ft.

PLAN DATA

Total Living Area: 3,315
Bedrooms: 4
Baths: 3 1/2
Garage: 2-car
Foundation Type:
Basement

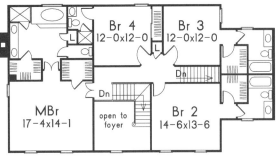

Second Floor
1,382 sq. ft.

Br 4
12-0x12-0

Br 3
12-0x12-0

MBr
17-4x14-1

open to foyer

Br 2
14-6x13-6

Dn

Dn

PLAN DATA

Total Living Area: 3,216
Bedrooms: 4
Baths: 4 1/2
Garage: 3-car
Foundation Type:
  Basement

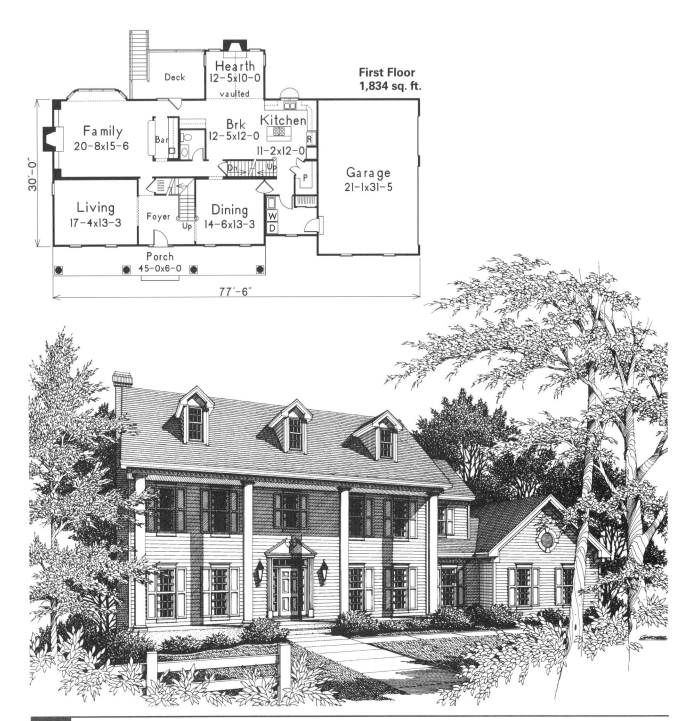

Deck

Hearth
12-5x10-0
vaulted

First Floor
1,834 sq. ft.

Family
20-8x15-6

Bar

Brk
12-5x12-0

Kitchen
11-2x12-0

R

Garage
21-1x31-5

Dn

Up

P

Living
17-4x13-3

Foyer

Up

Dining
14-6x13-3

W
D

Porch
45-0x6-0

30'-0"

77'-6"

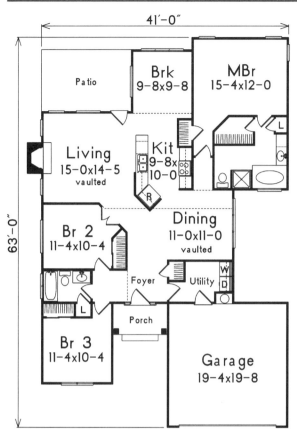

41'-0"

63'-0"

Patio

Brk
9-8x9-8

MBr
15-4x12-0

L

Living
15-0x14-5
vaulted

Kit
9-8x
10-0

R

Br 2
11-4x10-4

Dining
11-0x11-0
vaulted

Foyer

Utility

W
D

L

Porch

Br 3
11-4x10-4

Garage
19-4x19-8

PLAN DATA
Total Living Area: 1,560
Bedrooms: 3
Baths: 2
Garage: 2-car
Foundation Type:
Slab

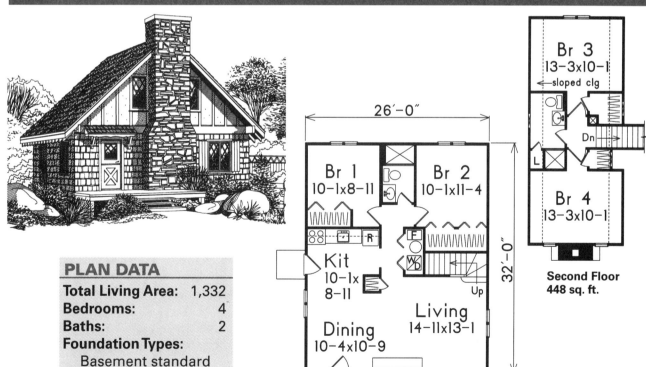

PLAN DATA
Total Living Area: 1,332
Bedrooms: 4
Baths: 2
Foundation Types:
Basement standard
Slab
Crawl space

26'-0"

Br 1
10-1x8-11

Br 2
10-1x11-4

R

F

W
D

Kit
10-1x
8-11

Up

Living
14-11x13-1

32'-0"

Dining
10-4x10-9

Deck

First Floor
832 sq. ft.

Br 3
13-3x10-1
←sloped clg

L

Dn

Br 4
13-3x10-1

Second Floor
448 sq. ft.

FOURNIER INC. #40

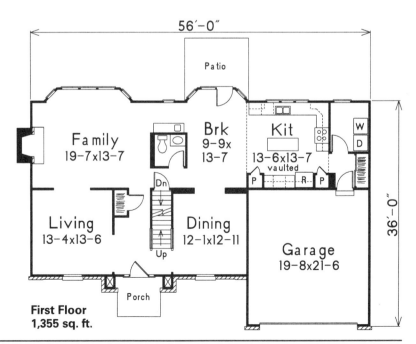

Second Floor
1,046 sq. ft.

vaulted

Br 3
12-1x11-0

MBr
15-0x17-0

Dn

Br 2
12-1x10-4

PLAN DATA

Total Living Area: 2,401
Bedrooms: 3
Baths: 2 1/2
Garage: 2-car
Foundation Types:
　Basement standard
　Slab
　Crawl space

56'-0"

Patio

Family
19-7x13-7

Brk
9-9x
13-7

Kit
13-6x13-7
vaulted

W
D

P　R　P

Dn

Living
13-4x13-6

Dining
12-1x12-11

Garage
19-8x21-6

Up

Porch

36'-0"

First Floor
1,355 sq. ft.

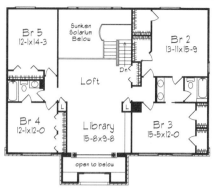

Second Floor
1,544 sq. ft.

PLAN DATA

Total Living Area:	3,850
Bedrooms:	5
Baths:	3 1/2
Garage:	3-car
Foundation Type:	
Basement	

First Floor
2,306 sq. ft.

Interior View

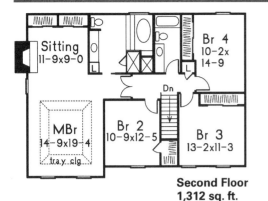

Second Floor
1,312 sq. ft.

71'-0"

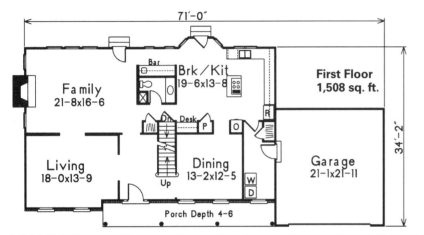

First Floor
1,508 sq. ft.

34'-2"

Porch Depth 4-6

PLAN DATA

Total Living Area: 2,820
Bedrooms: 4
Baths: 2 1/2
Garage: 2-car
Foundation Types:
  Basement standard
  Slab
  Crawl space

PLAN DATA

Total Living Area: 2,437
Bedrooms: 3
Baths: 2
Garage: 2-car
Foundation Types:
  Slab standard
  Crawl space

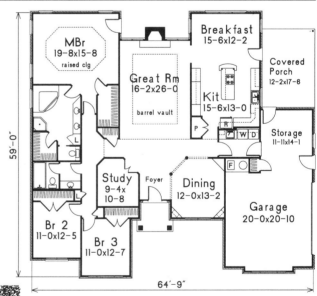

59'-0"

64'-9"

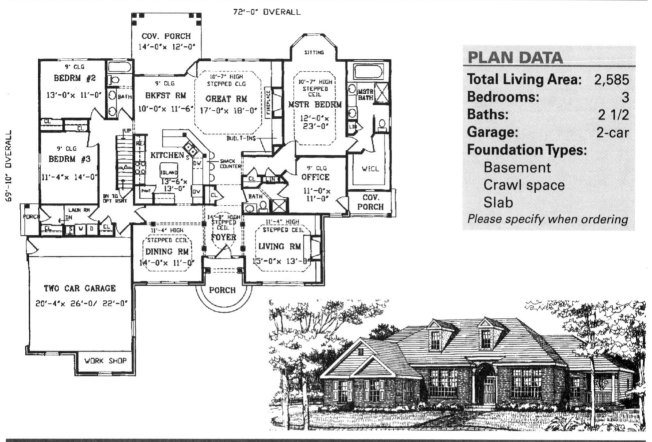

72'-0" OVERALL

COV. PORCH
14'-0"x 12'-0"

9' CLG
BEDRM #2
13'-0"x 11'-0"

BATH

9' CLG
BKFST RM
10'-0"x 11'-6"

10'-7" HIGH
STEPPED CLG
GREAT RM
17'-0"x 18'-0"

SITTING

FIREPLACE

10'-7" HIGH
STEPPED
CEIL
MSTR BEDRM
12'-0"x
23'-0"

MSTR
BATH

BUILT-INS

9' CLG
BEDRM #3
11'-4"x 14'-0"

69'-10" OVERALL

UP

KITCHEN

ISLAND
13'-6"x
13'-0"

DW

SNACK
COUNTER

DN TO
OPT BSMT

PANT

OV

9' CLG
OFFICE
11'-0"x
11'-0"

W.I.CL

COV.
PORCH

BATH

LAUN RM
DN

PORCH

CL

W

D

CL

11'-4" HIGH
STEPPED CEIL
DINING RM
14'-0"x 11'-0"

14'-0" HIGH
STEPPED
CEIL
FOYER

11'-4" HIGH
STEPPED CEIL
LIVING RM
15'-0"x 13'-0"

TWO CAR GARAGE
20'-4"x 26'-0/ 22'-0"

PORCH

WORK SHOP

PLAN DATA

Total Living Area: 2,585
Bedrooms: 3
Baths: 2 1/2
Garage: 2-car
Foundation Types:
  Basement
  Crawl space
  Slab
Please specify when ordering

PLAN DATA

Total Living Area: 1,915
Bedrooms: 4
Baths: 3
Garage: 2-car
Foundation Types:
  Basement
  Crawl space
Please specify when ordering

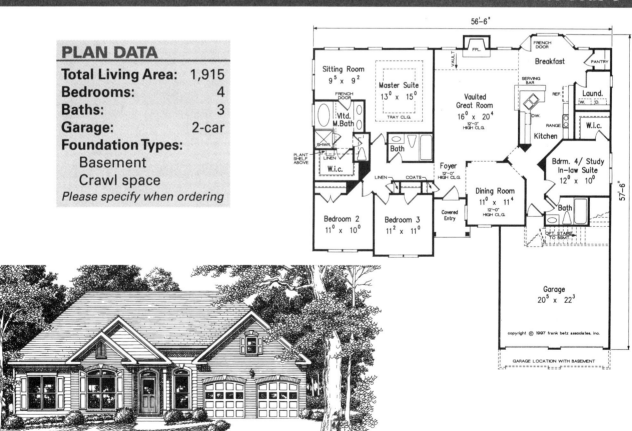

56'-6"

Sitting Room
9^5 x 9^2

FPL.

FRENCH
DOOR

Breakfast

PANTRY

FRENCH
DOOR

Master Suite
13^0 x 15^0
TRAY CLG.

VAULT

Vaulted
Great Room
16^0 x 20^4
12'-0"
HIGH CLG.

SERVING
BAR

REF.

Laund.
W. D.

Mtd.
M.Bath

SHWR

PLANT
SHELF
ABOVE

LINEN

W.i.c.

Bath

DW

RANGE

Kitchen

W.i.c.

Foyer
12'-0"
HIGH CLG.

LINEN

COATS

Bdrm. 4/ Study
In-law Suite
12^0 x 10^0

57'-6"

Bedroom 2
11^0 x 10^0

Bedroom 3
11^2 x 11^0

Covered
Entry

Dining Room
11^0 x 11^4
12'-0"
HIGH CLG.

Bath

OPT. STAIRS
TO BSMT.

Garage
20^5 x 22^3

copyright © 1997 frank betz associates, inc.

GARAGE LOCATION WITH BASEMENT

PLAN DATA

Total Living Area: 2,066
Bedrooms: 3
Baths: 2 1/2
Foundation Type:
  Slab

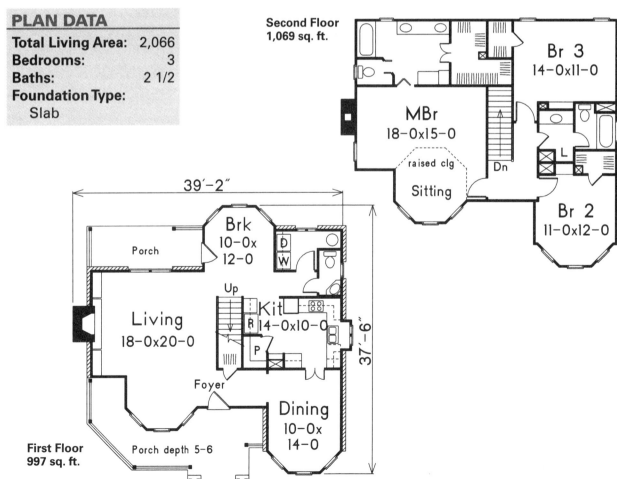

Second Floor
1,069 sq. ft.

Br 3
14-0x11-0

MBr
18-0x15-0

raised clg

Dn

Sitting

Br 2
11-0x12-0

39'-2"

Brk
10-0x
12-0

Porch

D

W

Up

Kit
14-0x10-0

R

Living
18-0x20-0

P

37'-6"

Foyer

Dining
10-0x
14-0

First Floor
997 sq. ft.

Porch depth 5-6

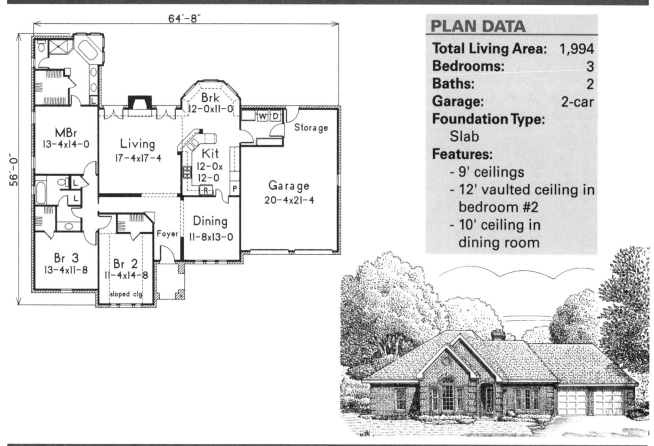

64′-8″

56′-0″

MBr
13-4x14-0

Living
17-4x17-4

Brk
12-0x11-0

Kit
12-0x
12-0

W D

Storage

Garage
20-4x21-4

Dining
11-8x13-0

Foyer

Br 3
13-4x11-8

Br 2
11-4x14-8

sloped clg.

PLAN DATA

Total Living Area:	1,994
Bedrooms:	3
Baths:	2
Garage:	2-car

Foundation Type:
Slab

Features:
- 9' ceilings
- 12' vaulted ceiling in bedroom #2
- 10' ceiling in dining room

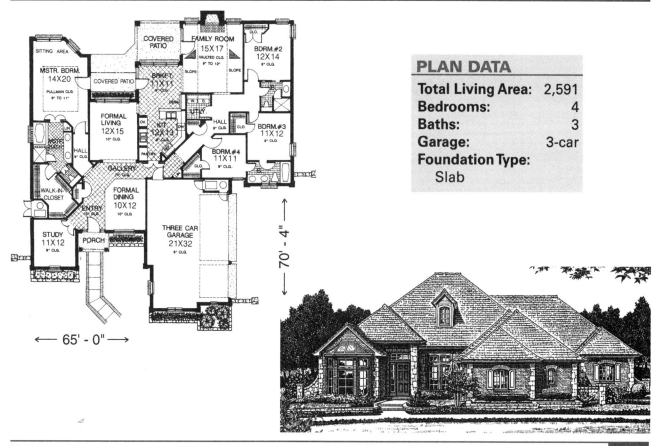

SITTING AREA

MSTR. BDRM.
14X20

PULLMAN CLG.
9' TO 11'

COVERED PATIO

COVERED
PATIO

FAMILY ROOM
15X17

VAULTED CLG.
9' TO 12'

SLOPE

SLOPE

BDRM.#2
12X14

9' CLG.

FORMAL
LIVING
12X15

10' CLG.

BRKFT.
11X11

KIT
12X13

UTLY.

W.D.

HALL

BDRM.#3
11X12

9' CLG.

MSTR
BATH

HALL
9' CLG.

GALLERY
10' CLG.

BDRM.#4
11X11

9' CLG.

WALK-IN
CLOSET

FORMAL
DINING
10X12

10' CLG.

ENTRY
10' CLG.

STUDY
11X12

9' CLG.

PORCH

THREE CAR
GARAGE
21X32

8' CLG.

65' - 0"

70' - 4"

PLAN DATA

Total Living Area:	2,591
Bedrooms:	4
Baths:	3
Garage:	3-car

Foundation Type:
Slab

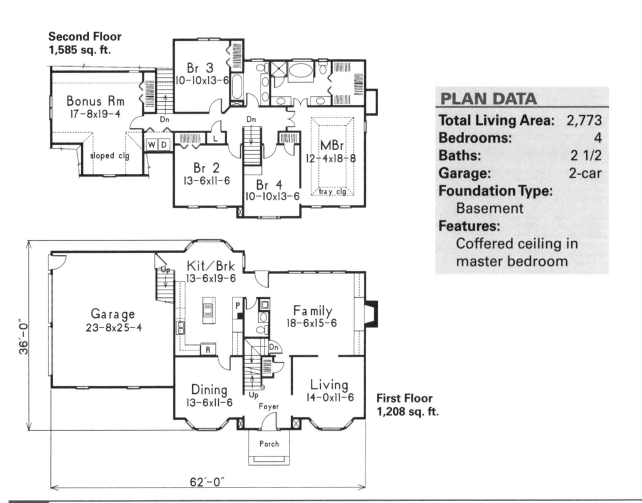

Second Floor
1,585 sq. ft.

Bonus Rm
17-8x19-4

sloped clg

Br 3
10-10x13-6

W D

L

Br 2
13-6x11-6

Br 4
10-10x13-6

MBr
12-4x18-8

tray clg

Dn

Dn

Garage
23-8x25-4

Up

Kit/Brk
13-6x19-6

P

Family
18-6x15-6

R

Dn

Dining
13-6x11-6

Up

Foyer

Living
14-0x11-6

Porch

36'-0"

62'-0"

First Floor
1,208 sq. ft.

PLAN DATA

Total Living Area: 2,773
Bedrooms: 4
Baths: 2 1/2
Garage: 2-car
Foundation Type:
   Basement
Features:
   Coffered ceiling in
   master bedroom

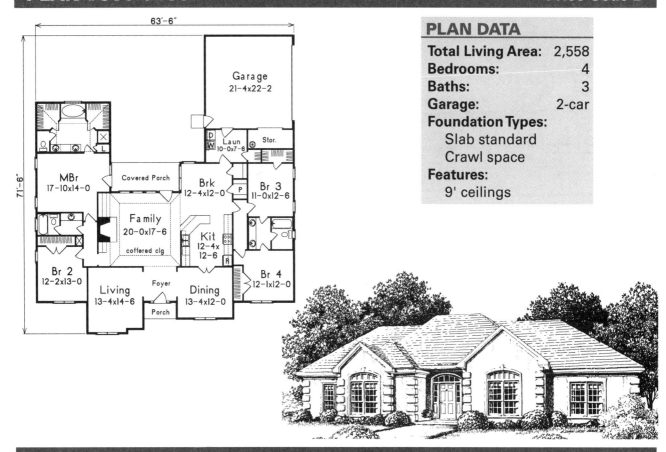

63'-6"

71'-6"

Garage
21-4x22-2

MBr
17-10x14-0

Covered Porch

Laun
10-0x7-6

D
W

Stor.

Brk
12-4x12-0

Br 3
11-0x12-6

P

Family
20-0x17-6
coffered clg

Kit
12-4x
12-6

Br 2
12-2x13-0

Living
13-4x14-6

Foyer

Dining
13-4x12-0

Br 4
12-1x12-0

Porch

PLAN DATA

Total Living Area: 2,558
Bedrooms: 4
Baths: 3
Garage: 2-car
Foundation Types:
  Slab standard
  Crawl space
Features:
  9' ceilings

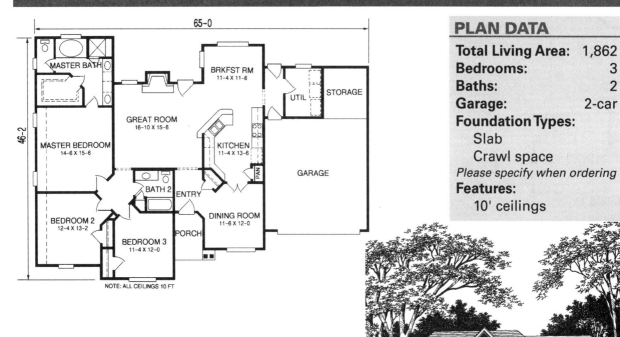

65-0

46-2

MASTER BATH

BRKFST RM
11-4 X 11-6

UTIL

STORAGE

GREAT ROOM
16-10 X 15-6

KITCHEN
11-4 X 13-6

MASTER BEDROOM
14-6 X 15-6

PAN

GARAGE

BATH 2

ENTRY

BEDROOM 2
12-4 X 13-2

DINING ROOM
11-6 X 12-0

BEDROOM 3
11-4 X 12-0

PORCH

NOTE: ALL CEILINGS 10 FT

PLAN DATA

Total Living Area: 1,862
Bedrooms: 3
Baths: 2
Garage: 2-car
Foundation Types:
  Slab
  Crawl space
  Please specify when ordering
Features:
  10' ceilings

PLAN #565-0512

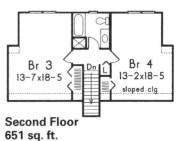

Second Floor
651 sq. ft.

Br 3
13-7x18-5

Dn

Br 4
13-2x18-5
sloped clg

PLAN DATA

Total Living Area: 1,827
Bedrooms: 4
Baths: 2
Garage: 2-car
Foundation Types:
   Crawl space standard
   Basement
   Slab

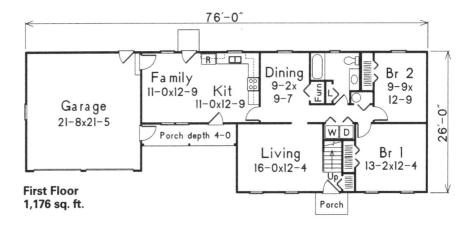

76'-0"

26'-0"

Garage
21-8x21-5

Family
11-0x12-9

Kit
11-0x12-9

Dining
9-2x 9-7

Fun

Br 2
9-9x 12-9

Porch depth 4-0

Living
16-0x12-4

Br 1
13-2x12-4

W D

Up

Porch

First Floor
1,176 sq. ft.

PLAN #565-JA-53394

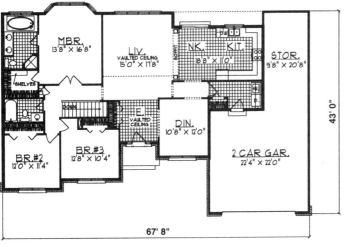

MBR.
13'8" X 16'8"

LIV.
VAULTED CEILING
15'0" X 17'8"

NK.
10'8" X 11'0"

KIT.

STOR.
9'8" X 20'8"

SHELVES

DOWN

E.
VAULTED CEILING

DIN.
10'8" X 12'0"

2 CAR GAR.
22'4" X 22'0"

BR.#2
12'0" X 11'4"

BR.#3
12'8" X 10'4"

43' 0"

67' 8"

PLAN DATA

Total Living Area: 1,763
Bedrooms: 3
Baths: 2
Garage: 2-car
Foundation Type:
   Basement

76   TO ORDER BLUEPRINTS USE THE FORM ON **PAGE 9** OR CALL TOLL-FREE **1-800-DREAM HOME** (373-2646)

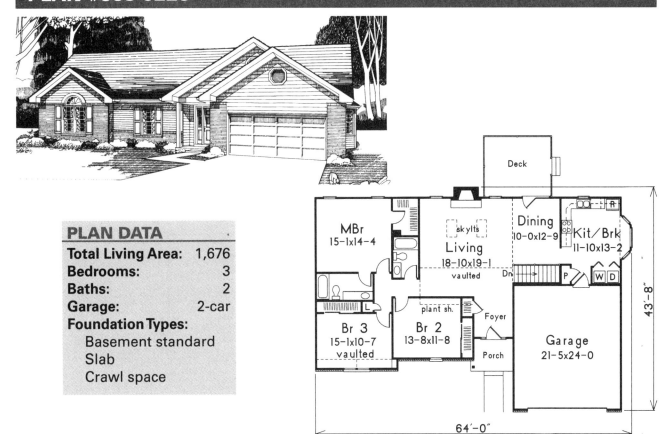

PLAN DATA

Total Living Area: 1,676
Bedrooms: 3
Baths: 2
Garage: 2-car
Foundation Types:
Basement standard
Slab
Crawl space

PLAN DATA

Total Living Area: 2,164
Bedrooms: 3
Baths: 2 1/2
Garage: 2-car
Foundation Type:
Basement

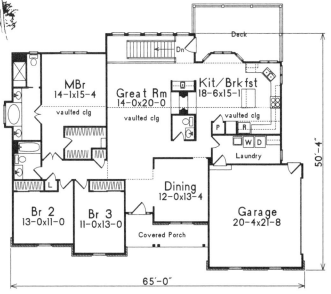

PLAN DATA

Total Living Area: 2,838
Bedrooms: 4
Baths: 2 1/2
Garage: 3-car
Foundation Type:
Basement
Features:
- 10' ceilings through-out first floor
- Vaulted ceiling in living room

Second Floor 1,236 sq. ft.

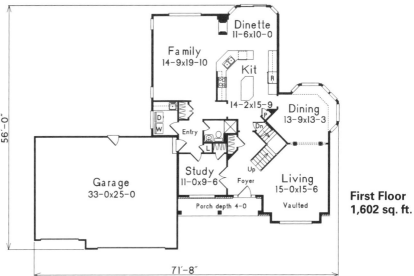

First Floor 1,602 sq. ft.

PLAN DATA

Total Living Area: 977
Bedrooms: 2
Baths: 1 1/2
Garage: 1-car
Foundation Type:
 Basement
Features:
 Vaulted ceiling in
 living room

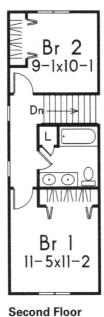

Second Floor
432 sq. ft.

Br 2
9–1x10–1

Dn

L

Br 1
11–5x11–2

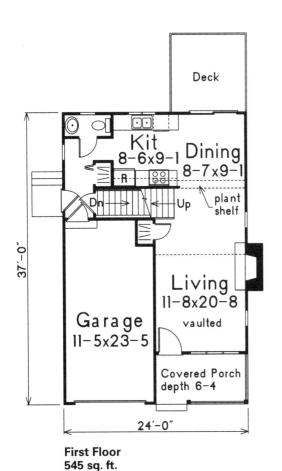

Deck

Kit
8–6x9–1

Dining
8–7x9–1

R

Dn

Up

plant shelf

37'–0"

Living
11–8x20–8
vaulted

Garage
11–5x23–5

Covered Porch
depth 6–4

24'–0"

First Floor
545 sq. ft.

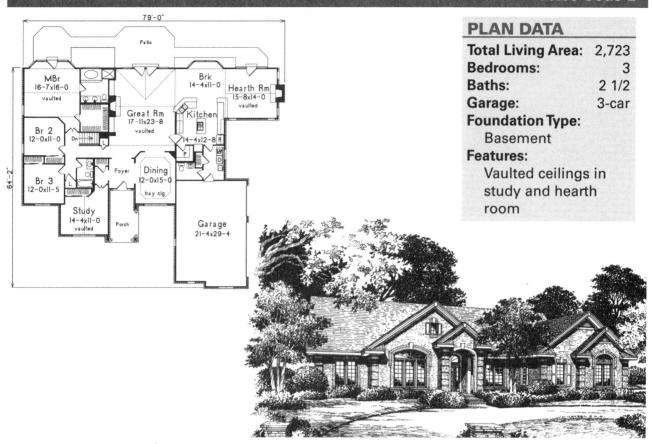

PLAN DATA

Total Living Area: 2,723
Bedrooms: 3
Baths: 2 1/2
Garage: 3-car
Foundation Type:
Basement
Features:
Vaulted ceilings in study and hearth room

PLAN DATA

Total Living Area: 2,729
Bedrooms: 3
Baths: 2 1/2
Garage: 2-car
Foundation Types:
Plan #565-1289-1
Basement
Plan #565-1289-2
Crawl space & slab

Width: 70'-10"
Depth: 64'-10"

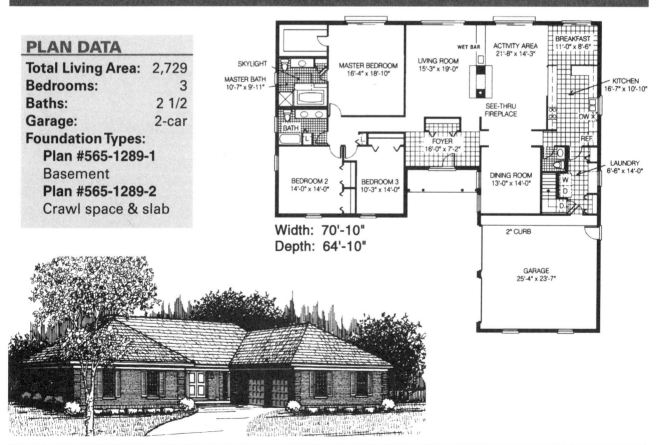

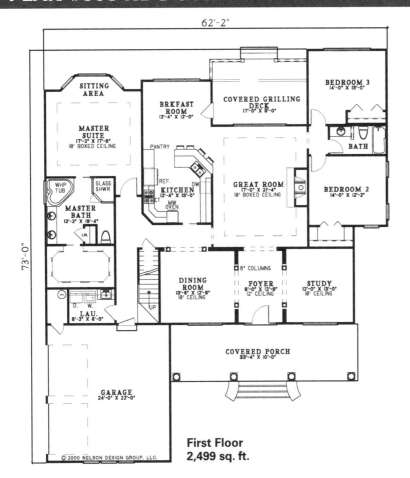

62'-2"

73'-0"

SITTING AREA

MASTER SUITE
17'-2" X 17'-8"
10' BOXED CEILING

BRKFAST ROOM
12'-4" X 12'-0"

COVERED GRILLING DECK
17'-0" X 8'-0"

BEDROOM 3
14'-0" X 13'-0"

BATH

PANTRY

WHP TUB

GLASS SHWR

MASTER BATH
12'-2" X 19'-4"

KITCHEN
12'-4" X 13'-0"

REF.

DW

MW OVEN

GREAT ROOM
17'-0" X 21'-4"
10' BOXED CEILING

BEDROOM 2
14'-0" X 12'-2"

LIN.

D. W.

LAU.
8'-2" X 6'-0"

UP

8' COLUMNS

DINING ROOM
13'-6" X 12'-8"
10' CEILING

FOYER
8'-0" X 12'-8"
12' CEILING

STUDY
12'-0" X 13'-0"
10' CEILING

COVERED PORCH
33'-4" X 10'-0"

GARAGE
24'-0" X 22'-0"

© 2000 NELSON DESIGN GROUP, LLC.

First Floor
2,499 sq. ft.

5' WALL

8' LINE

BONUS ROOM
20'-2" X 20'-10"

8' LINE

DN.

5' WALL

Optional
Second Floor

PLAN DATA

Total Living Area: 2,499
Bedrooms: 4
Baths: 2
Garage: 2-car
Foundation Types:
  Crawl space
  Slab
Please specify when ordering
Features:
  10' ceilings in study,
  great room and
  dining room

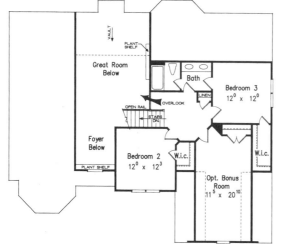

Second Floor
558 sq. ft.

Great Room Below

VAULT.

PLANT SHELF

Bath

Bedroom 3
12⁰ x 12⁰

LINEN

OPEN RAIL

OVERLOOK

STAIRS DN.

Foyer Below

Bedroom 2
12⁰ x 12³

W.i.c.

W.i.c.

PLANT SHELF

Opt. Bonus Room
11⁵ x 20¹⁰

54'-0"

RADIUS WINDOW

TRANSOM ABOVE

FPL

TRANSOM ABOVE

FRENCH DOOR

SEAT

SHWR

Vaulted M.Bath
13'-0" HIGH CLG.

Vaulted Great Room
15⁰ x 19⁰

Breakfast

Bedroom 4/ Study
11⁶ x 11⁰

PLANT SHELF ABOVE

FRENCH DOOR

W.S.

His

Hers

LINEN

PLANT SHELF ABOVE

SERVING BAR

ISLAND

DW.

RANGE

PANTRY

Bath

PLANT SHELF ABOVE

Kitchen

REF.

Laund.

TRAY CLG.

OPEN RAIL

STAIRS DN.

STAIRS DN.

COATS

SINK

W. D.

Master Suite
13⁰ x 15⁰

Two Story Foyer

Dining Room
12⁰ x 12³

Sitting Area
11⁰ x 6⁵

Covered Entry

Garage
19⁵ x 22³

48'-0"

copyright © 1998 frank betz associates, inc.

First Floor
1,688 sq. ft.

PLAN DATA

Total Living Area:	2,246
Bedrooms:	4
Baths:	3
Garage:	2-car

Foundation Types:
   Crawl space
   Basement
Please specify when ordering

Features:
   Optional bonus room
   has an additional 269
   square feet of living
   area

PLAN #565-0478

PLAN DATA

Total Living Area: 1,092
Bedrooms: 3
Baths: 1 1/2
Garage: 1-car
Foundation Type:
  Basement

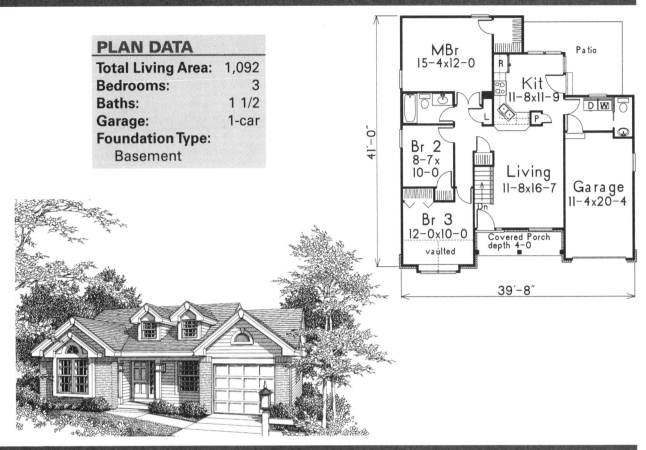

PLAN #565-JFD-10-1456-2

PLAN DATA

Total Living Area: 1,456
Bedrooms: 3
Baths: 2
Garage: 2-car
Foundation Type:
  Basement

Width: 49'-0"
Depth: 51'-8"

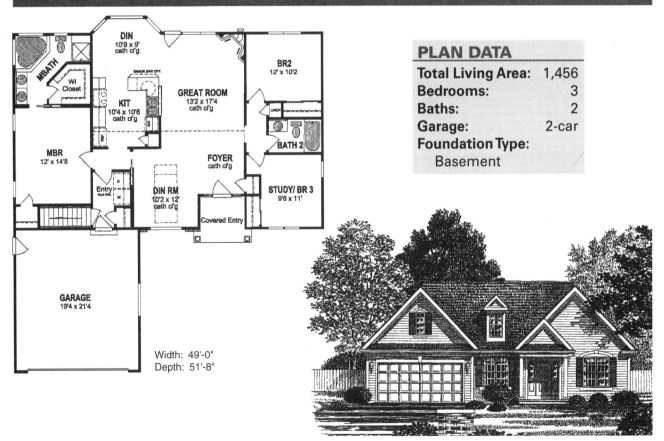

PLAN #565-0135

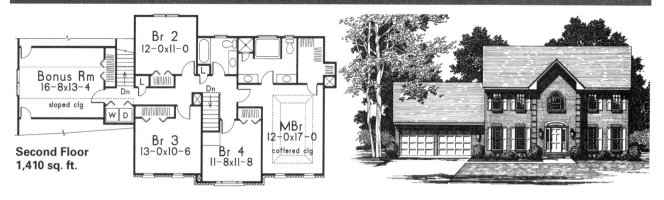

**Second Floor
1,410 sq. ft.**

Bonus Rm
16-8x13-4
sloped clg

Br 2
12-0x11-0

Br 3
13-0x10-6

Br 4
11-8x11-8

MBr
12-0x17-0
coffered clg

Dn

W D

L

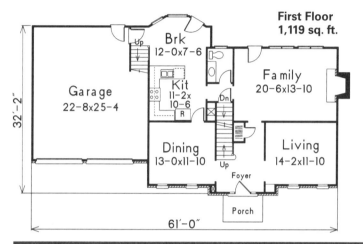

**First Floor
1,119 sq. ft.**

Garage
22-8x25-4

32'-2"

Up

Brk
12-0x7-6

Kit
11-2x
10-6
R

Dining
13-0x11-10

Up

Foyer

Family
20-6x13-10

Dn

Living
14-2x11-10

Porch

61'-0"

PLAN DATA

Total Living Area:	2,529
Bedrooms:	4
Baths:	2 1/2
Garage:	2-car
Foundation Type:	
Basement	

PLAN #565-DDI-98-106

PLAN DATA

Total Living Area:	1,588
Bedrooms:	3
Baths:	2
Garage:	2-car
Foundation Type:	
Basement	
Features:	
14' ceiling in vaulted great room	

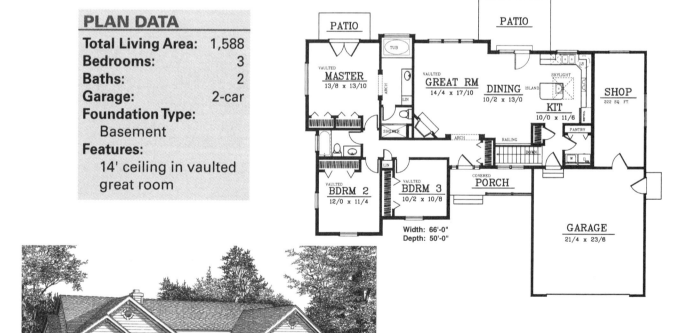

PATIO

PATIO

VAULTED
MASTER
13/8 x 13/10

TUB

VAULTED
GREAT RM
14/4 x 17/10

DINING
10/2 x 13/0

ISLAND

SKYLIGHT

KIT
10/0 x 11/6

SHOP
222 SQ. FT.

PANTRY

ARCH

LIN

SHOWER

ARCH

RAILING

DOWN

VAULTED
BDRM 2
12/0 x 11/4

LIN

VAULTED
BDRM 3
10/2 x 10/8

COVERED
PORCH

GARAGE
21/4 x 23/6

**Width: 66'-0"
Depth: 50'-0"**

Second Floor
690 sq. ft.

Br.#4
10x12

Br.#3
10x12

Br.#2
12x12/6

Attic

Roof

Roof

Down

Plant Ledge

Foyer Below

Attic

PLAN DATA

Total Living Area: 2,008
Bedrooms: 4
Baths: 2 1/2
Garage: 2-car
Foundation Type:
  Basement
Features:
  15' ceiling in family
  room

First Floor
1,318 sq. ft.

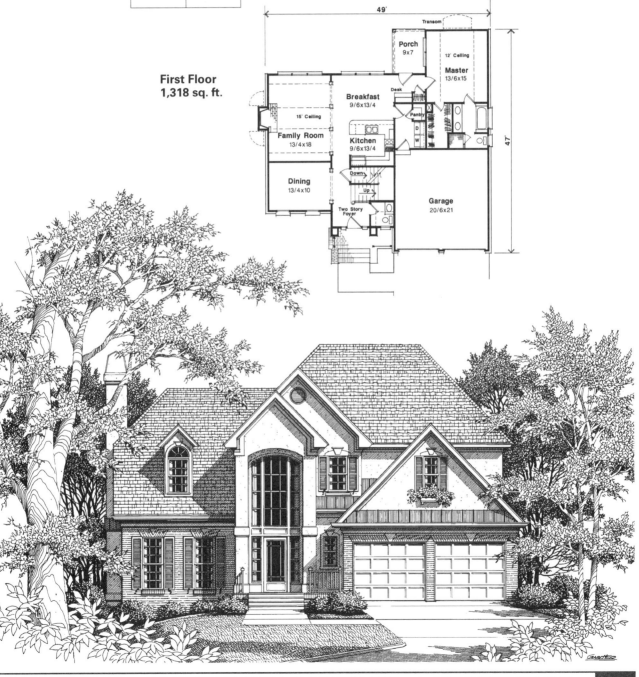

49'

47'

Transom

Porch
9x7

12' Ceiling

Master
13/6x15

Breakfast
9/6x13/4

Desk

Pantry

15' Ceiling

Family Room
13/4x18

Kitchen
9/6x13/4

D W

Dining
13/4x10

Down

Up

Two Story
Foyer

Garage
20/6x21

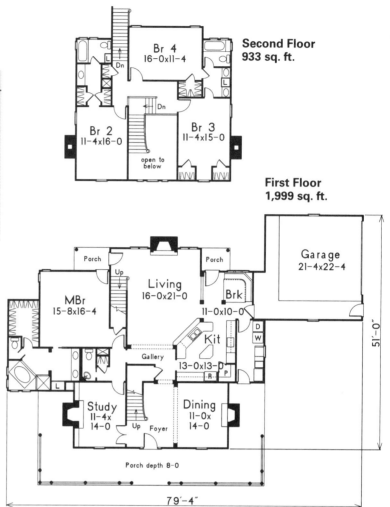

Second Floor
933 sq. ft.

Br 4
16-0x11-4

Br 2
11-4x16-0

Br 3
11-4x15-0

open to
below

First Floor
1,999 sq. ft.

PLAN DATA

Total Living Area: 2,932
Bedrooms: 4
Baths: 3 1/2
Garage: 2-car
Foundation Type:
  Slab
Features:
  9' ceilings

Garage
21-4x22-4

Porch

Porch

Living
16-0x21-0

Brk
11-0x10-0

MBr
15-8x16-4

Kit
13-0x13-0

Gallery

Study
11-4x
14-0

Dining
11-0x
14-0

Foyer

Porch depth 8-0

51'-0"

79'-4"

PLAN DATA

Total Living Area: 2,900
Bedrooms: 4
Baths: 2 1/2
Garage: 3-car
Foundation Type:
　Walk-out basement
Features:
　1,018 square feet of
　optional living area
　on lower level

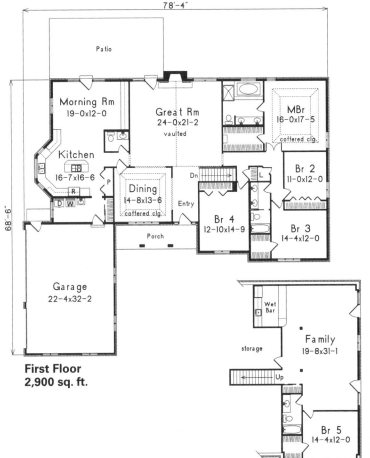

First Floor
2,900 sq. ft.

Optional
Lower Level

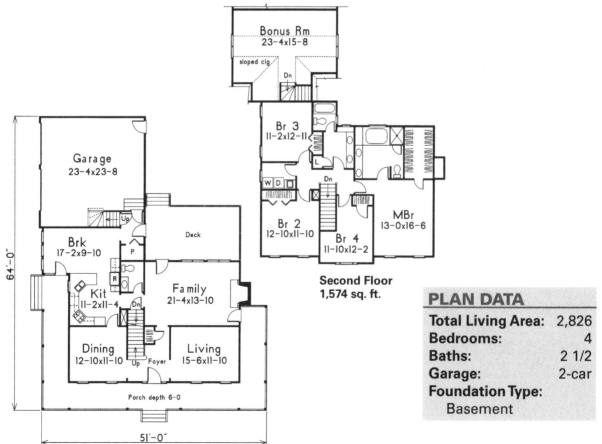

Bonus Rm
23-4x15-8

sloped clg.

Dn

Br 3
11-2x12-11

W D

Dn

Br 2
12-10x11-10

Br 4
11-10x12-2

MBr
13-0x16-6

Second Floor
1,574 sq. ft.

Garage
23-4x23-8

Up

Deck

Brk
17-2x9-10

P

Kit
11-2x11-4

R

Family
21-4x13-10

Dn

Dining
12-10x11-10

Up

Foyer

Living
15-6x11-10

64'-0"

Porch depth 6-0

51'-0"

First Floor
1,252 sq. ft.

PLAN DATA

Total Living Area:	2,826
Bedrooms:	4
Baths:	2 1/2
Garage:	2-car
Foundation Type:	
Basement	

PLAN DATA

Total Living Area:	1,958
Bedrooms:	3
Baths:	2
Garage:	2-car
Foundation Type:	
Basement	

PLAN #565-HDS-2454

Price Code D

PLAN DATA

Total Living Area:	2,458
Bedrooms:	4
Baths:	3
Garage:	2-car
Foundation Type:	
Slab	

Width: 65'-0"
Depth: 56'-8"

PLAN DATA

Total Living Area: 1,854
Bedrooms: 3
Baths: 2 1/2
Garage: 2-car
Foundation Type:
  Basement
Features:
  Sloped ceilings in
  family room

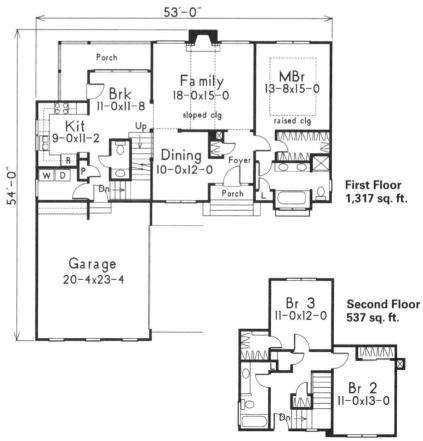

Porch

Brk
11-0x11-8

Family
18-0x15-0
sloped clg

MBr
13-8x15-0
raised clg

Kit
9-0x11-2

Up

Dining
10-0x12-0

Foyer

Dn

Porch

First Floor
1,317 sq. ft.

Garage
20-4x23-4

53'-0"

54'-0"

Br 3
11-0x12-0

Second Floor
537 sq. ft.

Br 2
11-0x13-0

Dn

PLAN DATA

Total Living Area: 2,967
Bedrooms: 4
Baths: 3 1/2
Garage: 3-car
Foundation Type:
Basement

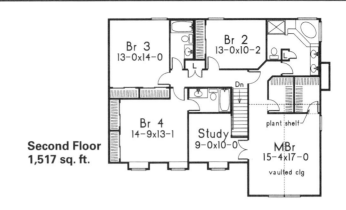

Second Floor
1,517 sq. ft.

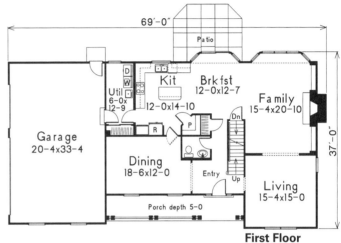

First Floor
1,450 sq. ft.

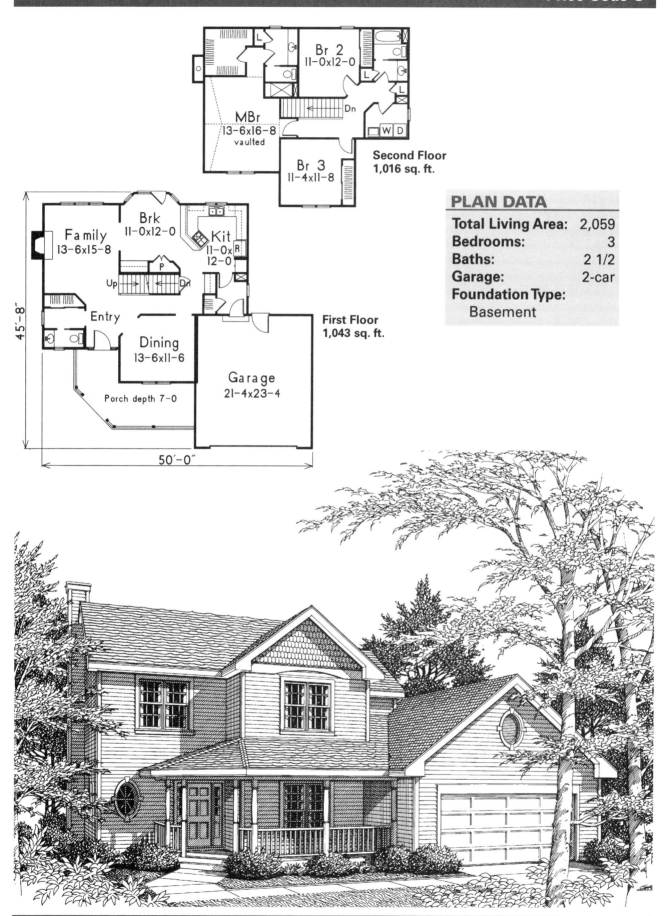

Br 2
11-0x12-0

MBr
13-6x16-8
vaulted

Dn

W D

Br 3
11-4x11-8

**Second Floor
1,016 sq. ft.**

Brk
11-0x12-0

Family
13-6x15-8

Kit
11-0x
12-0

R

P

Up

Dn

Entry

Dining
13-6x11-6

45'-8"

Porch depth 7-0

Garage
21-4x23-4

**First Floor
1,043 sq. ft.**

50'-0"

PLAN DATA

Total Living Area:	2,059
Bedrooms:	3
Baths:	2 1/2
Garage:	2-car
Foundation Type: Basement	

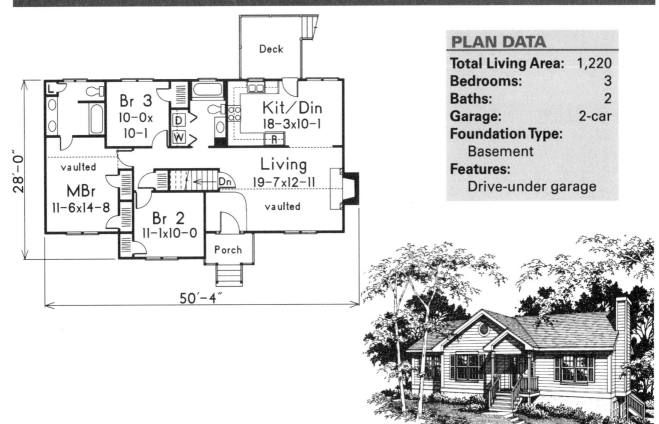

PLAN DATA

Total Living Area:	1,220
Bedrooms:	3
Baths:	2
Garage:	2-car
Foundation Type:	
Basement	
Features:	
Drive-under garage	

PLAN DATA

Total Living Area:	2,322
Bedrooms:	3
Baths:	2 1/2
Garage:	2-car
Foundation Types:	
Slab	
Basement	
Crawl space	
Please specify when ordering	

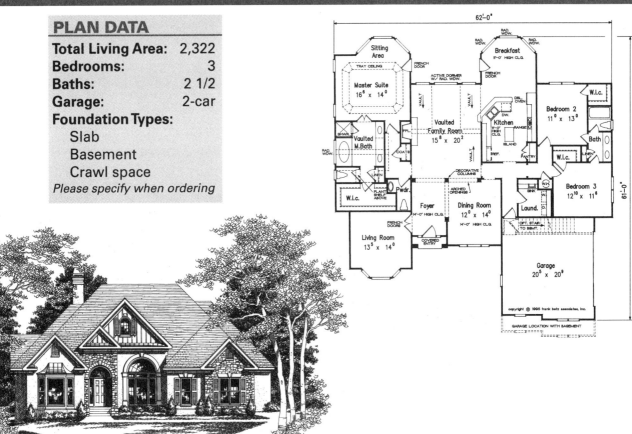

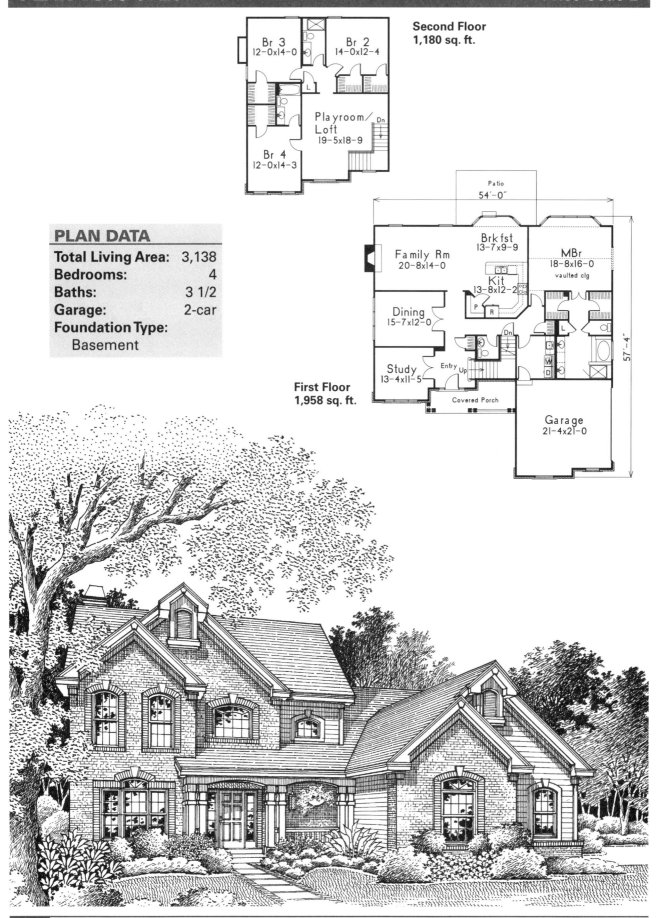

Second Floor
1,180 sq. ft.

Br 3
12-0x14-0

Br 2
14-0x12-4

Playroom/
Loft
19-5x18-9

Dn

Br 4
12-0x14-3

PLAN DATA

Total Living Area:	3,138
Bedrooms:	4
Baths:	3 1/2
Garage:	2-car
Foundation Type:	
Basement	

Patio
54'-0"

Family Rm
20-8x14-0

Brk fst
13-7x9-9

MBr
18-8x16-0
vaulted clg

Kit
13-8x12-2

Dining
15-7x12-0

P

R

Dn

L

Study
13-4x11-5

Entry

Up

W
D

57'-4"

First Floor
1,958 sq. ft.

Covered Porch

Garage
21-4x21-0

Second Floor 780 sq. ft.

open to below

Dn

Br 2
11-8x14-8

sloped clg

Game Rm
12-10x14-8

Br 3
11-4x14-8

desk

seat

seat

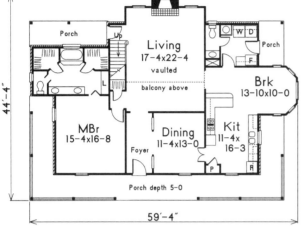

Porch

Up

Living
17-4x22-4
vaulted

balcony above

W D

F.

Porch

L

MBr
15-4x16-8

Dining
11-4x13-0

Foyer

Kit
11-4x
16-3

Brk
13-10x10-0

P

R

44'-4"

59'-4"

Porch depth 5-0

First Floor 1,669 sq. ft.

PLAN DATA

Total Living Area: 2,449
Bedrooms: 3
Baths: 2 1/2
Garage: detached 2-car
Foundation Types:
  Slab standard
  Crawl space

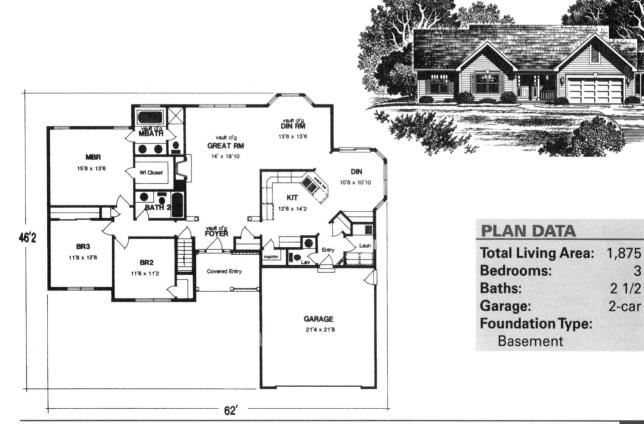

MBR
15'8 x 13'6

vault clg
MBATH

WI Closet

BATH 2

vault clg
GREAT RM
14' x 19'10

vault clg
FOYER

vault clg
DIN RM
13'6 x 13'6

KIT
12'6 x 14'2

DIN
10'8 x 10'10

Entry

Laun

BR3
11'8 x 12'8

BR2
11'6 x 11'2

PANTRY

Lav

Covered Entry

GARAGE
21'4 x 21'8

46'2

62'

PLAN DATA

Total Living Area: 1,875
Bedrooms: 3
Baths: 2 1/2
Garage: 2-car
Foundation Type:
  Basement

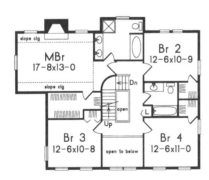

Second Floor
1,138 sq. ft.

MBr
17-8x13-0

Br 2
12-6x10-9

Br 3
12-6x10-8

Br 4
12-6x11-0

Dn

open

Up

open to below

slope clg

slope clg

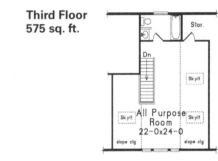

Third Floor
575 sq. ft.

Stor.

Dn

Skylt

Skylt

All Purpose
Room
22-0x24-0

slope clg

slope clg

PLAN DATA

Total Living Area: 3,006
Bedrooms: 4
Baths: 2 1/2
Garage: 2-car
Foundation Types:
  Basement standard
  Slab
Features:
  2" x 6" exterior walls

First Floor
1,293 sq. ft.

63'-4"

46'-4"

Patio

Garage
20-0x20-0

Dinette
9-4x11-0

Kit
12-6x
15-8

Family
19-10x13-0

D
W

Living
12-6x16-8

Up

Dining
12-6x14-0

Foyer

Porch depth 7-0

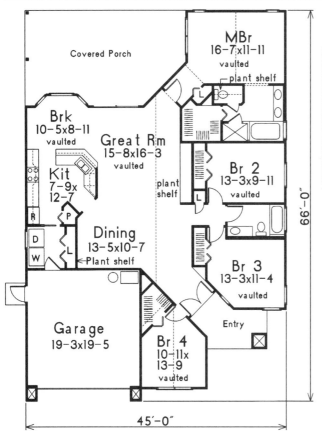

PLAN DATA

Total Living Area: 1,865
Bedrooms: 4
Baths: 2
Garage: 2-car
Foundation Types:
  Slab standard
  Crawl space
Features:
  Vaulted ceilings
  throughout

PLAN DATA

Total Living Area: 1,364
Bedrooms: 3
Baths: 2
Garage: 2-car
Foundation Types:
  Plan #565-ES-103-1
  Basement
  Plan #565-ES-103-2
  Crawl space & slab

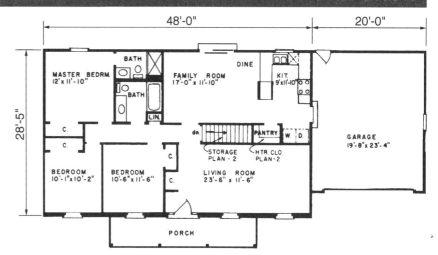

PLAN DATA

Total Living Area: 1,776
Bedrooms: 3
Baths: 2 1/2
Garage: 2-car
Foundation Type:
  Basement

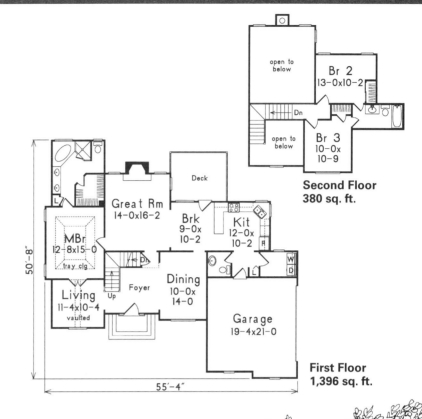

Second Floor
380 sq. ft.

Br 2
13-0x10-2

open to below

Dn

open to below

Br 3
10-0x
10-9

Deck

Great Rm
14-0x16-2

Brk
9-0x
10-2

Kit
12-0x
10-2

MBr
12-8x15-0
tray clg

Living
11-4x10-4
vaulted

Up

Foyer

Dining
10-0x
14-0

Garage
19-4x21-0

W
D

50'-8"

55'-4"

First Floor
1,396 sq. ft.

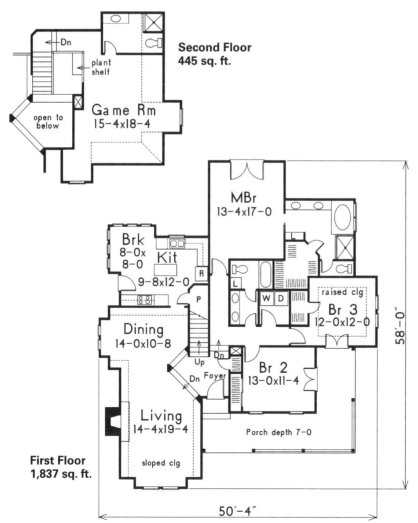

Second Floor
445 sq. ft.

Dn

plant shelf

open to below

Game Rm
15-4x18-4

PLAN DATA

Total Living Area: 2,282
Bedrooms: 3
Baths: 3
Garage: detached 2-car
Foundation Types:
  Slab standard
  Crawl space

MBr
13-4x17-0

Brk
8-0x
8-0

Kit
9-8x12-0

R

P

L

W D

raised clg

Br 3
12-0x12-0

Dining
14-0x10-8

Up

Dn Foyer

Dn

Br 2
13-0x11-4

58'-0"

Living
14-4x19-4

Porch depth 7-0

sloped clg

First Floor
1,837 sq. ft.

50'-4"

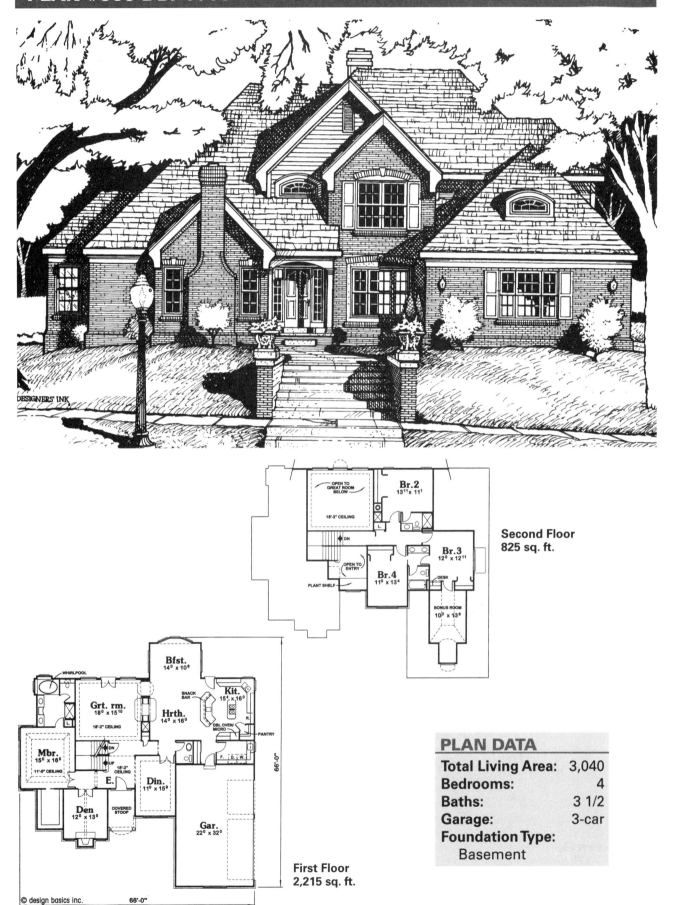

Second Floor
825 sq. ft.

Open to Great Room Below
18'-2" Ceiling

Br.2
13¹¹x 11¹

Br.3
12⁰ x 12¹¹

Open to Entry

Br.4
11⁰ x 13⁴

Plant Shelf

Desk

Bonus Room
10⁰ x 13⁸

Bfst.
14⁰ x 10⁸

Whirlpool

Grt. rm.
18⁰ x 15¹⁰
18'-2" Ceiling

Snack Bar

Kit.
15⁴ x 16⁰

Hrth.
14⁰ x 16⁰

Dbl Oven/Micro

Pantry

Mbr.
15⁰ x 16⁰
11'-0" Ceiling

E.

Din.
11⁰ x 15⁸

18'-2" Ceiling

Den
12⁰ x 13⁰

Covered Stoop

Gar.
22⁰ x 32⁰

66'-0"

© design basics inc.   66'-0"

First Floor
2,215 sq. ft.

PLAN DATA

Total Living Area:	3,040
Bedrooms:	4
Baths:	3 1/2
Garage:	3-car
Foundation Type:	
Basement	

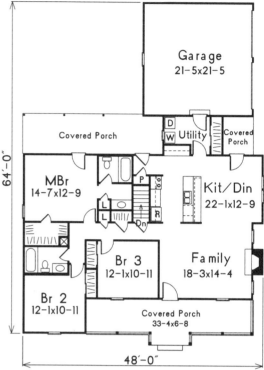

Garage
21-5x21-5

Covered Porch

Utility

D
W

Covered Porch

64'-0"

MBr
14-7x12-9

Kit/Din
22-1x12-9

P

L
L

R

Dn

Br 3
12-1x10-11

Family
18-3x14-4

Br 2
12-1x10-11

Covered Porch
33-4x6-8

48'-0"

PLAN DATA

Total Living Area:	1,501
Bedrooms:	3
Baths:	2
Garage:	2-car

Foundation Types:
　Basement standard
　Crawl space
　Slab

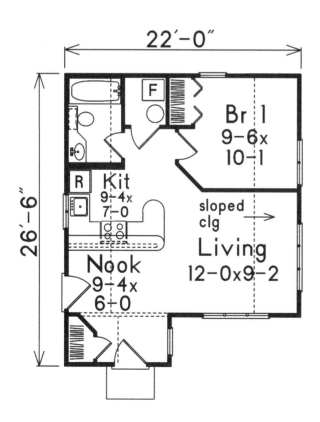

22'-0"

26'-6"

F

Br 1
9-6x
10-1

R

Kit
9-4x
7-0

sloped
clg

Nook
9-4x
6-0

Living
12-0x9-2

PLAN DATA

Total Living Area:	527
Bedrooms:	1
Baths:	1

Foundation Type:
　Crawl space

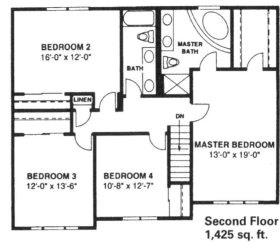

Second Floor 1,425 sq. ft.

BEDROOM 2
16'-0" x 12'-0"

MASTER BATH

BATH

LINEN

DN

MASTER BEDROOM
13'-0" x 19'-0"

BEDROOM 3
12'-0" x 13'-6"

BEDROOM 4
10'-8" x 12'-7"

PLAN DATA

Total Living Area: 2,617
Bedrooms: 4
Baths: 2 1/2
Garage: 2-car
Foundation Type:
  Basement

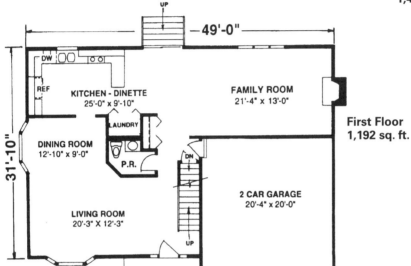

UP

— 49'-0" —

31'-10"

DW

REF

KITCHEN - DINETTE
25'-0" x 9'-10"

FAMILY ROOM
21'-4" x 13'-0"

First Floor 1,192 sq. ft.

LAUNDRY

DINING ROOM
12'-10" x 9'-0"

P.R.

DN

LIVING ROOM
20'-3" X 12'-3"

2 CAR GARAGE
20'-4" x 20'-0"

UP

mcLou

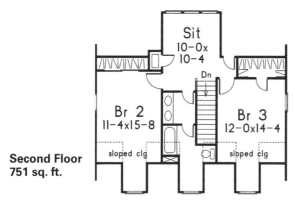

Sit
10-0x
10-4

Dn

Br 2
11-4x15-8

Br 3
12-0x14-4

sloped clg

sloped clg

Second Floor
751 sq. ft.

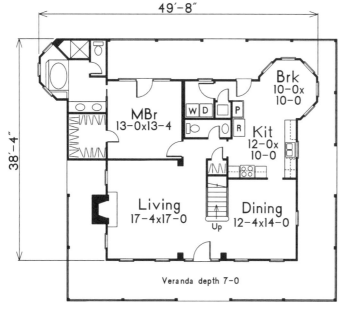

49'-8"

38'-4"

Brk
10-0x
10-0

MBr
13-0x13-4

W D   P

R

Kit
12-0x
10-0

Living
17-4x17-0

Up

Dining
12-4x14-0

First Floor
1,308 sq. ft.

Veranda depth 7-0

PLAN DATA

Total Living Area: 2,059
Bedrooms: 3
Baths: 2 1/2
Garage: detached 2-car
Foundation Types:
  Slab standard
  Basement
  Crawl space
Features:
  9' ceilings

PLAN DATA

Total Living Area: 1,539
Bedrooms: 3
Baths: 2
Garage: 2-car
Foundation Type:
  Slab
Features:
- 9' ceilings
- 10' tray ceiling in master bedroom

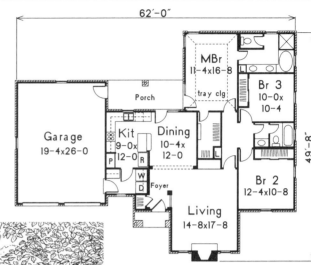

PLAN DATA

Total Living Area: 1,456
Bedrooms: 3
Baths: 2
Garage: 2-car
Foundation Type:
  Basement
Features:
  Vaulted ceilings throughout

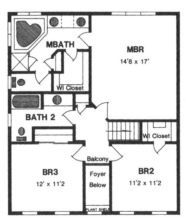

**Second Floor
926 sq. ft.**

PLAN DATA

Total Living Area:	1,887
Bedrooms:	3
Baths:	2 1/2
Garage:	2-car
Foundation Type:	
Basement	

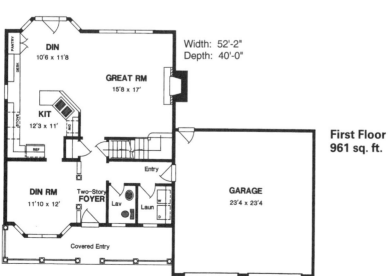

Width: 52'-2"
Depth: 40'-0"

**First Floor
961 sq. ft.**

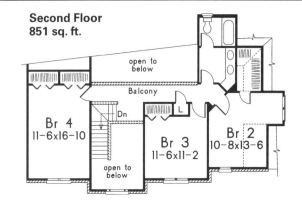

Second Floor
851 sq. ft.

open to below

Balcony

Br 4
11-6x16-10

Dn

open to below

L

Br 3
11-6x11-2

Br 2
10-8x13-6

PLAN DATA

Total Living Area: 2,282
Bedrooms: 4
Baths: 2 1/2
Garage: 2-car
Foundation Type:
Basement
Features:
Drive-under garage

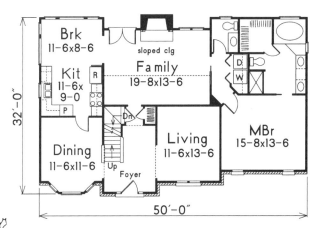

Brk
11-6x8-6

sloped clg

Family
19-8x13-6

D

W

Kit
11-6x
9-0

R

P

Dn

Dining
11-6x11-6

Up Foyer

Living
11-6x13-6

MBr
15-8x13-6

32'-0"

50'-0"

First Floor
1,431 sq. ft.

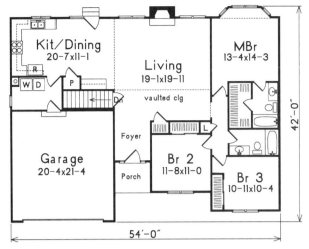

PLAN DATA

Total Living Area: 1,558
Bedrooms: 3
Baths: 2
Garage: 2-car
Foundation Type:
    Basement

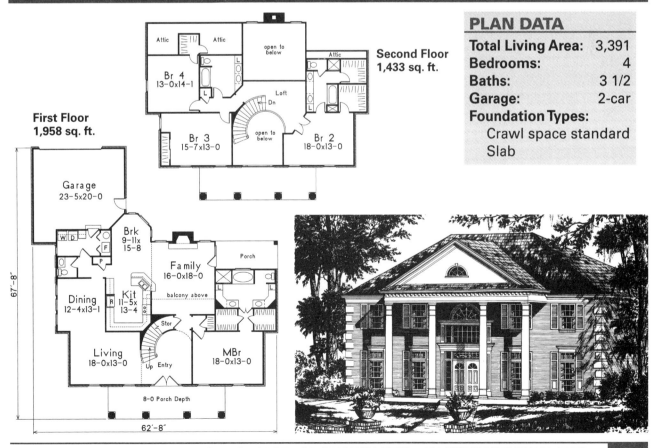

Second Floor
1,433 sq. ft.

First Floor
1,958 sq. ft.

PLAN DATA

Total Living Area: 3,391
Bedrooms: 4
Baths: 3 1/2
Garage: 2-car
Foundation Types:
    Crawl space standard
    Slab

PLAN DATA

Total Living Area: 1,600
Bedrooms: 3
Baths: 2
Garage: 2-car
Foundation Types:
  Crawl space standard
  Slab
Features:
  2" x 6" exterior walls

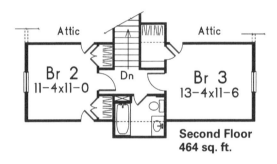

Attic   Attic

Br 2
11-4x11-0

Dn

Br 3
13-4x11-6

Second Floor
464 sq. ft.

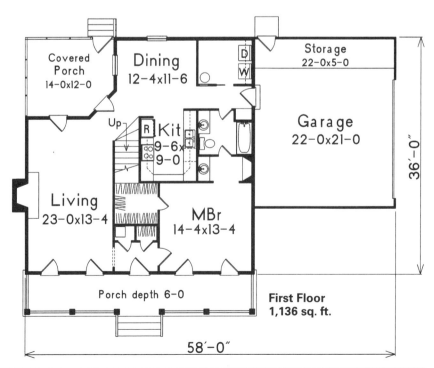

Covered Porch
14-0x12-0

Dining
12-4x11-6

Storage
22-0x5-0

Up

R Kit
9-6x
9-0

Garage
22-0x21-0

Living
23-0x13-4

MBr
14-4x13-4

36'-0"

Porch depth 6-0

First Floor
1,136 sq. ft.

58'-0"

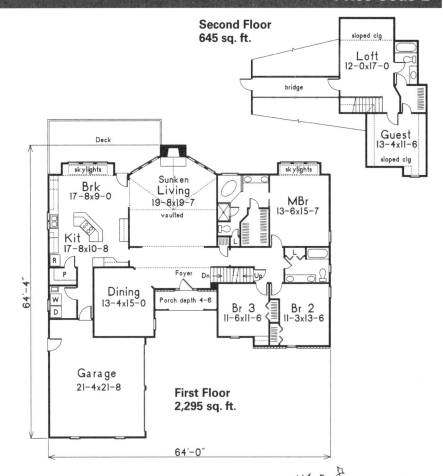

**Second Floor
645 sq. ft.**

Loft
12-0x17-0

sloped clg

bridge

Guest
13-4x11-6

sloped clg

PLAN DATA

Total Living Area:	2,940
Bedrooms:	4
Baths:	3
Garage:	2-car
Foundation Type:	
Basement	

Deck

skylights

Brk
17-8x9-0

Sunken
Living
19-8x19-7
vaulted

skylights

MBr
13-6x15-7

Kit
17-8x10-8

R

P

W

D

Dining
13-4x15-0

Foyer

Porch depth 4-6

Dn

Up

Br 3
11-6x11-6

Br 2
11-3x13-6

64'-4"

Garage
21-4x21-8

**First Floor
2,295 sq. ft.**

64'-0"

Second Floor
483 sq. ft.

open to below

Br 3
11-3x11-0

Dn

Br 2
9-11x10-0

Storage

open to below

Storage

63'-0"

43'-0"

Covered Porch

Family
20-4x13-0
vaulted

Deck

MBr
13-8x13-8

Kit
8-3x
11-3

Brk
10-6x
10-0

Dn

Dining
12-4x12-8

Up

Garage
21-4x21-4

Porch

First Floor
1,228 sq. ft.

PLAN DATA

Total Living Area:	1,711
Bedrooms:	3
Baths:	2 1/2
Garage:	2-car
Foundation Type:	
Basement	

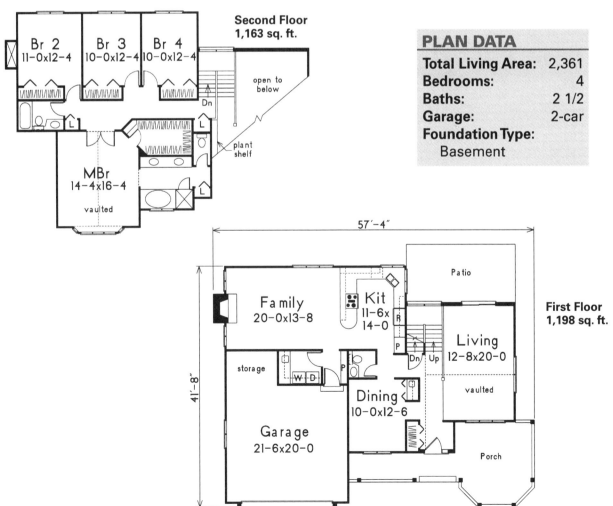

Second Floor
1,163 sq. ft.

Br 2
11-0x12-4

Br 3
10-0x12-4

Br 4
10-0x12-4

open to below

Dn

plant shelf

MBr
14-4x16-4

vaulted

L

PLAN DATA

Total Living Area:	2,361
Bedrooms:	4
Baths:	2 1/2
Garage:	2-car
Foundation Type:	
Basement	

57'-4"

41'-8"

Patio

Family
20-0x13-8

Kit
11-6x
14-0

R

P

Living
12-8x20-0

Dn   Up

vaulted

First Floor
1,198 sq. ft.

storage

W D

P

Dining
10-0x12-6

Garage
21-6x20-0

Porch

PLAN #565-0420

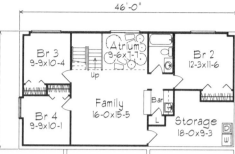

46'-0"

24'-4"

Br 3
9-9x10-4

Atrium
9-6x7-7

Br 2
12-3x11-6

Up

Family
16-0x15-5

Bar

Br 4
9-9x10-1

Storage
18-0x9-3

**Lower Level
945 sq. ft.**

PLAN DATA

Total Living Area: 1,941
Bedrooms: 4
Baths: 2 1/2
Garage: 2-car
Foundation Type:
  Walk-out basement
Features:
  Vaulted ceilings in
  kitchen and great
  room

Deck

Dining
10-8x12-0
vaulted

Skylts

W/D

Dn

plant shelf   vaulted

plant shelf

Kit
10-4x11-4
vaulted

Great Room
16-0x15-9
vaulted

MBr
12-5x15-0

46'-8"

Porch

**First Floor
996 sq. ft.**

Garage
18-4x20-4

46'-0"

PLAN #565-JA-79298

NK.
10'4" X 10'4"

DIN.
TRAY CEILING
11'4" X 12'6"

M.B.R.
CATHEDRAL CEILING
18'0" X 13'4"

GRT. RM.
CATHEDRAL CEILING
18'6" X 19'0"

ARCH 6'0" HT.

KIT.
12'8" X 15'8"

PANTRY   OVEN

11'-1 1/8" CEILING

BR.2
11'2" X 12'8"

BR.3
12'8" X 12'4"

2 CAR GAR.
21'6" X 25'8"

56'-0"

65'-0"

PLAN DATA

Total Living Area: 2,229
Bedrooms: 3
Baths: 2
Garage: 2-car
Foundation Type:
  Basement

PLAN DATA

Total Living Area: 1,816
Bedrooms: 3
Baths: 2 1/2
Garage: detached 2-car
Foundation Types:
  Slab standard
  Crawl space

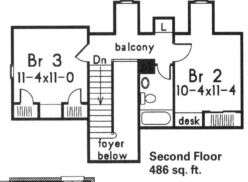

Br 3
11-4x11-0

balcony

Dn

Br 2
10-4x11-4

desk

foyer
below

**Second Floor
486 sq. ft.**

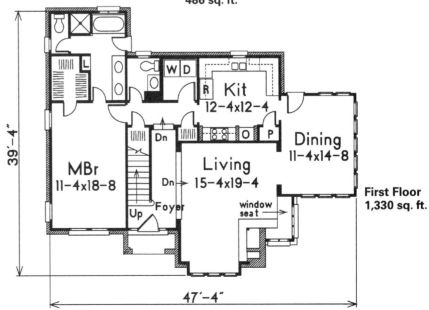

L

W|D

R

Kit
12-4x12-4

Dn

MBr
11-4x18-8

Dn

Living
15-4x19-4

Dining
11-4x14-8

O   P

Up   Foyer

window
seat

39'-4"

47'-4"

**First Floor
1,330 sq. ft.**

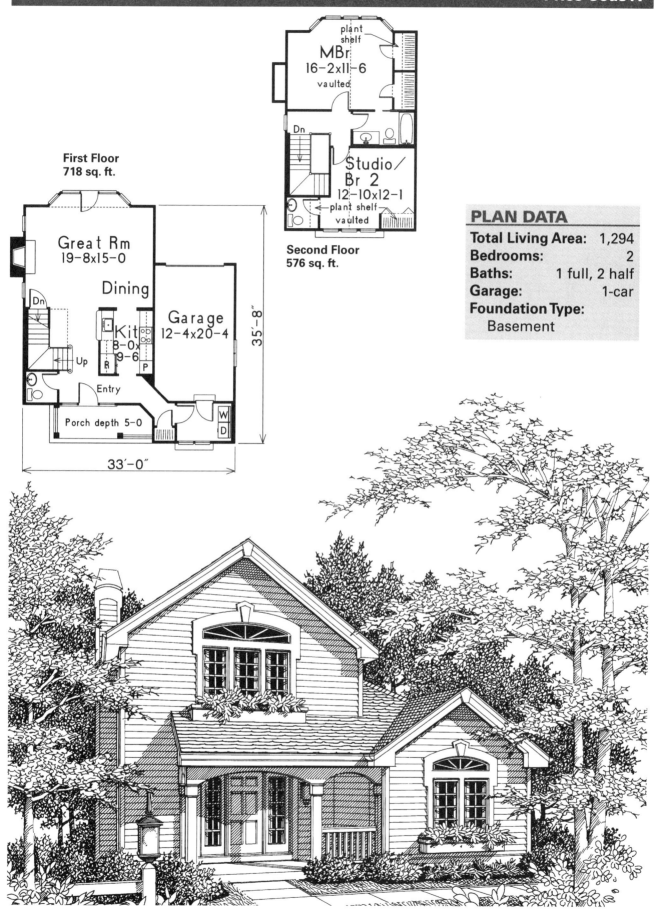

First Floor
718 sq. ft.

Great Rm
19-8x15-0

Dining

Kit
8-0x
9-6

Garage
12-4x20-4

Dn

Up

Entry

Porch depth 5-0

33'-0"

35'-8"

plant shelf

MBr
16-2x11-6
vaulted

Dn

Studio/
Br 2
12-10x12-1
plant shelf
vaulted

Second Floor
576 sq. ft.

PLAN DATA

Total Living Area: 1,294
Bedrooms: 2
Baths: 1 full, 2 half
Garage: 1-car
Foundation Type:
  Basement

Second Floor
470 sq. ft.

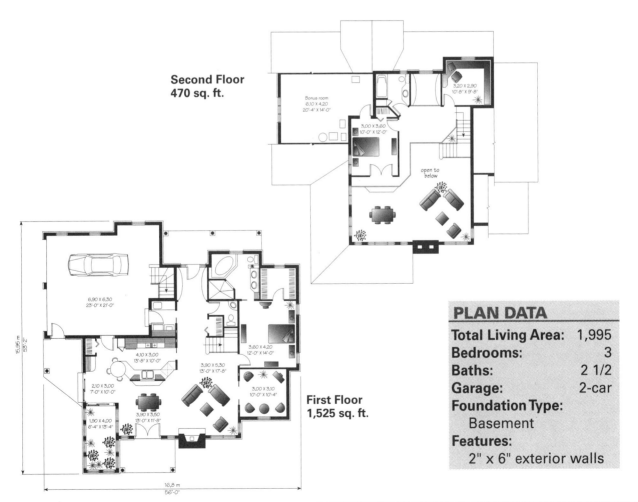

Bonus room
6,10 X 4,20
20'-4" X 14'-0"

3,20 X 2,90
10'-8" X 9'-8"

3,00 X 3,60
10'-0" X 12'-0"

open to below

6,90 X 6,30
23'-8" X 21'-0"

4,10 X 3,00
13'-8" X 10'-0"

3,60 X 4,20
12'-0" X 14'-0"

2,10 X 3,00
7'-0" X 10'-0"

3,90 X 5,30
13'-0" X 17'-8"

3,00 X 3,10
10'-0" X 10'-4"

1,90 X 4,00
6'-4" X 13'-4"

3,90 X 3,50
13'-0" X 11'-8"

15,95 m
55'-2"

16,8 m
56'-0"

First Floor
1,525 sq. ft.

PLAN DATA

Total Living Area:	1,995
Bedrooms:	3
Baths:	2 1/2
Garage:	2-car
Foundation Type:	
Basement	
Features:	
2" x 6" exterior walls	

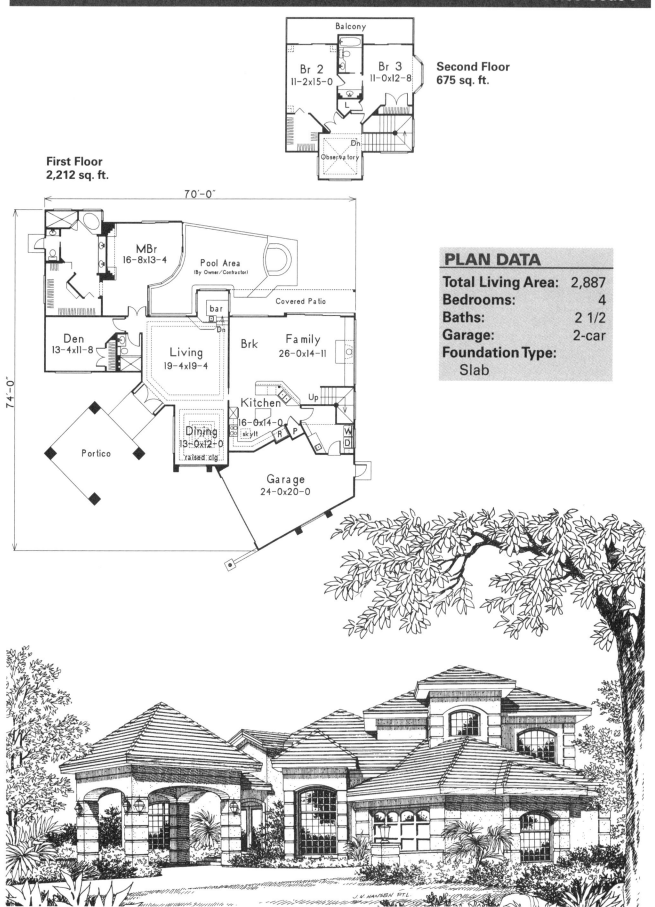

Balcony

Br 2
11-2x15-0

Br 3
11-0x12-8

Second Floor
675 sq. ft.

Dn
Observatory

First Floor
2,212 sq. ft.

70'-0"

74'-0"

MBr
16-8x13-4

Pool Area
(By Owner/Contractor)

Covered Patio

bar
Dn

Den
13-4x11-8

Living
19-4x19-4

Brk

Family
26-0x14-11

Up

Kitchen
16-0x14-0
skylt

Dining
13-0x12-0
raised clg.

R P

W D

Portico

Garage
24-0x20-0

PLAN DATA

Total Living Area:	2,887
Bedrooms:	4
Baths:	2 1/2
Garage:	2-car
Foundation Type:	
Slab	

J.V. HANSEN PTL.

PLAN DATA

Total Living Area: 1,104
Bedrooms: 3
Baths: 2
Foundation Types:
  Crawl space standard
  Basement
  Slab

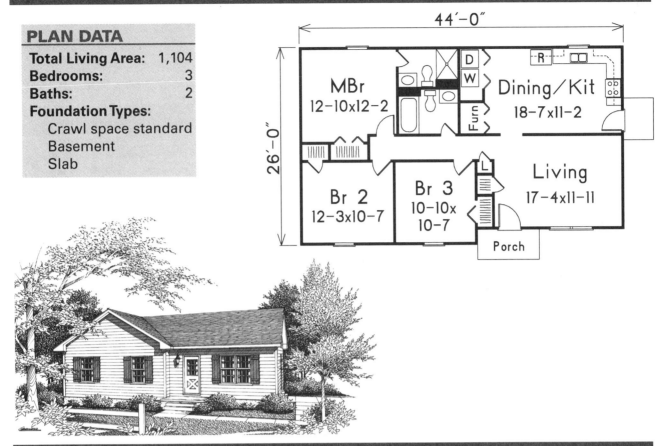

PLAN #565-HDS-1167

Price Code AA

PLAN DATA

Total Living Area: 1,167
Bedrooms: 3
Baths: 2
Garage: 2-car
Foundation Type:
  Slab

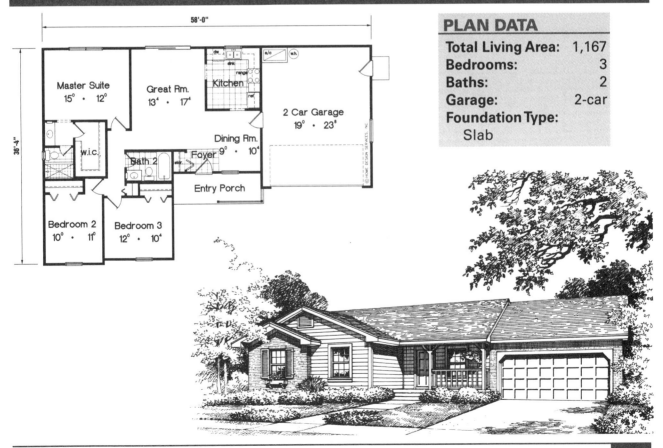

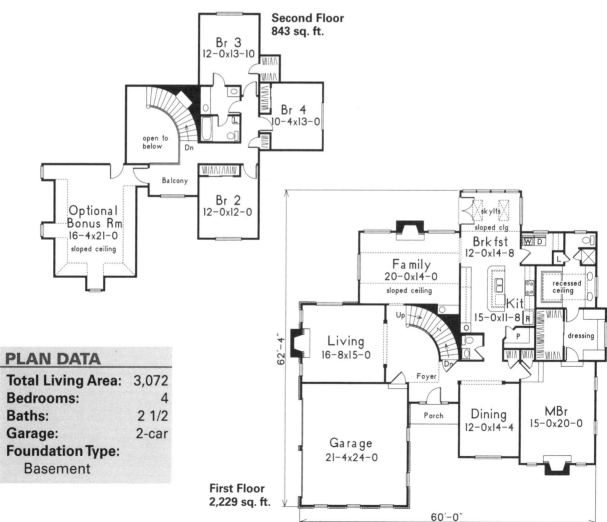

Second Floor
843 sq. ft.

Br 3
12-0x13-10

Br 4
10-4x13-0

open to
below

Dn

Balcony

Optional
Bonus Rm
16-4x21-0
sloped ceiling

Br 2
12-0x12-0

skylts
sloped clg

Brkfst
12-0x14-8

W D

Family
20-0x14-0
sloped ceiling

recessed
ceiling

Kit
15-0x11-8

R

L

P

dressing

Living
16-8x15-0

Up

Dn

Foyer

Porch

Dining
12-0x14-4

MBr
15-0x20-0

Garage
21-4x24-0

62'-4"

60'-0"

First Floor
2,229 sq. ft.

PLAN DATA

Total Living Area:	3,072
Bedrooms:	4
Baths:	2 1/2
Garage:	2-car
Foundation Type:	
Basement	

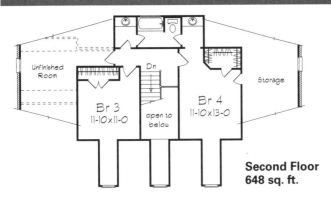

**Second Floor
648 sq. ft.**

Br 3
11-10x11-0

Br 4
11-10x13-0

Unfinished Room

Dn

open to below

Storage

PLAN DATA

Total Living Area:	2,333
Bedrooms:	4
Baths:	3
Garage:	2-car

Foundation Types:
Slab standard
Basement
Crawl space
Partial crawl space/
basement

Features:
9' ceilings on first
floor

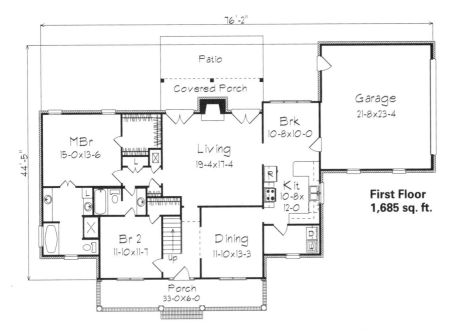

76'-2"

44'-5"

Patio

Covered Porch

MBr
15-0x13-6

Living
19-4x17-4

Brk
10-8x10-0

Garage
21-8x23-4

Kit
10-8x
12-0

Br 2
11-10x11-7

Dining
11-10x13-3

Up

Porch
33-0x6-0

**First Floor
1,685 sq. ft.**

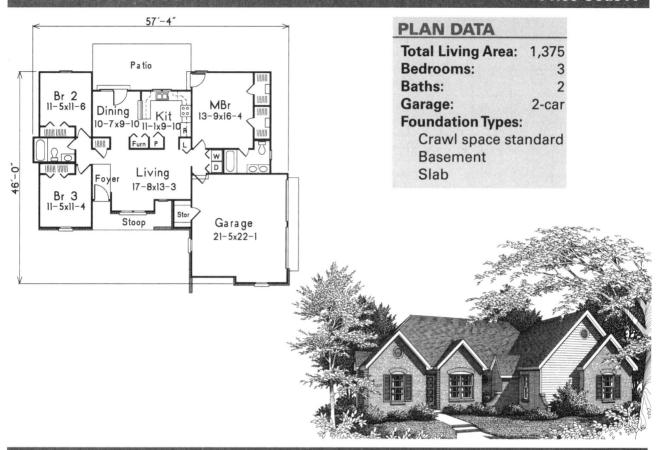

57'-4"

46'-0"

Patio

Br 2
11-5x11-6

Dining
10-7x9-10

Kit
11-1x9-10

MBr
13-9x16-4

Furn P

Foyer

Living
17-8x13-3

W D

Br 3
11-5x11-4

Stoop

Stor

Garage
21-5x22-1

PLAN DATA

Total Living Area: 1,375
Bedrooms: 3
Baths: 2
Garage: 2-car
Foundation Types:
   Crawl space standard
   Basement
   Slab

PLAN DATA

Total Living Area: 1,856
Bedrooms: 3
Baths: 2
Garage: 2-car
Foundation Types:
   Basement
   Crawl space
   Slab
   Please specify when ordering

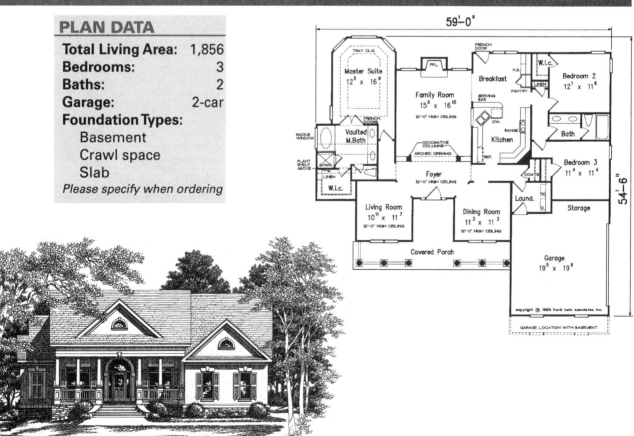

59'-0"

54'-6"

TRAY CLG.

FRENCH DOOR

Master Suite
12⁵ x 16⁸

FPL

K.S.

W.I.C.

Breakfast

LINEN

Bedroom 2
12¹ x 11⁸

Family Room
15⁰ x 16¹⁰
12'-0" HIGH CEILING

SERVING BAR

PANTRY

DW.

RADIUS WINDOW

Vaulted M.Bath

FRENCH DOORS

Kitchen

RANGE

Bath

DECORATIVE COLUMNS

REF.

PLANT SHELF ABOVE

SHWR

ARCHED OPENING

Foyer
12'-0" HIGH CEILING

Bedroom 3
11⁴ x 11⁴

LINEN

COATS

W.I.C.

Laund.

W

Storage

Living Room
10¹¹ x 11⁷
12'-0" HIGH CEILING

Dining Room
11³ x 11³
12'-0" HIGH CEILING

Covered Porch

Garage
19⁵ x 19⁹

copyright ® 1995 frank betz associates, inc.

GARAGE LOCATION WITH BASEMENT

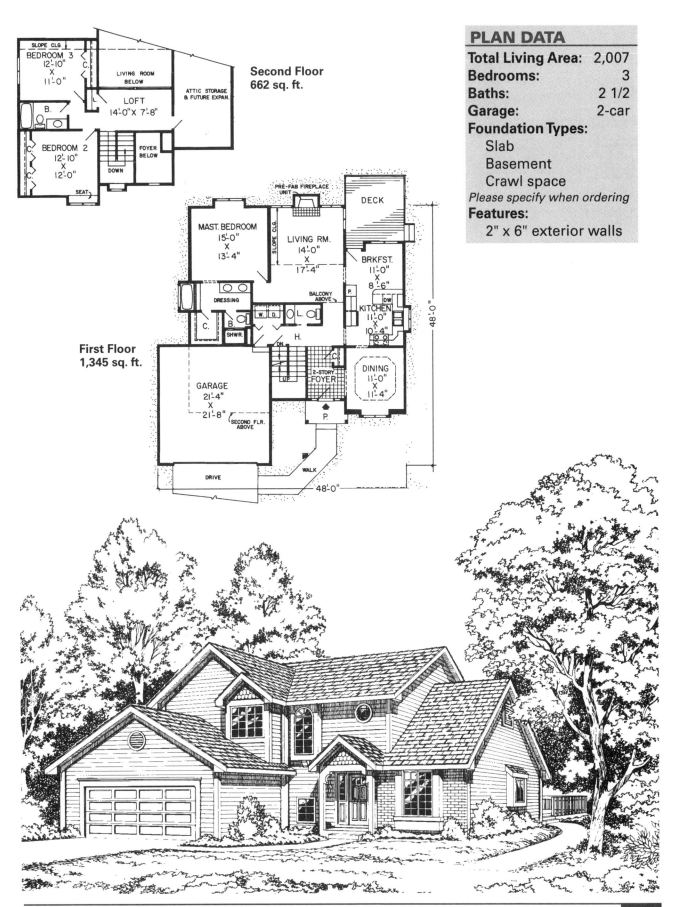

SLOPE CLG.

BEDROOM 3
12'-10"
X
11'-0"

C.

LIVING ROOM
BELOW

ATTIC STORAGE
& FUTURE EXPAN.

**Second Floor
662 sq. ft.**

B.

LOFT
14'-0" X 7'-8"

BEDROOM 2
12'-10"
X
12'-0"

C.

C.

FOYER
BELOW

DOWN

SEAT

PRE-FAB FIREPLACE
UNIT

DECK

MAST. BEDROOM
15'-0"
X
13'-4"

SLOPE CLG.

LIVING RM.
14'-0"
X
17'-4"

BRKFST.
11'-0"
X
8'-6"

P.

DRESSING

BALCONY
ABOVE

DW

KITCHEN
11'-0"
X
10'-4"

C.

B.

W. D.

L.

SHWR.

H.

48'-0"

**First Floor
1,345 sq. ft.**

DN.

C.

UP

2-STORY
FOYER

DINING
11'-0"
X
11'-4"

GARAGE
21'-4"
X
21'-8"

SECOND FLR.
ABOVE

P.

DRIVE

WALK

48'-0"

PLAN DATA

Total Living Area: 2,007
Bedrooms: 3
Baths: 2 1/2
Garage: 2-car
Foundation Types:
  Slab
  Basement
  Crawl space
Please specify when ordering
Features:
  2" x 6" exterior walls

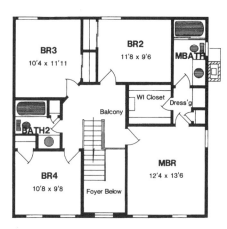

BR3
10'4 x 11'11

BR2
11'8 x 9'6

MBATH

WI Closet

Dress'g

Balcony

BATH2

BR4
10'8 x 9'8

Foyer Below

MBR
12'4 x 13'6

Second Floor
892 sq. ft.

Width: 52'-8"
Depth: 41'-8"

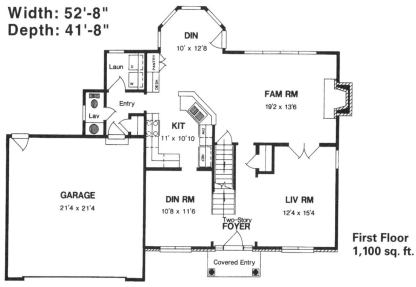

DIN
10' x 12'8

Laun

D

W

PANTRY

DESK

Entry

Lav

KIT
11' x 10'10

FAM RM
19'2 x 13'6

GARAGE
21'4 x 21'4

DIN RM
10'8 x 11'6

Two-Story
FOYER

LIV RM
12'4 x 15'4

First Floor
1,100 sq. ft.

Covered Entry

PLAN DATA	
Total Living Area:	1,992
Bedrooms:	4
Baths:	2 1/2
Garage:	2-car
Foundation Type: Basement	

Second Floor
1,589 sq. ft.

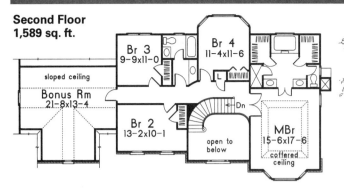

Br 3
9-9x11-0

Br 4
11-4x11-6

sloped ceiling

Bonus Rm
21-8x13-4

Br 2
13-2x10-1

open to below

Dn

MBr
15-6x17-6

coffered ceiling

First Floor
1,277 sq. ft.

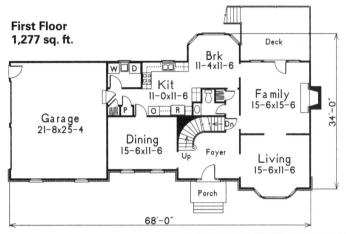

W D

Brk
11-4x11-6

Deck

Kit
11-0x11-6

Family
15-6x15-6

P O R

Garage
21-8x25-4

Dining
15-6x11-6

Up   Foyer

Dn

Living
15-6x11-6

34'-0"

Porch

68'-0"

PLAN DATA

Total Living Area: 2,846
Bedrooms: 4
Baths: 2 1/2
Garage: 2-car
Foundation Types:
  Basement standard
  Slab
  Crawl space
Features:
  9' ceilings on first
  floor

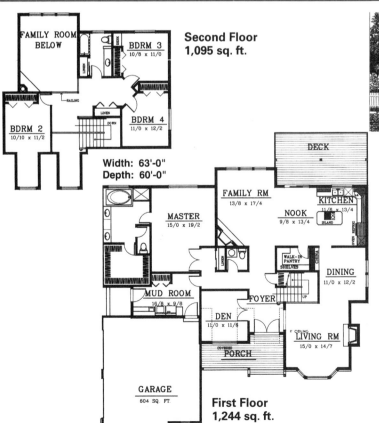

FAMILY ROOM BELOW

BDRM 3
10/8 x 11/0

Second Floor
1,095 sq. ft.

BDRM 2
10/10 x 11/2

BDRM 4
11/0 x 12/2

Width: 63'-0"
Depth: 60'-0"

DECK

FAMILY RM
13/8 x 17/4

KITCHEN
11/6 x 13/4

MASTER
15/0 x 19/2

NOOK
9/8 x 13/4

ISLAND

WALK-IN PANTRY
SHELVES

DINING
11/0 x 12/2

MUD ROOM
16/8 x 9/8

FOYER

UP

DEN
11/0 x 11/6

LIVING RM
15/0 x 14/7

COVERED PORCH

GARAGE
604 SQ. FT.

First Floor
1,244 sq. ft.

PLAN DATA

Total Living Area: 2,995
Bedrooms: 4
Baths: 2 1/2
Garage: 2-car
Foundation Types:
  Crawl space
  Slab
Please specify when ordering

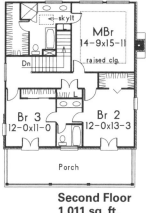

Second Floor
1,011 sq. ft.

First Floor
1,316 sq. ft.

PLAN DATA

Total Living Area: 2,327
Bedrooms: 3
Baths: 2 1/2
Garage: 2-car
Foundation Type:
   Basement
Features:
   9' ceilings

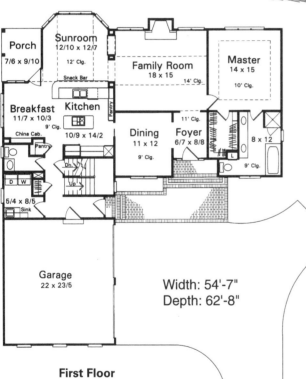

PLAN DATA

Total Living Area: 2,148
Bedrooms: 3
Baths: 2 1/2
Garage: 2-car
Foundation Type:
  Basement
Features:
  Varied ceiling heights

Porch
7/6 x 9/10

Sunroom
12/10 x 12/7
12' Clg.

Snack Bar

Family Room
18 x 15
14' Clg.

Master
14 x 15
10' Clg.

Breakfast
11/7 x 10/3
9' Clg.

Kitchen

China Cab.

Pantry

Dining
11 x 12
9' Clg.

Foyer
6/7 x 8/8

11' Clg.

8 x 12

9' Clg.

10/9 x 14/2

Pantry

Dn.

Up.

D W

5/4 x 8/5

Sink

Garage
22 x 23/5

Width: 54'-7"
Depth: 62'-8"

First Floor
1,626 sq. ft.

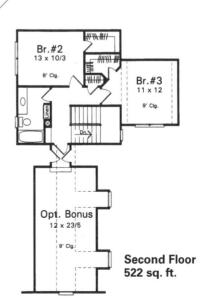

Br.#2
13 x 10/3
8' Clg.

Br.#3
11 x 12
9' Clg.

Linen

Dn.

Opt. Bonus
12 x 23/5
9' Clg.

Second Floor
522 sq. ft.

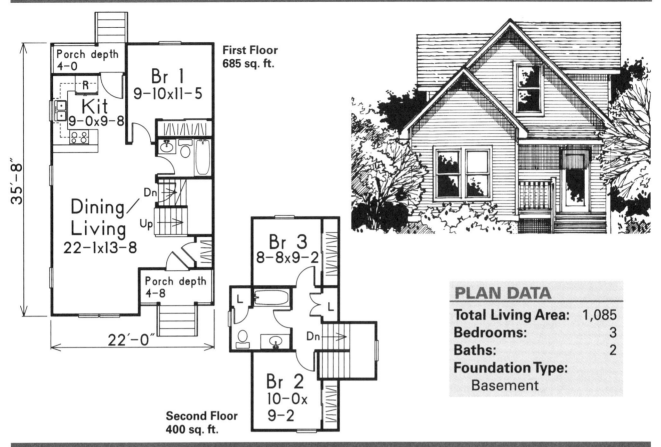

First Floor
685 sq. ft.

Porch depth
4-0

Kit
9-0x9-8

R

Br 1
9-10x11-5

35'-8"

Dn

Up

Dining/
Living
22-1x13-8

Porch depth
4-8

22'-0"

Br 3
8-8x9-2

L

L

Dn

Br 2
10-0x
9-2

Second Floor
400 sq. ft.

PLAN DATA

Total Living Area: 1,085
Bedrooms: 3
Baths: 2
Foundation Type:
  Basement

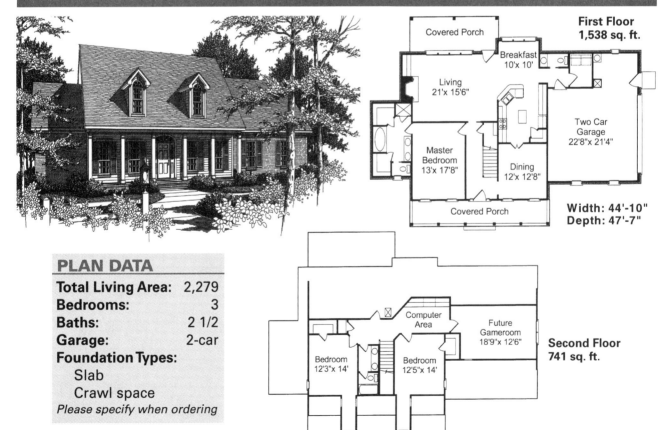

First Floor
1,538 sq. ft.

Covered Porch

Breakfast
10'x 10'

Living
21'x 15'6"

Two Car
Garage
22'8"x 21'4"

Master
Bedroom
13'x 17'8"

Dining
12'x 12'8"

Covered Porch

Width: 44'-10"
Depth: 47'-7"

Computer
Area

Future
Gameroom
18'9"x 12'6"

Bedroom
12'3"x 14'

Bedroom
12'5"x 14'

Second Floor
741 sq. ft.

PLAN DATA

Total Living Area: 2,279
Bedrooms: 3
Baths: 2 1/2
Garage: 2-car
Foundation Types:
  Slab
  Crawl space
Please specify when ordering

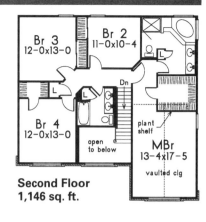

Second Floor
1,146 sq. ft.

Br 3
12-0x13-0

Br 2
11-0x10-4

Br 4
12-0x13-0

Dn

plant shelf

open to below

MBr
13-4x17-5

vaulted clg

PLAN DATA

Total Living Area: 2,521
Bedrooms: 4
Baths: 2 1/2
Garage: 2-car
Foundation Type:
  Basement

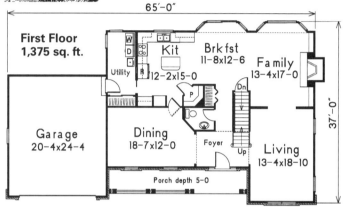

First Floor
1,375 sq. ft.

65'-0"

37'-0"

Kit
12-2x15-0

Brkfst
11-8x12-6

Family
13-4x17-0

Utility

Garage
20-4x24-4

Dining
18-7x12-0

Foyer

Dn

Up

Living
13-4x18-10

Porch depth 5-0

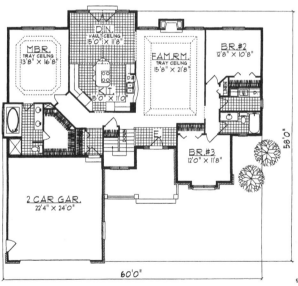

MBR.
TRAY CEILING
13'8" X 16'8"

DIN.
VAULT CEILING
15'0" X 11'8"

FAM.RM.
TRAY CEILING
15'8" X 21'8"

BR.#2
12'8" X 10'8"

KIT.
15'0" X 11'0"

BR.#3
12'0" X 11'8"

2 CAR GAR.
22'4" X 24'0"

58'0"

60'0"

PLAN DATA

Total Living Area: 1,919
Bedrooms: 3
Baths: 2
Garage: 2-car
Foundation Type:
  Basement

PLAN DATA

Total Living Area: 1,954
Bedrooms: 3
Baths: 2 1/2
Garage: 2-car
Foundation Type:
Basement
Features:
Vaulted ceilings in living and dining rooms

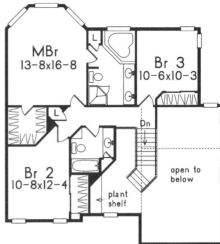

**Second Floor
902 sq. ft.**

MBr
13-8x16-8

Br 3
10-6x10-3

Br 2
10-8x12-4

Dn

open to below

plant shelf

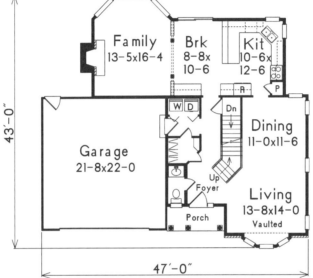

Family
13-5x16-4

Brk
8-8x
10-6

Kit
10-6x
12-6

**First Floor
1,052 sq. ft.**

Garage
21-8x22-0

W D

Dn

R

P

Dining
11-0x11-6

Up
Foyer

Living
13-8x14-0
Vaulted

Porch

43'-0"

47'-0"

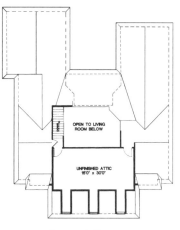

Second Floor
450 sq. ft.

PLAN DATA

Total Living Area: 2,123
Bedrooms: 3
Baths: 2 1/2
Garage: 2-car
Foundation Types:
  Slab
  Basement
  Crawl space
Please specify when ordering
Features:
  2" x 6" exterior walls

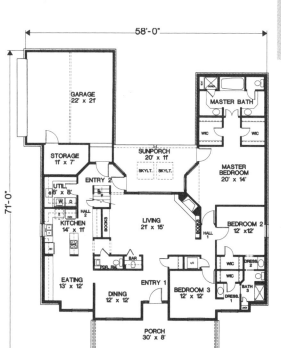

First Floor
2,123 sq. ft.

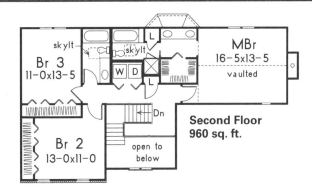

Second Floor
960 sq. ft.

Br 3
11-0x13-5

MBr
16-5x13-5
vaulted

Br 2
13-0x11-0

open to below

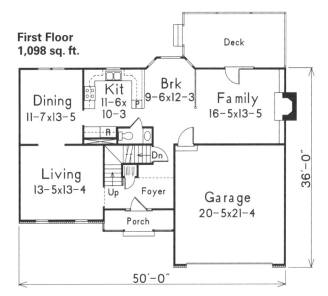

First Floor
1,098 sq. ft.

Deck

Dining
11-7x13-5

Kit
11-6x
10-3

Brk
9-6x12-3

Family
16-5x13-5

Living
13-5x13-4

Foyer

Garage
20-5x21-4

Porch

36'-0"

50'-0"

PLAN DATA

Total Living Area: 2,058
Bedrooms: 3
Baths: 2 1/2
Garage: 2-car
Foundation Types:
  Basement standard
  Slab
  Crawl space

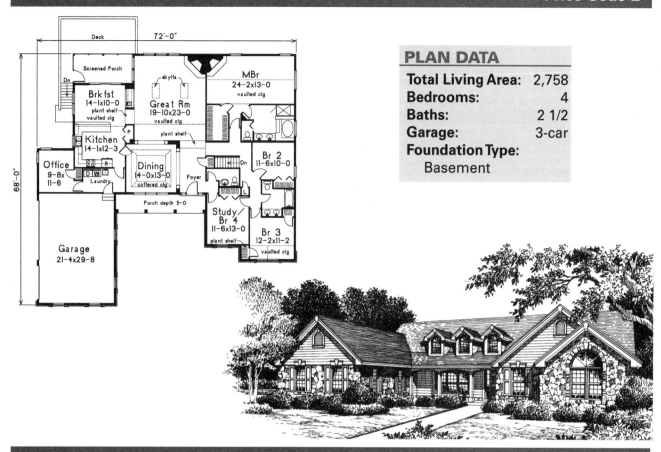

PLAN DATA

Total Living Area: 2,758
Bedrooms: 4
Baths: 2 1/2
Garage: 3-car
Foundation Type:
  Basement

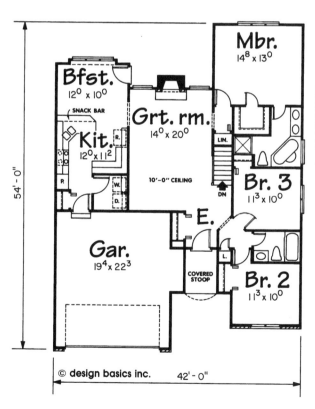

PLAN DATA

Total Living Area: 1,392
Bedrooms: 3
Baths: 2
Garage: 2-car
Foundation Type:
  Basement

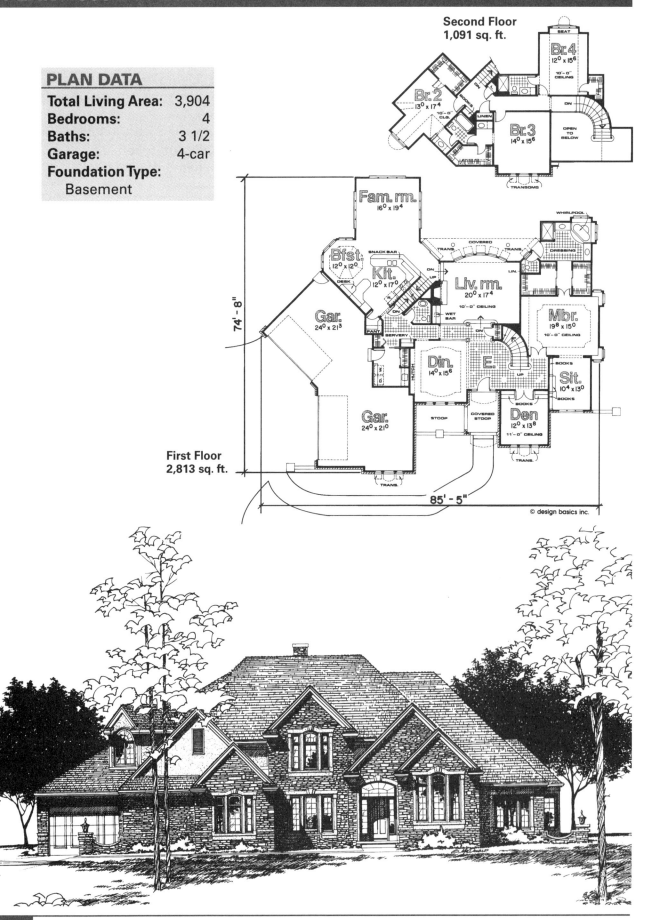

Second Floor
1,091 sq. ft.

SEAT

Br. 4
12⁰ x 15⁶
10'-0" CEILING

Br. 2
13⁰ x 17⁴

LINEN

Br. 3
14⁰ x 15⁶

DN

OPEN TO BELOW

TRANSOMS

PLAN DATA

Total Living Area:	3,904
Bedrooms:	4
Baths:	3 1/2
Garage:	4-car
Foundation Type:	
Basement	

Fam. rm.
16⁰ x 19⁴

Bfst.
12⁰ x 12⁰

SNACK BAR

Kit.
12⁰ x 17⁰

DESK

Liv. rm.
20⁰ x 17⁴
10'-0" CEILING

COVERED

TRANS.

WHIRLPOOL

DRESSING

LIN.

Gar.
24⁰ x 21³

PANT.

SERVERY

WET BAR

Mbr.
19⁸ x 15⁰
10'-0" CEILING

Din.
14⁰ x 15⁶

E.

BOOKS

Sit.
10⁴ x 13⁰

BOOKS

Gar.
24⁰ x 21⁰

STOOP

COVERED STOOP

Den
12⁰ x 13⁸
11'-0" CEILING

TRANS.

74'-8"

85'-5"

First Floor
2,813 sq. ft.

© design basics inc.

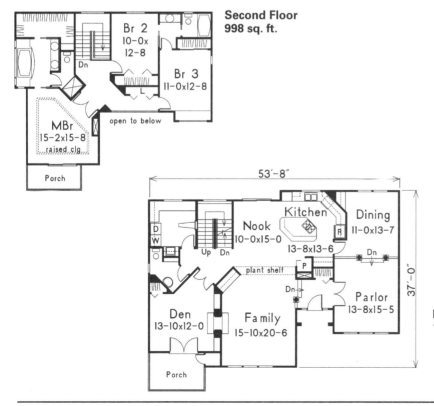

Second Floor
998 sq. ft.

Br 2
10-0x
12-8

Br 3
11-0x12-8

Dn

L

MBr
15-2x15-8
raised clg

open to below

Porch

PLAN DATA

Total Living Area:	2,813
Bedrooms:	3
Baths:	2 1/2
Garage:	3-car

Foundation Type:
Partial basement/
crawl space

Features:
- Drive-under garage
- 102 square feet of
  living area on the
  garage level

53′-8″

37′-0″

Kitchen
13-8x13-6

Dining
11-0x13-7

Nook
10-0x15-0

Up Dn

D
W

R

Dn

plant shelf

P

Dn

Den
13-10x12-0

Family
15-10x20-6

Parlor
13-8x15-5

Porch

First Floor
1,713 sq. ft.

Rear View

PLAN DATA

Total Living Area: 2,397
Bedrooms: 4
Baths: 3
Garage: 2-car
Foundation Type:
  Slab
Features:
  Varied ceiling heights
  throughout

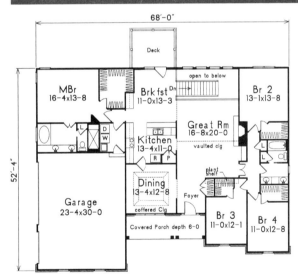

PLAN DATA

Total Living Area: 2,412
Bedrooms: 4
Baths: 2
Garage: 3-car
Foundation Types:
  Walk-out basement
Features:
  Vaulted ceiling in
  great room

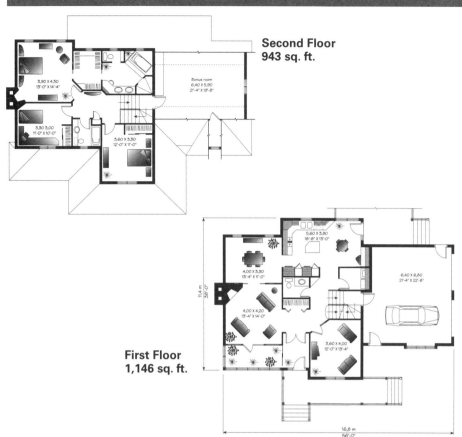

Second Floor
943 sq. ft.

First Floor
1,146 sq. ft.

PLAN DATA

Total Living Area: 2,089
Bedrooms: 3
Baths: 2 1/2
Garage: 2-car
Foundation Type:
  Basement
Features:
  - 9' ceilings on first floor
  - 2" x 6" exterior walls

Second Floor
488 sq. ft.

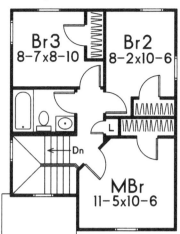

Br3
8-7 x 8-10

Br2
8-2 x 10-6

MBr
11-5 x 10-6

First Floor
488 sq. ft.

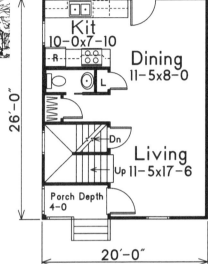

Kit
10-0 x 7-10

Dining
11-5 x 8-0

Living
11-5 x 17-6

Porch Depth
4-0

26'-0"

20'-0"

PLAN DATA

Total Living Area:	976
Bedrooms:	3
Baths:	1 1/2
Foundation Type:	
Basement	

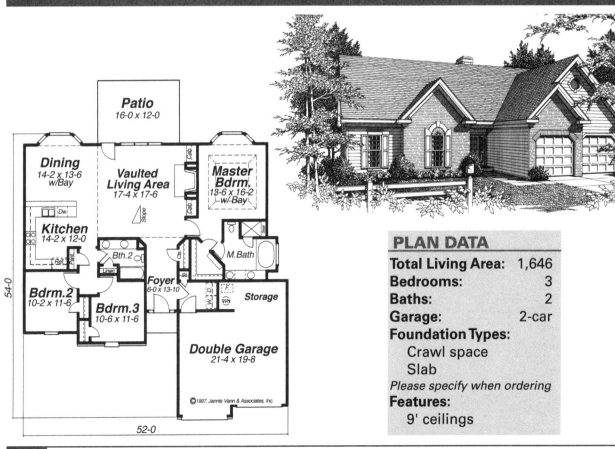

Patio
16-0 x 12-0

Dining
14-2 x 13-6
w/Bay

Vaulted
Living Area
17-4 x 17-6

Master
Bdrm.
13-6 x 16-2
w/Bay

Kitchen
14-2 x 12-0

Bth.2

M.Bath

Linen

Foyer
6-0 x 13-10

Bdrm.2
10-2 x 11-6

Bdrm.3
10-6 x 11-6

Storage

Double Garage
21-4 x 19-8

©1997, Jannis Vann & Associates, Inc.

54-0

52-0

PLAN DATA

Total Living Area:	1,646
Bedrooms:	3
Baths:	2
Garage:	2-car
Foundation Types:	
Crawl space	
Slab	
Please specify when ordering	
Features:	
9' ceilings	

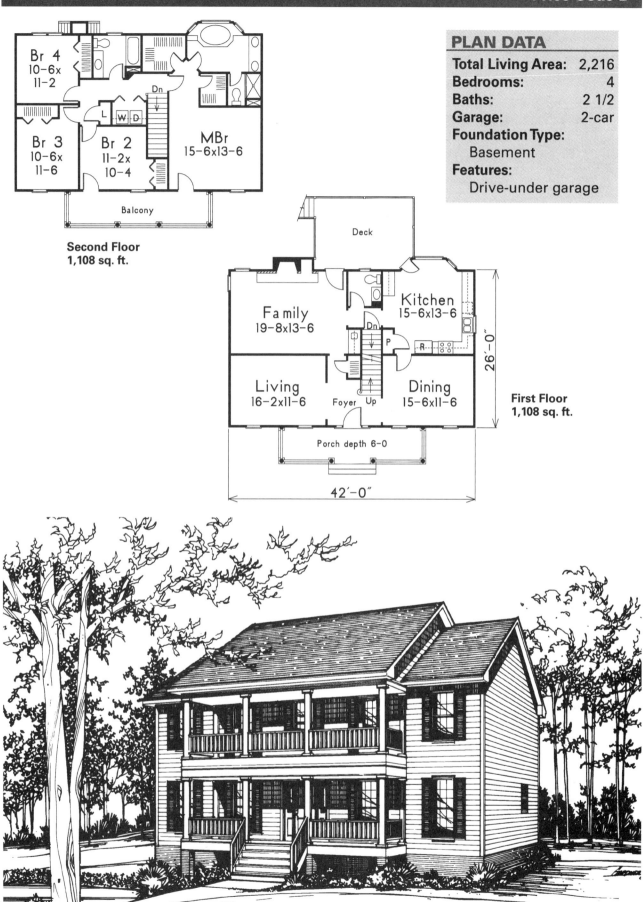

Second Floor
1,108 sq. ft.

Br 4
10-6x
11-2

Br 3
10-6x
11-6

Br 2
11-2x
10-4

MBr
15-6x13-6

L W D Dn

Balcony

PLAN DATA

Total Living Area:	2,216
Bedrooms:	4
Baths:	2 1/2
Garage:	2-car
Foundation Type:	
Basement	
Features:	
Drive-under garage	

Deck

Family
19-8x13-6

Kitchen
15-6x13-6

Dn P R

Living
16-2x11-6

Dining
15-6x11-6

Foyer Up

Porch depth 6-0

26'-0"

42'-0"

First Floor
1,108 sq. ft.

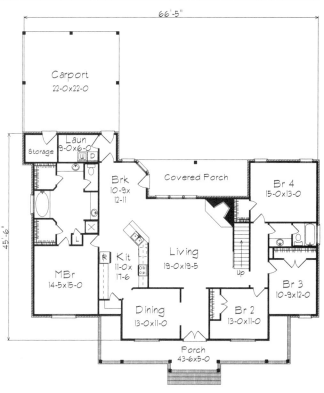

PLAN DATA

Total Living Area: 2,365
Bedrooms: 4
Baths: 2
Garage: 2-car carport
Foundation Type:
Slab
Features:
9' ceilings

PLAN DATA

Total Living Area: 1,084
Bedrooms: 2
Baths: 2
Foundation Type:
Basement

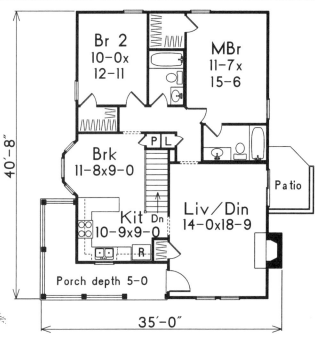

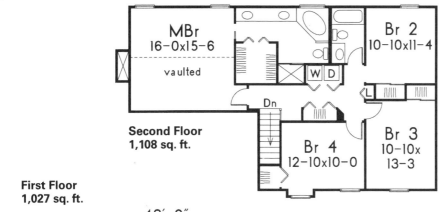

MBr
16-0x15-6

vaulted

Br 2
10-10x11-4

W D

L

**Second Floor
1,108 sq. ft.**

Dn

Br 4
12-10x10-0

Br 3
10-10x
13-3

**First Floor
1,027 sq. ft.**

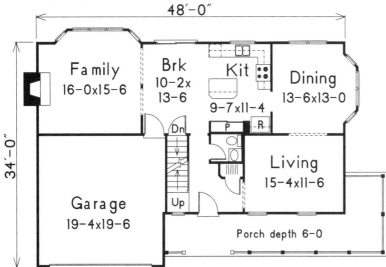

48'-0"

Family
16-0x15-6

Brk
10-2x
13-6

Kit
9-7x11-4

Dining
13-6x13-0

34'-0"

Dn

P   R

Living
15-4x11-6

Garage
19-4x19-6

Up

Porch depth 6-0

PLAN DATA

Total Living Area:	2,135
Bedrooms:	4
Baths:	2 1/2
Garage:	2-car
Foundation Type:	
Basement	

PLAN DATA

Total Living Area: 2,024
Bedrooms: 4
Baths: 2 1/2
Garage: 2-car
Foundation Type:
Basement

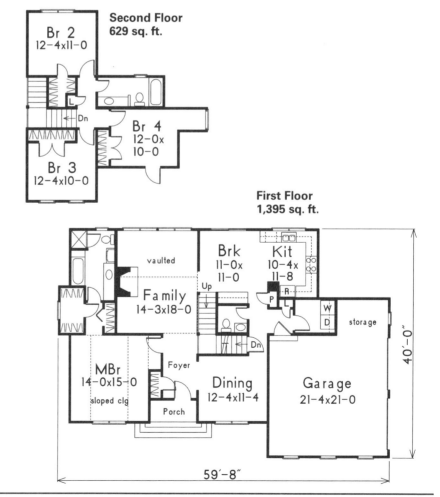

Second Floor
629 sq. ft.

Br 2
12-4x11-0

Br 4
12-0x
10-0

Br 3
12-4x10-0

Dn

First Floor
1,395 sq. ft.

vaulted

Brk
11-0x
11-0

Kit
10-4x
11-8

Family
14-3x18-0

Up

P

R

W
D

storage

MBr
14-0x15-0

Foyer

Dining
12-4x11-4

Garage
21-4x21-0

Dn

sloped clg

Porch

40'-0"

59'-8"

PLAN DATA

Total Living Area: 1,989
Bedrooms: 4
Baths: 3
Garage: 2-car
Foundation Types:
  Crawl space
  Slab
Please specify when ordering

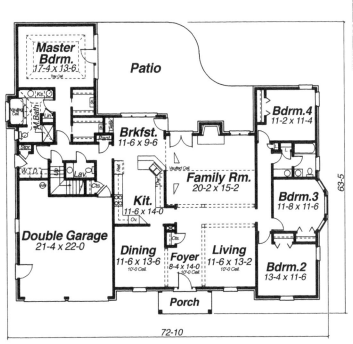

PLAN DATA

Total Living Area: 2,542
Bedrooms: 4
Baths: 2 1/2
Garage: 2-car
Foundation Types:
  Basement
  Crawl space
  Slab
Please specify when ordering

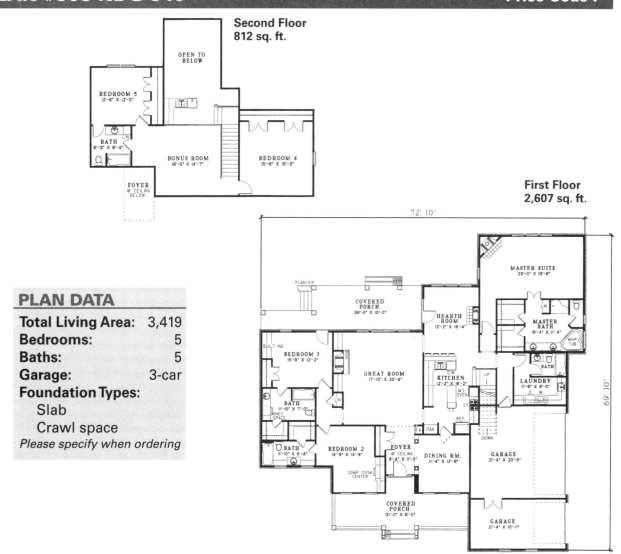

Second Floor
812 sq. ft.

BEDROOM 5
12'-6" X 12'-0"

OPEN TO BELOW

BATH
8'-3" X 8'-4"

LIN

BONUS ROOM
18'-0" X 14'-7"

BEDROOM 4
15'-6" X 15'-3"

FOYER
10' CEILING BELOW

First Floor
2,607 sq. ft.

72' 10"

69' 10"

PLANTER

MASTER SUITE
23'-0" X 13'-8"

COVERED PORCH
36'-5" X 10'-0"

HEARTH ROOM
12'-2" X 16'-4"

LIN

MASTER BATH
18'-4" X 11'-4"

WHP TUB

BATH

BUILT-INS

BEDROOM 3
15'-8" X 12'-2"

GREAT ROOM
17'-10" X 20'-6"

KITCHEN
12'-2" X 16'-2"

D W

UP

LAUNDRY
11'-8" X 6'-0"

D W

BATH
11'-10" X 7'-0"

LIN

M.C. OVEN

TC

CT

REF

DOWN

GARAGE
21'-4" X 20'-6"

KNEE SPACE

BATH
11'-10" X 5'-4"

BEDROOM 2
15'-8" X 14'-6"

FOYER
10' CEILING
6'-4" X 11'-0"

R A

PAN

DINING RM.
11'-4" X 12'-8"

COMP. DESK CENTER

COVERED PORCH
31'-0" X 8'-0"

GARAGE
21'-4" X 10'-11"

PLAN DATA

Total Living Area:	3,419
Bedrooms:	5
Baths:	5
Garage:	3-car

Foundation Types:
Slab
Crawl space
Please specify when ordering

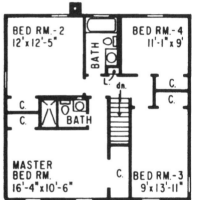

Second Floor - 4 bedroom plan
870 sq. ft.

BED RM.-2
12'x12'-5"

BED RM.-4
11'-1" x 9'

BATH

dn.

C.
C.

C.
C.

BATH

MASTER
BED RM.
16'-4"x10'-6"

C.

BED RM.-3
9'x13'-11"

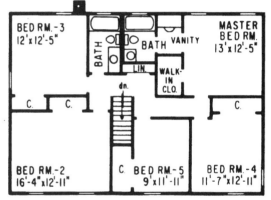

Second Floor - 5 bedroom plan
1,218 sq. ft.

BED RM.-3
12'x12'-5"

BATH

VANITY

MASTER
BED RM.
13'x12'-5"

BATH

LIN.

WALK-
IN
CLO.

dn.

C.
C.

C.

BED RM.-2
16'-4"x12'-11"

C. BED RM.-5
9'x11'-11"

BED RM.-4
11'-7"x12'-11"

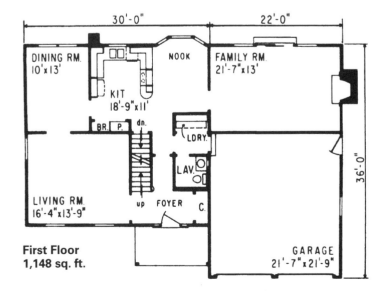

30'-0" 22'-0"

DINING RM.
10'x13'

NOOK

FAMILY RM.
21'-7"x13'

KIT
18'-9"x11"

BR. P.

dn.

LDRY.

LAV.

36'-0"

LIVING RM.
16'-4"x13'-9"

up FOYER

C.

First Floor
1,148 sq. ft.

GARAGE
21'-7"x21'-9"

PLAN DATA

Total Living Area: 2,366
Bedrooms: 4
Baths: 2 1/2
Garage: 2-car
Foundation Type:
  Basement
Features:
  5 bedroom plan
  includes an additional
  348 square feet of
  living area

Second Floor
825 sq. ft.

Br 3
11-6x11-6

MBr
15-10x12-8
vaulted

Dn

open to below

Br 2
12-4x11-0

raised ceiling

46'0"

Deck

Screened Porch

Dinette
9-0x10-4

Kitchen
11-4x11-8

Family
12-0x19-0

36'8"

Dn

Up

Living
12-4x12-4

Garage
21-0x22-0

Porch Depth 5-0

Window Seat

First Floor
870 sq. ft.

PLAN DATA

Total Living Area:	1,695
Bedrooms:	3
Baths:	2 1/2
Garage:	2-car
Foundation Type:	
Basement	

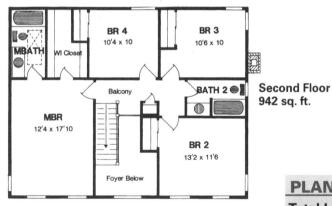

**Second Floor
942 sq. ft.**

BR 4
10'4 x 10

BR 3
10'6 x 10

MBATH

WI Closet

Balcony

BATH 2

MBR
12'4 x 17'10

BR 2
13'2 x 11'6

Foyer Below

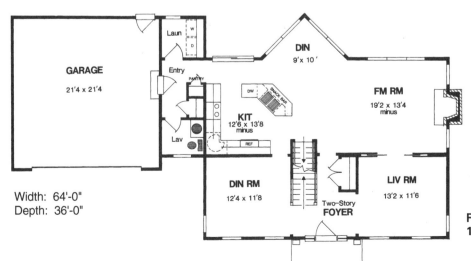

GARAGE
21'4 x 21'4

Laun

Entry

PANTRY

DIN
9' x 10'

FM RM
19'2 x 13'4
minus

KIT
12'6 x 13'8
minus

Lav

REF

DIN RM
12'4 x 11'8

Two-Story
FOYER

LIV RM
13'2 x 11'6

Width: 64'-0"
Depth: 36'-0"

**First Floor
1,108 sq. ft.**

PLAN DATA

Total Living Area:	2,050
Bedrooms:	4
Baths:	2 1/2
Garage:	2-car
Foundation Type:	
Basement	

PLAN DATA

Total Living Area: 1,833
Bedrooms: 3
Baths: 2
Garage: 2-car
Foundation Type:
  Basement
Features:
  Drive-under garage

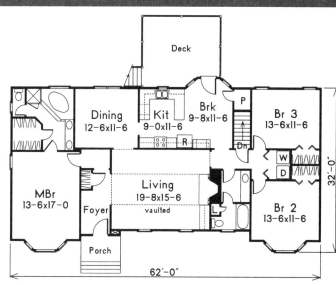

PLAN #565-0748

Price Code D

PLAN DATA

Total Living Area: 2,514
Bedrooms: 3
Baths: 2
Garage: 3-car
Foundation Types:
  Walk-out basement
Features:
  Extra storage in
  garage

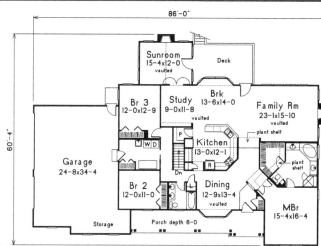

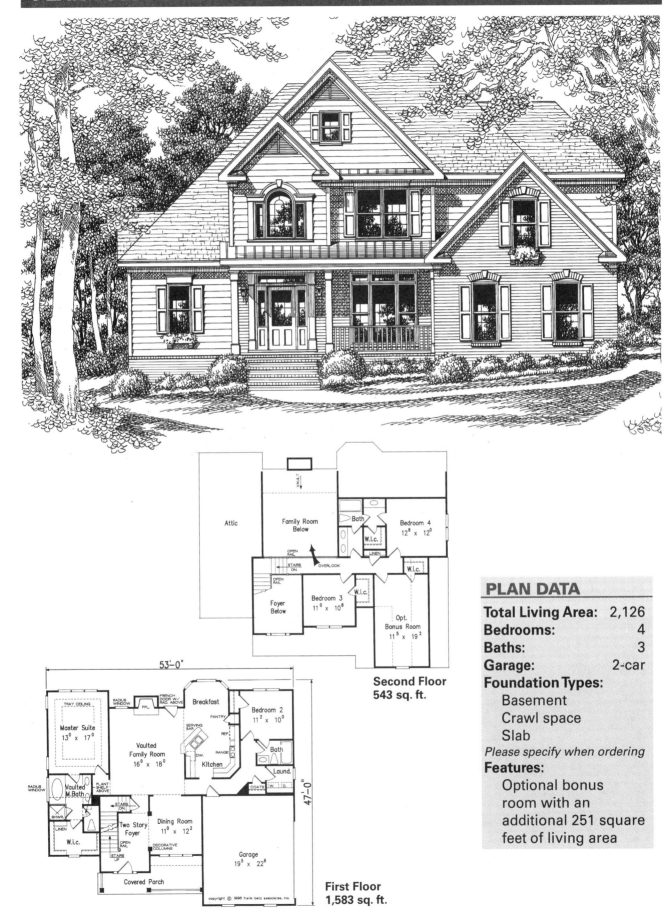

Second Floor
543 sq. ft.

First Floor
1,583 sq. ft.

PLAN DATA

Total Living Area:	2,126
Bedrooms:	4
Baths:	3
Garage:	2-car

Foundation Types:
Basement
Crawl space
Slab
Please specify when ordering

Features:
Optional bonus room with an additional 251 square feet of living area

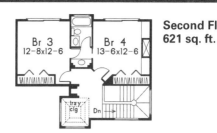

Second Floor
621 sq. ft.

Br 3
12-8x12-6

Br 4
13-6x12-6

tray
clg

Dn

First Floor
2,669 sq. ft.

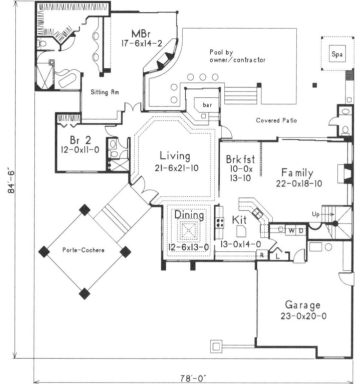

MBr
17-6x14-2

Pool by owner/contractor

Spa

Sitting Rm

bar

Covered Patio

Br 2
12-0x11-0

Living
21-6x21-10

Brk fst
10-0x
13-10

Family
22-0x18-10

Dining
12-6x13-0

Kit
13-0x14-0

Up

W D

R   L

Porte-Cochere

Garage
23-0x20-0

84'-6"

78'-0"

PLAN DATA

Total Living Area: 3,290
Bedrooms: 4
Baths: 3 1/2
Garage: 2-car
Foundation Type:
Slab
Features:
Varied ceiling heights throughout

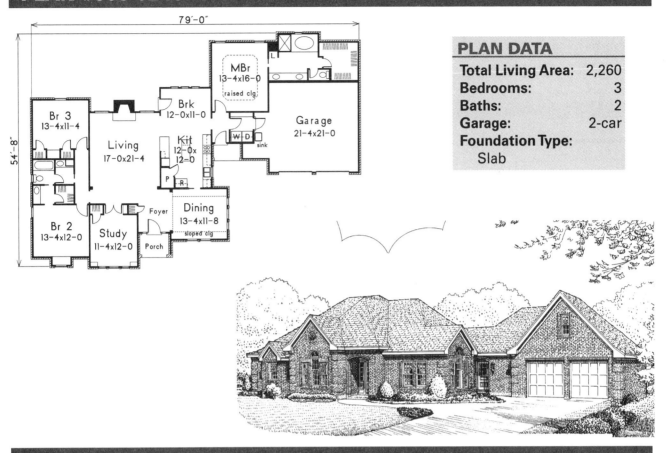

PLAN DATA	
Total Living Area:	2,260
Bedrooms:	3
Baths:	2
Garage:	2-car
Foundation Type:	
Slab	

PLAN #565-FDG-9035

Price Code B

PLAN DATA	
Total Living Area:	1,760
Bedrooms:	3
Baths:	2
Garage:	2-car
Foundation Type:	
Slab	

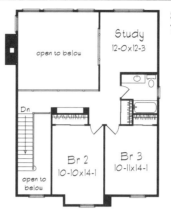

Second Floor
772 sq. ft.

Study
12-0x12-3

open to below

Dn

Br 2
10-10x14-1

Br 3
10-11x14-1

open to below

PLAN DATA

Total Living Area:	2,444
Bedrooms:	3
Baths:	2 1/2
Garage:	2-car
Foundation Type:	
Basement	

64'-0"

48'-0"

Great Rm
17-0x15-9

Brk
11-8x11-6

Patio

skylt

Kitchen
11-8x11-0

Dn

MBr
13-8x20-0

Dining
14-1x11-11

Up

Garage
19-8x19-5

Porch

First Floor
1,672 sq. ft.

J.N. HANSEN

COPYRIGHT LARRY E. BELK

Second Floor
558 sq. ft.

PLAN DATA

Total Living Area:	2,586
Bedrooms:	4
Baths:	3
Garage:	2-car

Foundation Types:
Basement
Crawl space
Slab
Please specify when ordering

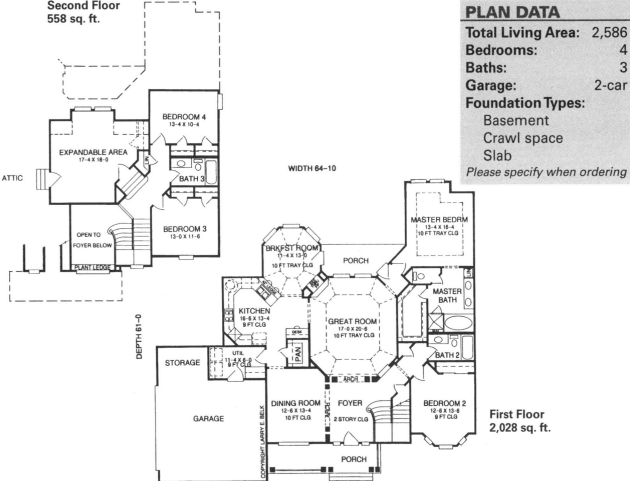

BEDROOM 4
13-4 X 10-4

EXPANDABLE AREA
17-4 X 18-0

ATTIC

BATH 3

OPEN TO
FOYER BELOW

BEDROOM 3
13-0 X 11-6

PLANT LEDGE

WIDTH 64-10

DEPTH 61-0

MASTER BEDRM
13-4 X 16-4
10 FT TRAY CLG

BRKFST ROOM
11-4 X 13-0
10 FT TRAY CLG

PORCH

MASTER
BATH

KITCHEN
16-6 X 13-4
9 FT CLG

GREAT ROOM
17-0 X 20-6
10 FT TRAY CLG

STORAGE

UTIL
11-4 X 6-0
9 FT CLG

DESK

PAN

BATH 2

GARAGE

DINING ROOM
12-6 X 13-4
10 FT CLG

ARCH

FOYER
2 STORY CLG

ARCH

BEDROOM 2
12-6 X 13-6
9 FT CLG

COPYRIGHT LARRY E. BELK

PORCH

First Floor
2,028 sq. ft.

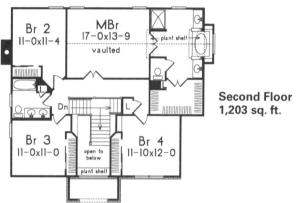

Second Floor
1,203 sq. ft.

Br 2
11-0x11-4

MBr
17-0x13-9
vaulted

plant shelf

Dn

L

Br 3
11-0x11-0

open to
below

plant shelf

Br 4
11-10x12-0

55'-0"

Deck

Family
19-0x19-3

Brk
10-0x
14-6

Kit

9-10x12-6

P

W D

R

43'-0"

Dn

Up

Entry

shelves

Up

Dining
14-0x12-0

tray clg

Garage
19-4x21-0

Parlor
11-0x13-4

vaulted

plant shelf

Porch

First Floor
1,412 sq. ft.

PLAN DATA

Total Living Area:	2,615
Bedrooms:	4
Baths:	2 1/2
Garage:	2-car
Foundation Type:	
Basement	

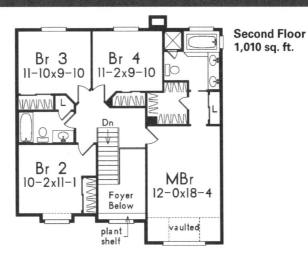

**Second Floor
1,010 sq. ft.**

Br 3
11-10x9-10

Br 4
11-2x9-10

Dn

Br 2
10-2x11-1

Foyer
Below

plant
shelf

MBr
12-0x18-4

vaulted

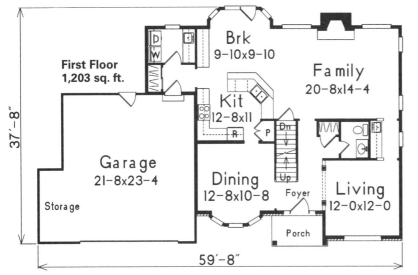

**First Floor
1,203 sq. ft.**

37'-8"

59'-8"

Brk
9-10x9-10

Family
20-8x14-4

Kit
12-8x11

Garage
21-8x23-4

Storage

Dining
12-8x10-8

Foyer

Porch

Living
12-0x12-0

PLAN DATA

Total Living Area:	2,213
Bedrooms:	4
Baths:	2 1/2
Garage:	2-car
Foundation Type:	
Basement	

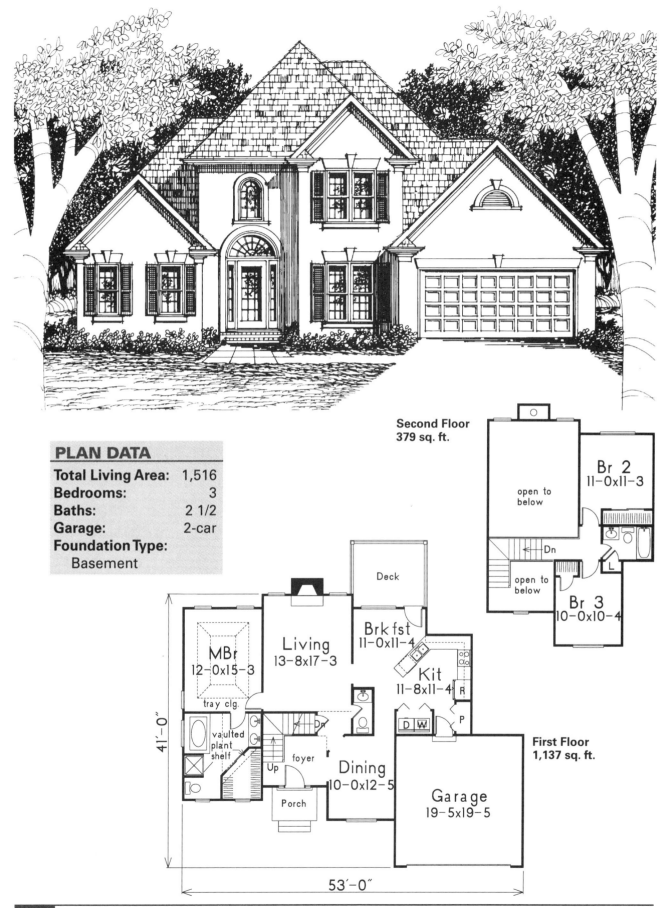

PLAN DATA

Total Living Area: 1,516
Bedrooms: 3
Baths: 2 1/2
Garage: 2-car
Foundation Type:
　Basement

Second Floor
379 sq. ft.

open to
below

Br 2
11-0x11-3

Dn

open to
below

L

Br 3
10-0x10-4

Deck

Brk fst
11-0x11-4

MBr
12-0x15-3

Living
13-8x17-3

Kit
11-8x11-4

R

tray clg.

vaulted
plant
shelf

Dn

D W

P

Up

foyer

First Floor
1,137 sq. ft.

Dining
10-0x12-5

Garage
19-5x19-5

Porch

41'-0"

53'-0"

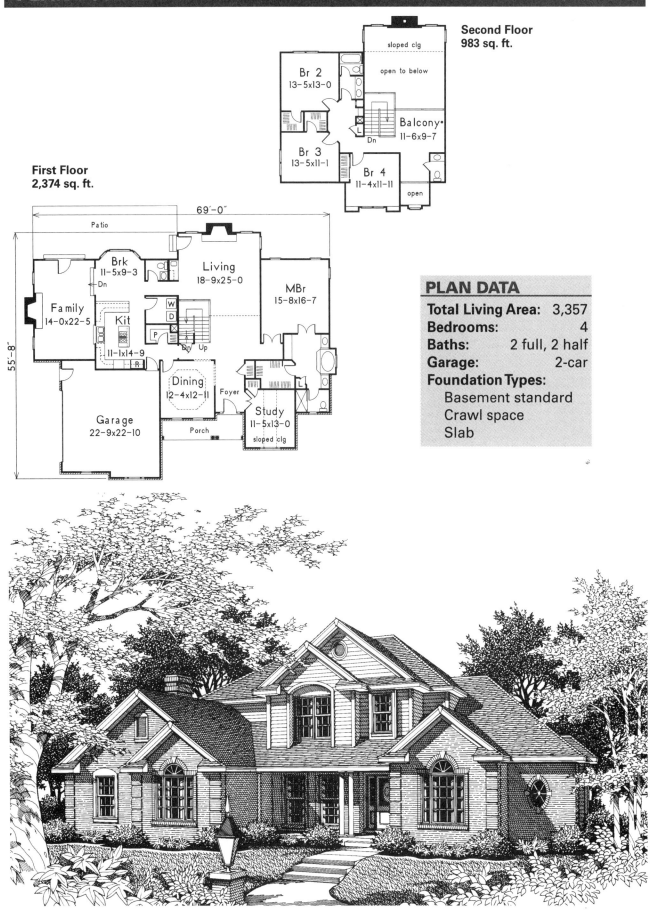

Second Floor
983 sq. ft.

sloped clg

open to below

Br 2
13-5x13-0

Balcony
11-6x9-7

Br 3
13-5x11-1

Dn

L

Br 4
11-4x11-11

open

First Floor
2,374 sq. ft.

69'-0"

Patio

55'-8"

Brk
11-5x9-3

Dn

Living
18-9x25-0

MBr
15-8x16-7

Family
14-0x22-5

Kit
11-1x14-9

W
D
P

Dn Up

R

Dining
12-4x12-11

Foyer

Garage
22-9x22-10

Porch

Study
11-5x13-0

sloped clg

PLAN DATA

Total Living Area: 3,357
Bedrooms: 4
Baths: 2 full, 2 half
Garage: 2-car
Foundation Types:
  Basement standard
  Crawl space
  Slab

Second Floor
952 sq. ft.

First Floor
1,228 sq. ft.

PLAN DATA

Total Living Area:	2,180
Bedrooms:	3
Baths:	2 1/2
Garage:	2-car
Foundation Type:	
Basement	

Second Floor
1,233 sq. ft.

5,40 X 4,30
18'-0" X 14'-4"

4,50 X 4,50
15'-0" X 15'-0"

3,80 X 4,80
12'-8" X 16'-0"

3,00 X 4,20
10'-0" X 14'-0"

3,00 X 3,60
10'-0" X 12'-0"

PLAN DATA

Total Living Area:	2,300
Bedrooms:	3
Baths:	2 1/2
Garage:	2-car

Foundation Type:
 Basement

Features:
- 9' ceilings on first floor
- 2" x 6" exterior walls

First Floor
1,067 sq. ft.

6,80 X 4,20
22'-0" X 14'-0"

6,00 X 6,00
20'-0" X 20'-0"

3,90 X 5,10
13'-0" X 17'-0"

6,00 X 6,00
20'-0" X 20'-0"

3,00 X 3,60
10'-0" X 12'-0"

3,00 X 1,80
10'-0" X 6'-0"

9,9 m
33'-0"

17,4 m
58'-0"

First Floor
2,182 sq. ft.

PLAN DATA

Total Living Area: 3,411
Bedrooms: 3
Baths: 3
Garage: 3-car
Foundation Type:
  Basement

Lower Level
1,229 sq. ft.

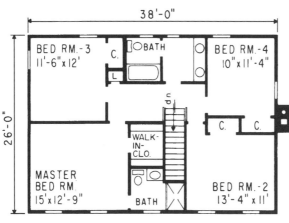

38'-0"

BED RM.-3
11'-6"x12'

C.

BATH

BED RM.-4
10"x11'-4"

26'-0"

up

dn

WALK-IN-CLO.

C.

C.

MASTER
BED RM.
15'x12'-9"

BATH

BED RM.-2
13'-4"x11'

Second Floor
988 sq. ft.

PLAN DATA

Total Living Area:	2,137
Bedrooms:	4
Baths:	2 1/2
Garage:	2-car
Foundation Type:	
Partial basement/ crawl space	

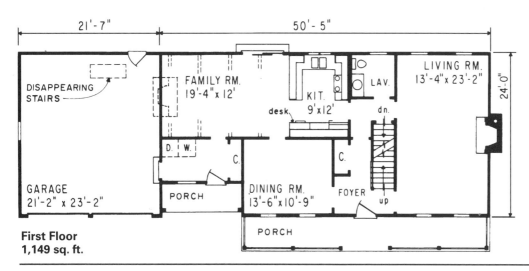

21'-7"

50'- 5"

DISAPPEARING
STAIRS

FAMILY RM.
19'-4"x 12'

KIT.
9'x12'

LAV.

LIVING RM.
13'-4"x 23'-2"

24'-0"

desk

dn.

D. W.

C.

C.

up

GARAGE
21'-2" x 23'-2"

PORCH

DINING RM.
13'-6"x10'-9"

FOYER

PORCH

First Floor
1,149 sq. ft.

Second Floor
1,455 sq. ft.

Br 2
18-9x13-3

Br 3
18-9x13-3

Dn→   Dn→   L

Loft
14-9x12-0

open to
below

Br 4
14-2x12-0

PLAN DATA

Total Living Area:	3,657
Bedrooms:	4
Baths:	3 1/2
Garage:	3-car
Foundation Type:	
Basement	

First Floor
2,202 sq. ft.

61'-0"

Patio

vaulted clg

Brk fst
11-0x13-8

Kit
10-6x
15-0

Family
21-1x19-3

bar

MBr
15-0x17-0
vaulted clg

Dn→

Up

W D

Dining
14-0x12-0
raised clg

Up

Parlor
13-0x15-0

Porch

Garage
21-4x31-8

vaulted clg

vaulted clg

73'-0"

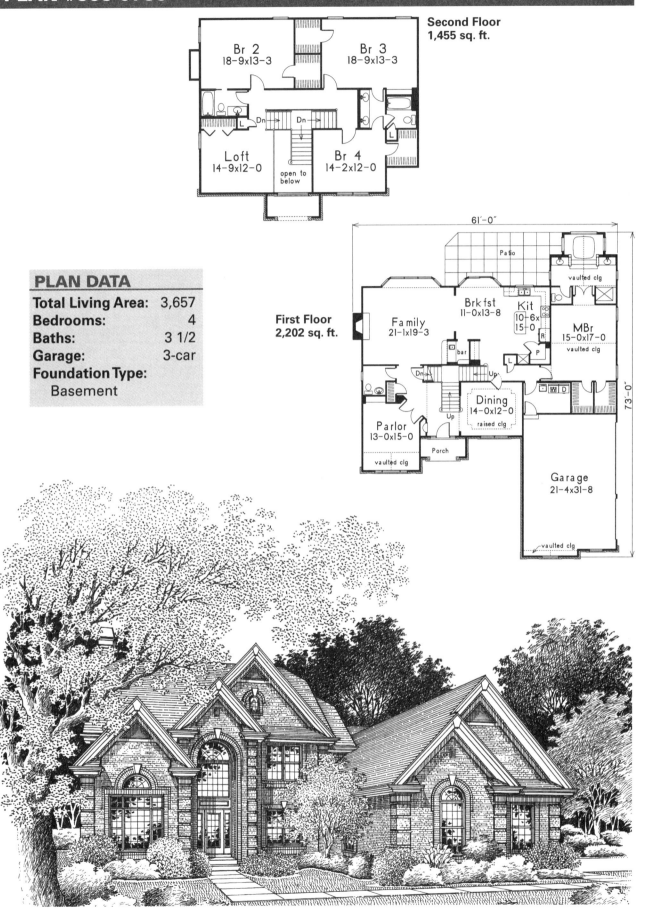

Second Floor
880 sq. ft.

4,00 X 2,70
13'-4" X 9'-0"

3,30 X 3,30
11'-0" X 11'-0"

BONUS ROOM
4,70 X 4,60
15'-8" X 15'-4"

3,80 X 4,70
12'-8" X 15'-8"

First Floor
880 sq. ft.

6,20 X 3,40
20'-8" X 11'-4"

5,10 X 3,30
17'-0" X 11'-0"

4,60 X 6,80
15'-4" X 22'-8"

3,80 X 4,70
12'-8" X 15'-8"

12,0 m
40'-0"

12,6 m
42'-0"

PLAN DATA

Total Living Area:	1,760
Bedrooms:	3
Baths:	2 1/2
Garage:	1-car

Foundation Type:
Basement

Features:
- 9' ceilings on first floor
- 2" x 6" exterior walls

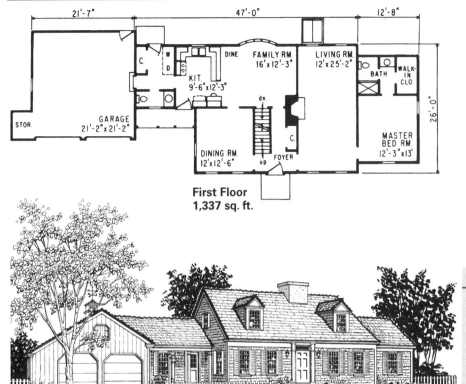

First Floor
1,337 sq. ft.

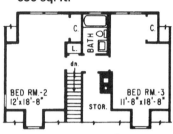

Second Floor
636 sq. ft.

PLAN DATA

Total Living Area:	1,973
Bedrooms:	3
Baths:	2 1/2
Garage:	2-car
Foundation Type:	Partial basement/ crawl space

PLAN DATA

Total Living Area:	1,710
Bedrooms:	4
Baths:	2
Garage:	2-car
Foundation Type:	Slab

Features:
- Bedrooms have sloped ceilings
- 10' ceiling in family room

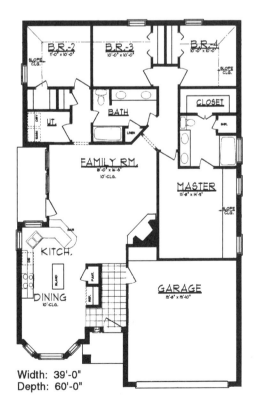

Width: 39'-0"
Depth: 60'-0"

Second Floor
598 sq. ft.

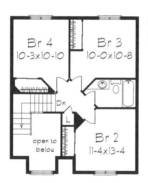

Br 4
10-3x10-10

Br 3
10-0x10-8

Dn

open to below

Br 2
11-4x13-4

First Floor
1,861 sq. ft.

PLAN DATA	
Total Living Area:	2,459
Bedrooms:	4
Baths:	2 1/2
Garage:	2-car
Foundation Type:	
Basement	
Features:	
2" x 6" exterior walls	

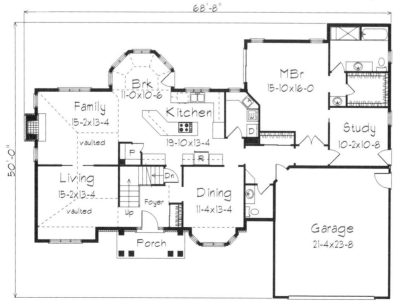

68'-8"

50'-0"

Brk
11-0x10-6

Family
15-2x13-4
vaulted

Kitchen
19-10x13-4

MBr
15-10x16-0

Study
10-2x10-8

Living
15-2x13-4
vaulted

P

Dn

Up   Foyer

Dining
11-4x13-4

Garage
21-4x23-8

Porch

PLAN DATA

Total Living Area:	2,012
Bedrooms:	5
Baths:	2 1/2
Garage:	2-car
Foundation Type:	
Basement	

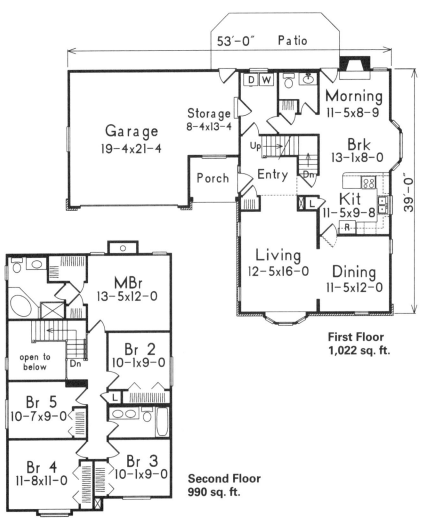

53'-0" Patio

Garage
19-4x21-4

Storage
8-4x13-4

Morning
11-5x8-9

Brk
13-1x8-0

D W

Up

Porch

Entry

Dn

Kit
11-5x9-8

L

R

Living
12-5x16-0

Dining
11-5x12-0

39'-0"

First Floor
1,022 sq. ft.

MBr
13-5x12-0

Br 2
10-1x9-0

open to
below

Dn

Br 5
10-7x9-0

L

Br 4
11-8x11-0

Br 3
10-1x9-0

Second Floor
990 sq. ft.

PLAN DATA

Total Living Area: 2,096
Bedrooms: 3
Baths: 2 1/2
Garage: 2-car
Foundation Type:
  Basement

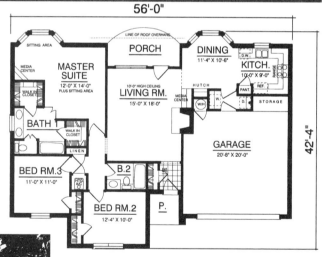

PLAN DATA

Total Living Area: 1,429
Bedrooms: 3
Baths: 2
Garage: 2-car
Foundation Types:
  Crawl space
  Slab
Please specify when ordering

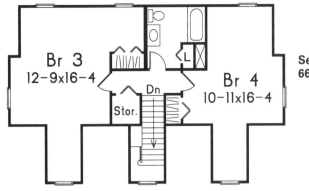

Second Floor
665 sq. ft.

Br 3
12-9x16-4

Br 4
10-11x16-4

Dn

Stor.

L

PLAN DATA

Total Living Area:	1,705
Bedrooms:	4
Baths:	2
Foundation Types:	
Crawl space standard	
Basement	
Slab	

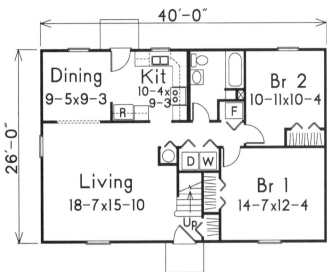

40'-0"

26'-0"

First Floor
1,040 sq. ft.

Dining
9-5x9-3

Kit
10-4x
9-3

R

Br 2
10-11x10-4

F

D W

Living
18-7x15-10

Br 1
14-7x12-4

Up

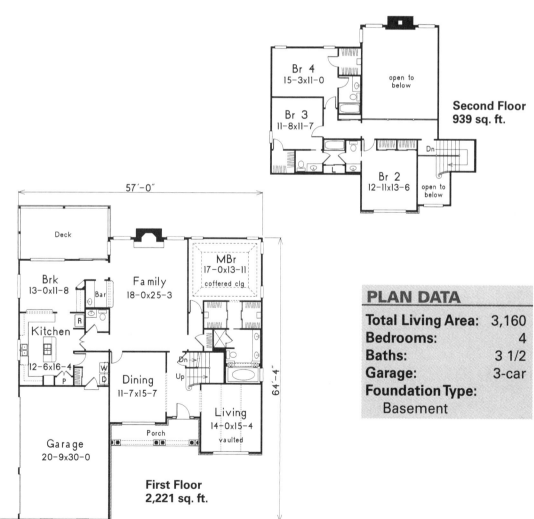

Second Floor
939 sq. ft.

Br 4
15-3x11-0

open to below

Br 3
11-8x11-7

Br 2
12-11x13-6

Dn

open to below

57'-0"

Deck

Brk
13-0x11-8

Bar

Kitchen
12-6x16-4

R

Family
18-0x25-3

MBr
17-0x13-11
coffered clg.

Dn

Up

W
D

P

Dining
11-7x15-7

64'-4"

Living
14-0x15-4
vaulted

Garage
20-9x30-0

Porch

First Floor
2,221 sq. ft.

PLAN DATA

Total Living Area: 3,160
Bedrooms: 4
Baths: 3 1/2
Garage: 3-car
Foundation Type:
  Basement

PLAN DATA

Total Living Area: 2,760
Bedrooms: 4
Baths: 2 1/2
Garage: 2-car
Foundation Type:
  Basement

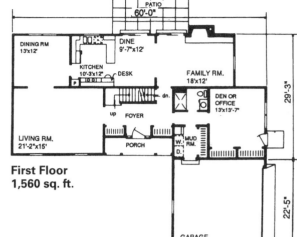

First Floor
1,560 sq. ft.

Second Floor
1,200 sq. ft.

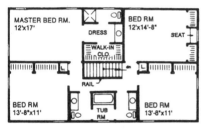

PLAN DATA

Total Living Area: 1,307
Bedrooms: 3
Baths: 2
Garage: 2-car
Foundation Types:
  Slab
  Basement
  Crawl space
Please specify when ordering
Features:
  2" x 6" exterior walls

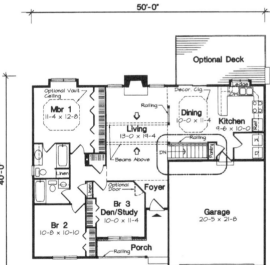

Rear View

Second Floor Above Garage

Home Office
13-4x17-0
sloped clg

Main House First Floor 1,213 sq. ft.

Main House Second Floor 932 sq. ft.

Br 2
10-8x12-0

Br 3
10-8x12-0

dn

MBr
13-4x14-0
vaulted

Porch

Brk
10-4x12-0

Utility
8-8x8-0

Kitchen
13-0x14-0

Dining
11-4x13-8

R

Alcove
7-0x10-0

Foyer

up

Living
13-4x21-0

Porch

50'-4"

33'-0"

Garage Apartment 738 sq. ft.

22'-0"

Studio
17-8x12-0

R

up

L

45'-4"

Garage
21-4x21-8

PLAN DATA

Total Living Area:	2,883
Bedrooms:	3
Baths:	3 1/2
Garage:	2-car
Foundation Type:	
Slab	
Features:	
9' ceilings	

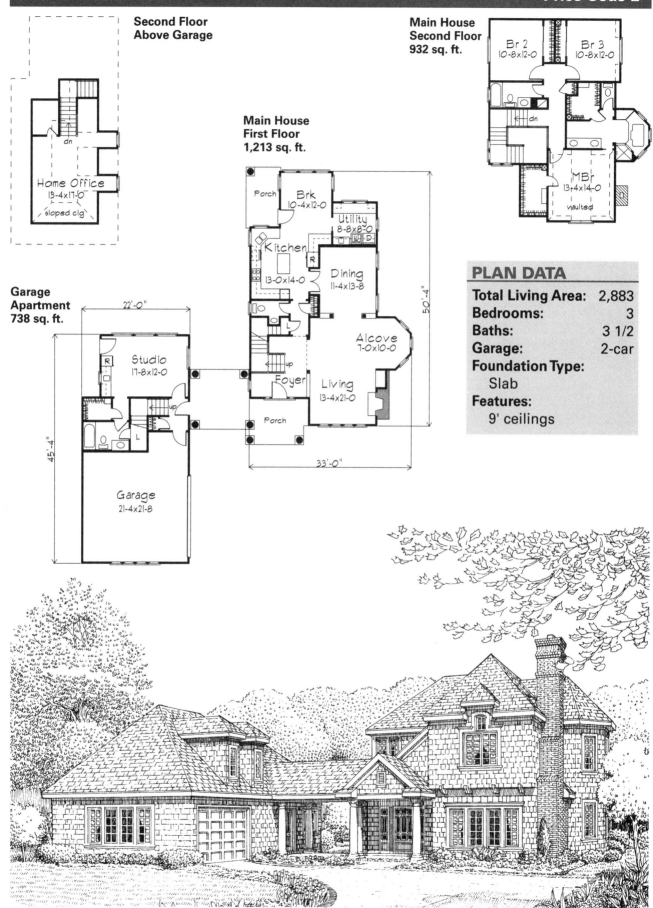

PLAN DATA

Total Living Area:	2,204
Bedrooms:	3
Baths:	2 1/2
Garage:	2-car
Foundation Type:	
Basement	

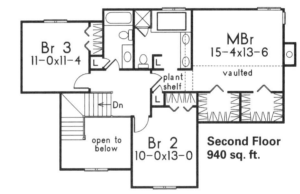

Br 3
11-0x11-4

MBr
15-4x13-6
vaulted

plant shelf

Dn

open to below

Br 2
10-0x13-0

**Second Floor
940 sq. ft.**

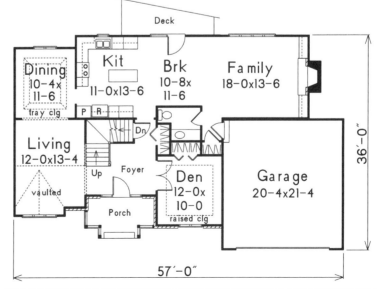

Deck

Dining
10-4x
11-6
tray clg

Kit
11-0x13-6

Brk
10-8x
11-6

Family
18-0x13-6

P R

Dn

Living
12-0x13-4

Up

Foyer

Den
12-0x
10-0
raised clg

Garage
20-4x21-4

vaulted

Porch

**First Floor
1,264 sq. ft.**

36'-0"

57'-0"

Second Floor
940 sq. ft.

MASTER BEDROOM
14'-4" x 16'-4"

BEDROOM
11'-1" x 14'-0"

BEDROOM
12'-0" x 10'-9"

BATH 2

BATH 1

LINEN

DN.

PLAN DATA

Total Living Area: 1,858
Bedrooms: 3
Baths: 2 1/2
Garage: 2-car
Foundation Type:
  Basement

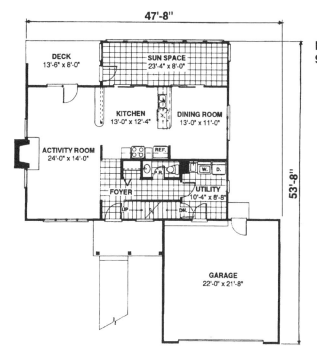

47'-8"

53'-8"

First Floor
918 sq. ft.

DECK
13'-6" x 8'-0"

SUN SPACE
23'-4" x 8'-0"

KITCHEN
13'-0" x 12'-4"

DINING ROOM
13'-0" x 11'-0"

ACTIVITY ROOM
24'-0" x 14'-0"

REF.

W. D.

P.R.

FOYER

UTILITY
10'-4" x 8'-8"

UP

DN.

GARAGE
22'-0" x 21'-8"

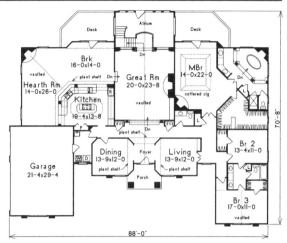

PLAN DATA

Total Living Area: 3,814
Bedrooms: 3
Baths: 2 1/2
Garage: 3-car
Foundation Type:
  Walk-out basement
Features:
  3,566 square feet on
  the first floor and 248
  square feet on the
  lower level atrium

Rear View

PLAN DATA

Total Living Area: 1,849
Bedrooms: 3
Baths: 2
Garage: 2-car
Foundation Types:
  Crawl space
  Slab
Please specify when ordering

Width: 66'-5"
Depth: 60'-0"

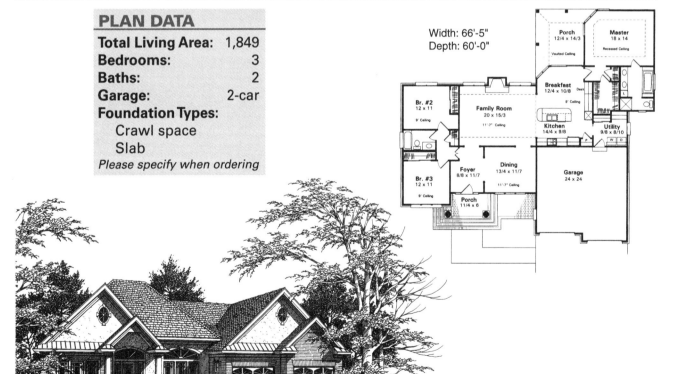

PLAN DATA

Total Living Area:	1,595
Bedrooms:	3
Baths:	2
Garage:	2-car

Foundation Types:
- Basement
- Slab
- Crawl space

Please specify when ordering

Features:
- Vaulted ceiling in master suite

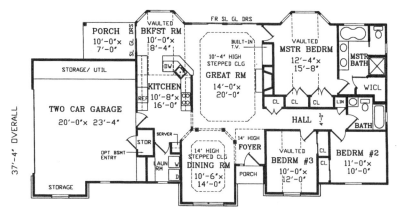

PLAN DATA

Total Living Area:	1,525
Bedrooms:	3
Baths:	2
Garage:	2-car

Foundation Types:
- Crawl space
- Slab

Please specify when ordering

PLAN DATA

Total Living Area: 2,414
Bedrooms: 4
Baths: 2 1/2
Garage: 2-car
Foundation Types:
   Plan #565-1303-1
   Basement
   Plan #565-1303-2
   Crawl space

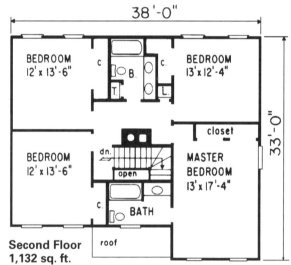

BEDROOM
12' x 13'-6"

c

B.

c.

BEDROOM
13' x 12'-4"

T.

L.

closet

BEDROOM
12' x 13'-6"

dn.

open

MASTER
BEDROOM
13' x 17'-4"

c.

BATH

Second Floor
1,132 sq. ft.

roof

38'-0"

33'-0"

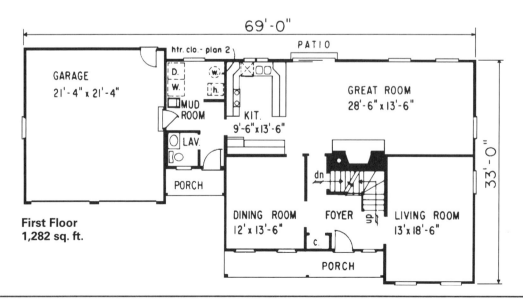

38'-0"...

GARAGE
21'-4" x 21'-4"

htr. clo. - plan 2

PATIO

D.
W.

W.

h.

MUD
ROOM

KIT.
9'-6" x 13'-6"

GREAT ROOM
28'-6" x 13'-6"

LAV.

PORCH

DINING ROOM
12' x 13'-6"

dn

FOYER

up

LIVING ROOM
13' x 18'-6"

c.

First Floor
1,282 sq. ft.

PORCH

69'-0"

33'-0"

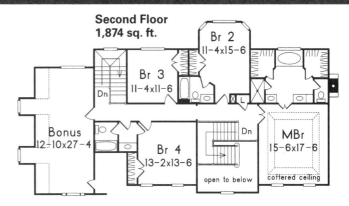

Second Floor
1,874 sq. ft.

Br 2
11-4x15-6

Br 3
11-4x11-6

Dn

Bonus
12-10x27-4

Br 4
13-2x13-6

Dn

open to below

MBr
15-6x17-6

coffered ceiling

L

PLAN DATA

Total Living Area:	3,427
Bedrooms:	4
Baths:	3 1/2
Garage:	2-car
Foundation Type:	
Basement	
Features:	
10' ceilings	

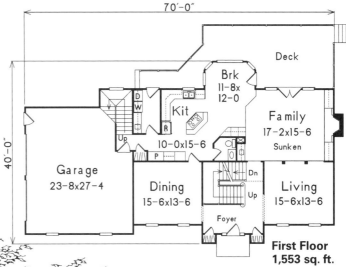

70'-0"

40'-0"

Deck

Brk
11-8x
12-0

Kit

Family
17-2x15-6
Sunken

Garage
23-8x27-4

10-0x15-6

Dining
15-6x13-6

Dn

Up

Living
15-6x13-6

Up

P

Foyer

First Floor
1,553 sq. ft.

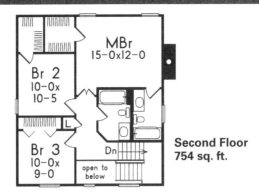

Second Floor
754 sq. ft.

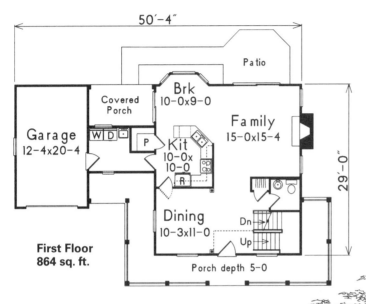

First Floor
864 sq. ft.

PLAN DATA

Total Living Area:	1,618
Bedrooms:	3
Baths:	2 1/2
Garage:	1-car
Foundation Type:	
Basement	

Second Floor 1,000 sq. ft.

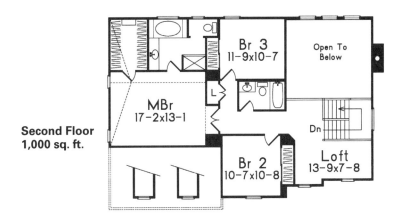

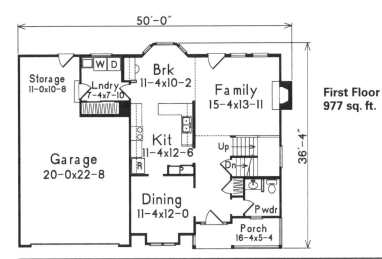

First Floor 977 sq. ft.

PLAN DATA

Total Living Area:	1,977
Bedrooms:	3
Baths:	2 1/2
Garage:	2-car
Foundation Type:	
Basement	
Features:	
Extra storage in garage	

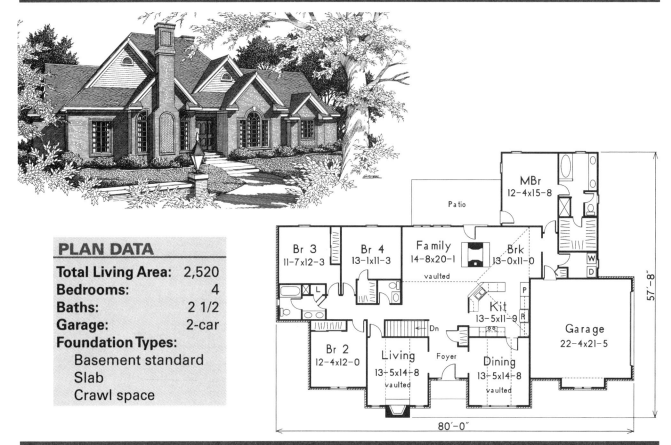

PLAN DATA

Total Living Area: 2,520
Bedrooms: 4
Baths: 2 1/2
Garage: 2-car
Foundation Types:
   Basement standard
   Slab
   Crawl space

PLAN #565-FDG-8729-L

Price Code D

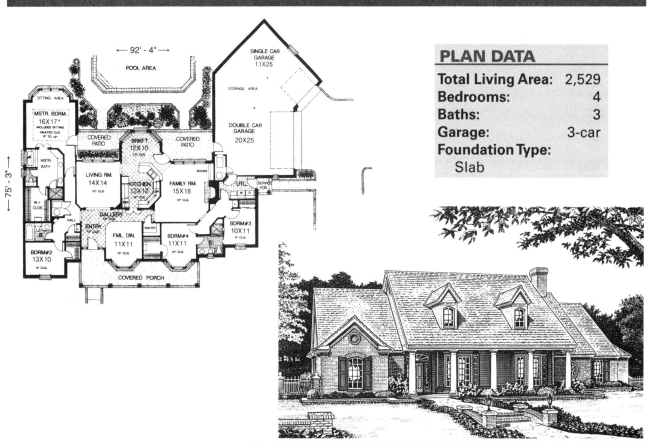

PLAN DATA

Total Living Area: 2,529
Bedrooms: 4
Baths: 3
Garage: 3-car
Foundation Type:
   Slab

64'-6"

59'-0"

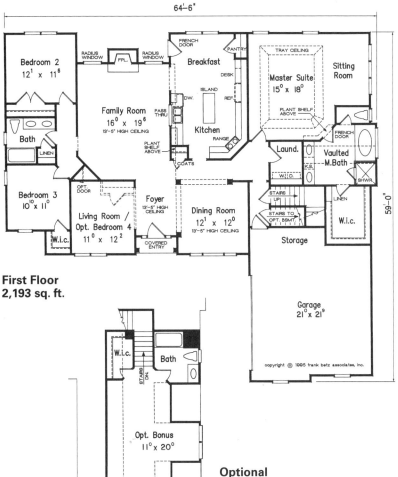

Bedroom 2
12¹ x 11⁶

RADIUS WINDOW

FPL

RADIUS WINDOW

FRENCH DOOR

Breakfast

PANTRY

TRAY CEILING

Master Suite
15⁰ x 18⁰

Sitting Room

DESK

Bath

LINEN

Family Room
16⁰ x 19⁶
13'-5" HIGH CEILING

PLANT SHELF ABOVE

DW.

ISLAND

REF.

Kitchen

RANGE

PLANT SHELF ABOVE

FRENCH DOOR

Bedroom 3
10¹⁰ x 11⁰

COATS

OPT. DOOR

Laund.

Vaulted M. Bath

W. D.

K.S.

SHWR.

W.i.c.

Foyer
13'-5" HIGH CEILING

Living Room / Opt. Bedroom 4
11⁰ x 12²

COVERED ENTRY

Dining Room
12¹ x 12⁰
13'-5" HIGH CEILING

STAIRS UP

STAIRS TO OPT. BSMT.

LINEN

W.i.c.

Storage

Garage
21⁰ x 21⁹

copyright © 1995 frank betz associates, inc.

**First Floor
2,193 sq. ft.**

W.i.c.

STAIRS DN.

Bath

Opt. Bonus
11⁰ x 20⁰

**Optional
Second Floor**

PLAN DATA

Total Living Area:	2,193
Bedrooms:	3
Baths:	3
Garage:	2-car

Foundation Types:

Slab

Basement

Crawl space

Please specify when ordering

Features:

Optional bonus room with bath on second floor has an additional 400 square feet

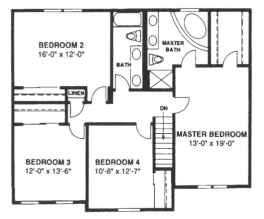

Second Floor
1,418 sq. ft.

BEDROOM 2
16'-0" x 12'-0"

BATH

MASTER BATH

LINEN

DN

MASTER BEDROOM
13'-0" x 19'-0"

BEDROOM 3
12'-0" x 13'-6"

BEDROOM 4
10'-8" x 12'-7"

PLAN DATA

Total Living Area:	2,586
Bedrooms:	4
Baths:	2 1/2
Garage:	2-car
Foundation Type:	
Basement	

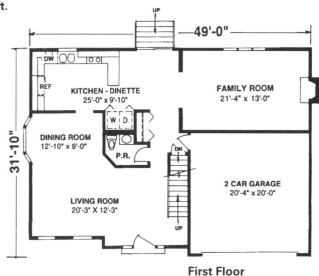

First Floor
1,168 sq. ft.

UP

—49'-0"—

DW

REF

KITCHEN - DINETTE
25'-0" x 9'-10"

FAMILY ROOM
21'-4" x 13'-0"

31'-10"

W. D.

DINING ROOM
12'-10" x 9'-0"

P.R.

DN

LIVING ROOM
20'-3" X 12'-3"

2 CAR GARAGE
20'-4" x 20'-0"

UP

Width: 50'-0"
Depth: 55'-0"

PLAN DATA

Total Living Area:	1,735
Bedrooms:	3
Baths:	2
Garage:	2-car
Foundation Type:	
Basement	

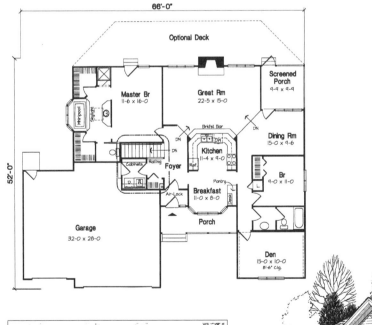

PLAN DATA

Total Living Area:	1,738
Bedrooms:	2
Baths:	2
Garage:	3-car
Foundation Types:	
Basement	
Crawl space	
Slab	
Please specify when ordering	

Rear View

**Second Floor
489 sq. ft.**

PLAN DATA

Total Living Area: 2,009
Bedrooms: 3
Baths: 2
Garage: 2-car
Foundation Type:
Basement

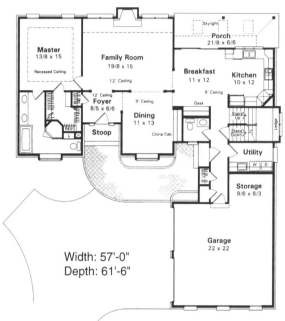

Width: 57'-0"
Depth: 61'-6"

**First Floor
1,520 sq. ft.**

MBr
14-2x14-10

skylt

open to
below

**Second Floor
1,136 sq. ft.**

open to
below

Dn

Br 2
11-4x12-2

Br 3
11-4x12-2

Br 4
9-8x13-0

PLAN DATA

Total Living Area:	2,321
Bedrooms:	4
Baths:	2 1/2
Garage:	2-car
Foundation Type:	
Basement	

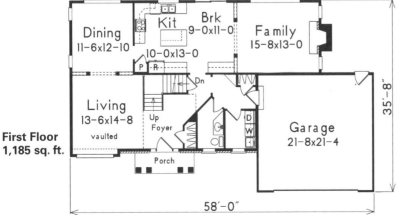

Dining
11-6x12-10

Kit

Brk
9-0x11-0

Family
15-8x13-0

10-0x13-0

P R

Dn

Living
13-6x14-8
vaulted

Up
Foyer

D
W

Garage
21-8x21-4

Porch

**First Floor
1,185 sq. ft.**

35'-8"

58'-0"

PLAN DATA

Total Living Area: 1,477
Bedrooms: 3
Baths: 2
Garage: 2-car
Foundation Type:
  Basement
Features:
  Extra storage in garage

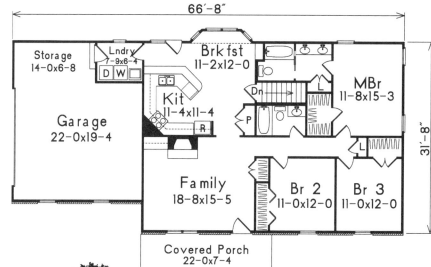

Storage
14-0x6-8

Lndry
7-9x6-4

D W

Brk fst
11-2x12-0

Kit
11-4x11-4

Dn

P

R

MBr
11-8x15-3

L

L

Garage
22-0x19-4

Family
18-8x15-5

Br 2
11-0x12-0

Br 3
11-0x12-0

66'-8"

31'-8"

Covered Porch
22-0x7-4

PLAN #565-FDG-7963-L

Price Code C

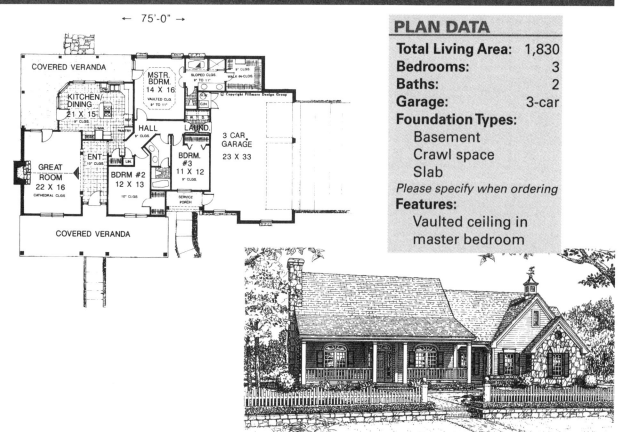

COVERED VERANDA

MSTR.
BDRM.
14 X 16
VAULTED CLG.
9' TO 11'

SLOPED CLGS.
9' TO 11'

WALK IN-CLOS.

KITCHEN/
DINING
21 X 15

© Copyright Fillmore Design Group

HALL

LAUND.

3 CAR
GARAGE
23 X 33

ENT.

GREAT
ROOM
22 X 16
CATHEDRAL CLGS.

BDRM #2
12 X 13

BDRM.
#3
11 X 12

SERVICE
PORCH

COVERED VERANDA

75'-0"

52'-3"

PLAN DATA

Total Living Area: 1,830
Bedrooms: 3
Baths: 2
Garage: 3-car
Foundation Types:
  Basement
  Crawl space
  Slab
  Please specify when ordering
Features:
  Vaulted ceiling in master bedroom

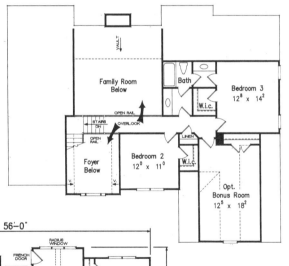

Second Floor
588 sq. ft.

Family Room Below

VAULT

Bath

Bedroom 3
12⁸ x 14²

W.i.c.

OPEN RAIL

STAIRS DN

OVERLOOK

OPEN RAIL

Foyer Below

Bedroom 2
12⁰ x 11⁰

LINEN

W.i.c.

Opt. Bonus Room
12⁵ x 18²

56'-0"

RADIUS WINDOW

FRENCH DOOR

FRENCH DOOR

FPL

Master Suite
13⁵ x 17⁰¹

Vaulted Breakfast
VAULT   VAULT

Bedroom 4/ Den
11⁵ x 12⁰

SERVING BAR

PANTRY

Vaulted Family Room
18⁰ x 17⁹

TRAY CLG.

PLANT SHELF ABOVE

Kitchen

D.W.

REF.

SURFACE UNIT

Bath

RADIUS WDW.

Vaulted M.Bath

OVENS

Laund.

SHWR.

STAIRS DN

COATS

SINK

W. D.

LINEN

W.i.c.

OPEN RAIL

STAIRS

Dining Room
12⁰ x 14⁵

Two Story Foyer

Garage
20⁵ x 20⁵

47'-6"

First Floor
1,761 sq. ft.

copyright © 1995 frank betz associates, inc.

PLAN DATA
Total Living Area: 2,349
Bedrooms: 4
Baths: 3
Garage: 2-car
Foundation Types:
   Crawl space
   Basement
Please specify when ordering
Features:
   Optional bonus room
   has an additional 276
   square feet of living
   area

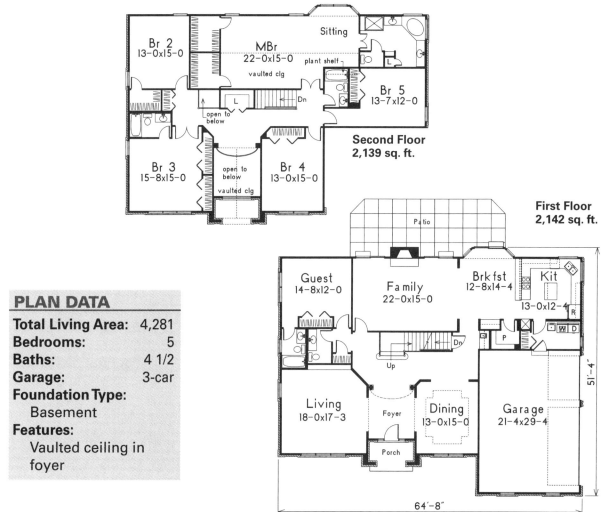

Br 2
13-0x15-0

MBr
22-0x15-0

Sitting

plant shelf

vaulted clg

L

Dn

open to
below

Br 5
13-7x12-0

**Second Floor
2,139 sq. ft.**

Br 3
15-8x15-0

open to
below

vaulted clg

Br 4
13-0x15-0

**First Floor
2,142 sq. ft.**

Patio

Guest
14-8x12-0

Family
22-0x15-0

Brkfst
12-8x14-4

Kit
13-0x12-4

Up

Dn

W D

P

51'-4"

Living
18-0x17-3

Foyer

Dining
13-0x15-0

Garage
21-4x29-4

Porch

64'-8"

PLAN DATA

Total Living Area: 4,281
Bedrooms: 5
Baths: 4 1/2
Garage: 3-car
Foundation Type:
   Basement
Features:
   Vaulted ceiling in
   foyer

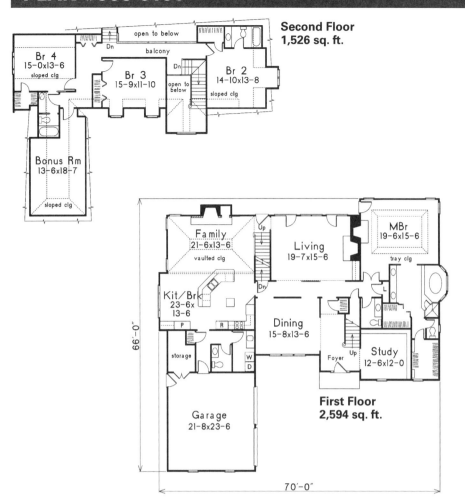

Second Floor
1,526 sq. ft.

Br 4
15-0x13-6
sloped clg

open to below
Dn
balcony

Br 3
15-9x11-10

Dn
open to below
Up

Br 2
14-10x13-8
sloped clg

Bonus Rm
13-6x18-7
sloped clg

PLAN DATA

Total Living Area: 4,120
Bedrooms: 4
Baths: 3 full, 2 half
Garage: 2-car
Foundation Type:
  Partial basement/
  crawl space
Features:
  Vaulted ceiling in
  kitchen

Family
21-6x13-6
vaulted clg

Living
19-7x15-6

MBr
19-6x15-6
tray clg

Kit/Brk
23-6x
13-6

Dining
15-8x13-6

Foyer

Study
12-6x12-0

storage

Garage
21-8x23-6

First Floor
2,594 sq. ft.

66'-0"

70'-0"

PLAN DATA

Total Living Area: 1,800
Bedrooms: 3
Baths: 2
Garage: 2-car
Foundation Types:
  Crawl space
  Slab
Please specify when ordering
Features:
  - 10' ceiling in foyer
  - 9' ceiling in great
    room

PLAN DATA

Total Living Area: 2,115
Bedrooms: 3
Baths: 2 1/2
Garage: 2-car
Foundation Types:
  Basement
  Crawl space
  Slab
Please specify when ordering

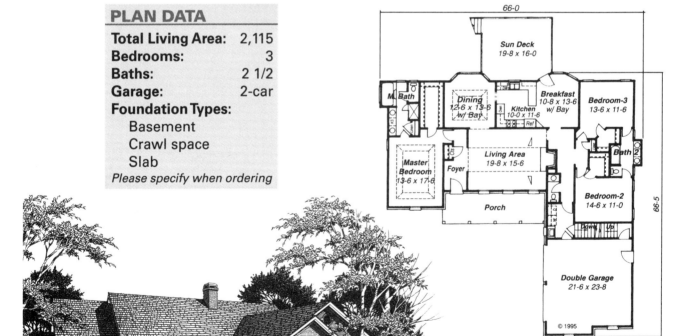

PLAN #565-RJ-A1390

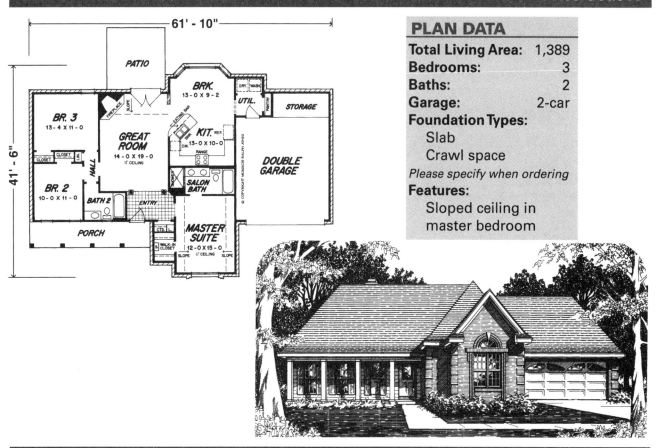

PLAN DATA

Total Living Area: 1,389
Bedrooms: 3
Baths: 2
Garage: 2-car
Foundation Types:
   Slab
   Crawl space
Please specify when ordering
Features:
   Sloped ceiling in
   master bedroom

PLAN #565-1114-1 & 2

PLAN DATA

Total Living Area: 2,851
Bedrooms: 4
Baths: 3
Garage: 2-car
Foundation Types:
   Plan #565-1114-1
   Basement
   Plan #565-1114-2
   Crawl space & slab

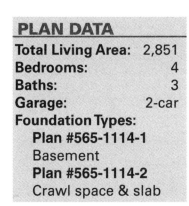

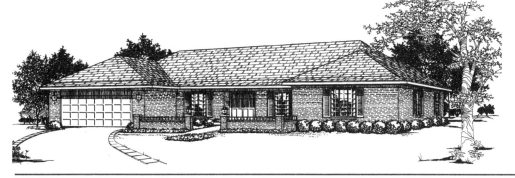

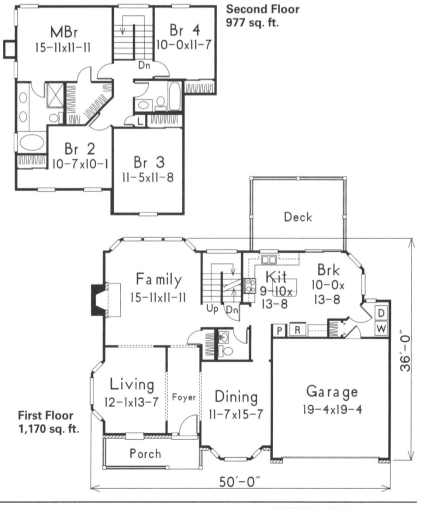

Second Floor
977 sq. ft.

MBr
15-11x11-11

Br 4
10-0x11-7

Dn

Br 2
10-7x10-1

Br 3
11-5x11-8

Deck

Family
15-11x11-11

Kit
9-10x
13-8

Brk
10-0x
13-8

Up   Dn

Living
12-1x13-7

Foyer

Dining
11-7x15-7

Garage
19-4x19-4

36'-0"

First Floor
1,170 sq. ft.

Porch

50'-0"

PLAN DATA

Total Living Area: 2,147
Bedrooms: 4
Baths: 2 1/2
Garage: 2-car
Foundation Type:
Basement

**Second Floor
1,310 sq. ft.**

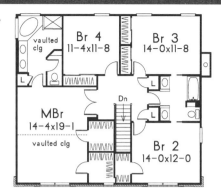

Br 4
11-4x11-8

Br 3
14-0x11-8

vaulted clg

L

Dn

MBr
14-4x19-1

L

L

vaulted clg

Br 2
14-0x12-0

**First Floor
1,420 sq. ft.**

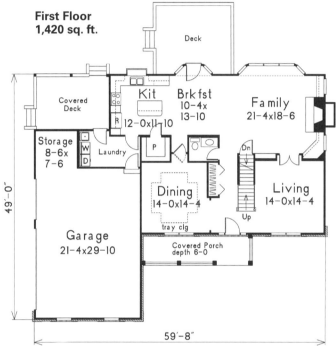

Deck

Covered
Deck

Kit
12-0x11-10

Brkfst
10-4x
13-10

Family
21-4x18-6

R

Storage
8-6x
7-6

W D

Laundry

P

Dn

Dining
14-0x14-4

Up

Living
14-0x14-4

tray clg

Garage
21-4x29-10

Covered Porch
depth 6-0

49'-0"

59'-8"

PLAN DATA

Total Living Area: 2,730
Bedrooms: 4
Baths: 2 1/2
Garage: 3-car
Foundation Type:
  Basement
Features:
  Extra storage in
  garage

J.N. HANSEN S.D.G.

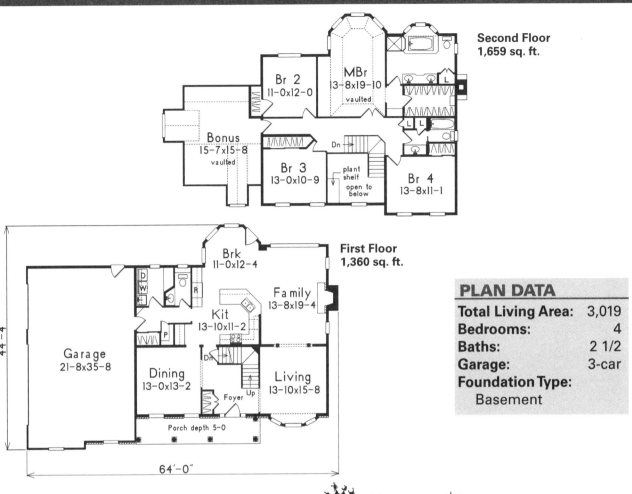

Second Floor
1,659 sq. ft.

Br 2
11-0x12-0

MBr
13-8x19-10
vaulted

Bonus
15-7x15-8
vaulted

Br 3
13-0x10-9

plant shelf
open to below

Dn

Br 4
13-8x11-1

First Floor
1,360 sq. ft.

Brk
11-0x12-4

Family
13-8x19-4

Kit
13-10x11-2

Garage
21-8x35-8

Dining
13-0x13-2

Living
13-10x15-8

Foyer

Up

Dn

P

R

44'-4"

64'-0"

Porch depth 5-0

PLAN DATA

Total Living Area:	3,019
Bedrooms:	4
Baths:	2 1/2
Garage:	3-car
Foundation Type:	
Basement	

PLAN DATA

Total Living Area: 1,872
Bedrooms: 4
Baths: 2
Garage: 2-car
Foundation Types:
  Plan #565-T-109-1
  Basement
  Plan #565-T-109-2
  Crawl space & slab

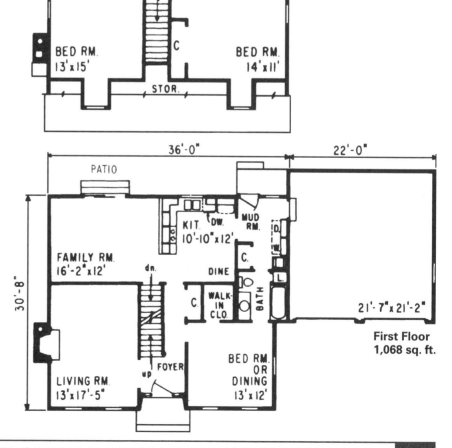

Second Floor
804 sq. ft.

BED RM.
11'-6" x 11'-6"

C.
DRESS.
AREA

BATH

BED RM.
13' x 15'

BED RM.
14' x 11'

dn

STOR.

First Floor
1,068 sq. ft.

36'-0"

22'-0"

PATIO

KIT.
10'-10" x 12'

DW.

MUD RM.

FAMILY RM.
16'-2" x 12'

DINE

dn

WALK-IN CLO.

BATH

30'-8"

21'-7" x 21'-2"

LIVING RM.
13' x 17'-5"

FOYER

up

BED RM.
OR
DINING
13' x 12'

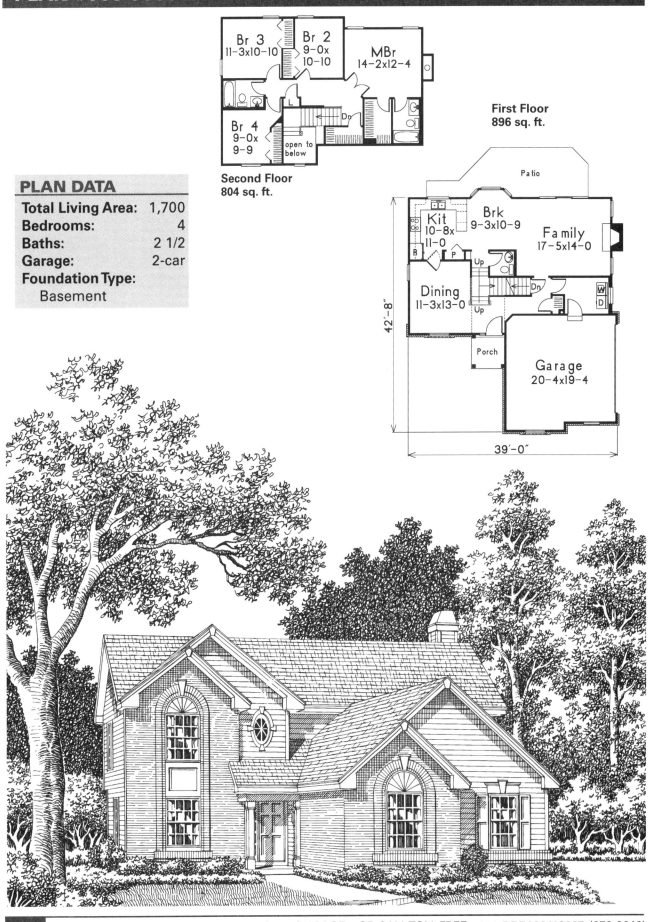

Br 3
11-3x10-10

Br 2
9-0x
10-10

MBr
14-2x12-4

Br 4
9-0x
9-9

open to
below

Dn

L

Second Floor
804 sq. ft.

First Floor
896 sq. ft.

Patio

Kit
10-8x
11-0

Brk
9-3x10-9

Family
17-5x14-0

Dining
11-3x13-0

Up

P

R

Up

Dn

W
D

42'-8"

Porch

Garage
20-4x19-4

39'-0"

PLAN DATA

Total Living Area:	1,700
Bedrooms:	4
Baths:	2 1/2
Garage:	2-car
Foundation Type:	
Basement	

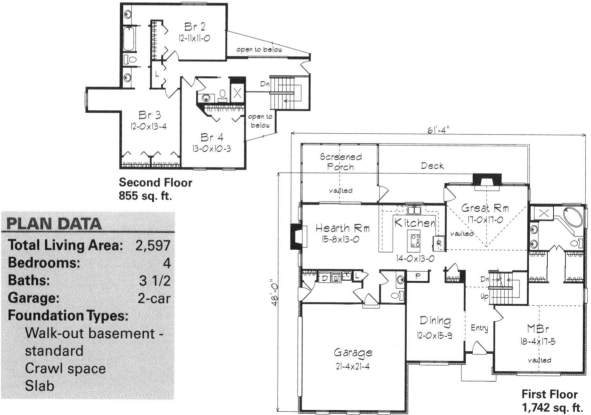

Second Floor
855 sq. ft.

Br 2
12-11x11-0

open to below

Br 3
12-0x13-4

Br 4
13-0x10-3

Dn

open to below

PLAN DATA

Total Living Area: 2,597
Bedrooms: 4
Baths: 3 1/2
Garage: 2-car
Foundation Types:
   Walk-out basement -
   standard
   Crawl space
   Slab

61'-4"

48'-0"

Screened Porch
vaulted

Deck

Great Rm
17-0x17-0
vaulted

Hearth Rm
15-8x13-0

Kitchen
14-0x13-0

Dn

Up

Garage
21-4x21-4

Dining
12-0x15-9

Entry

MBr
18-4x17-5
vaulted

First Floor
1,742 sq. ft.

PLAN DATA

Total Living Area: 2,050
Bedrooms: 3
Baths: 2 1/2
Garage: 2-car
Foundation Types:
   Basement standard
   Crawl space
   Slab

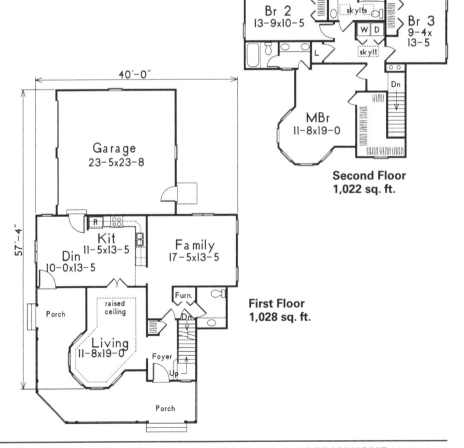

40'-0"

Garage
23-5x23-8

57'-4"

Kit
11-5x13-5

Din
10-0x13-5

Family
17-5x13-5

R

raised
ceiling

Furn.

Dn

Porch

Living
11-8x19-0

Foyer

Up

Porch

First Floor
1,028 sq. ft.

Br 2
13-9x10-5

skylts

W D

Br 3
9-4x
13-5

L

skylt

Dn

MBr
11-8x19-0

Second Floor
1,022 sq. ft.

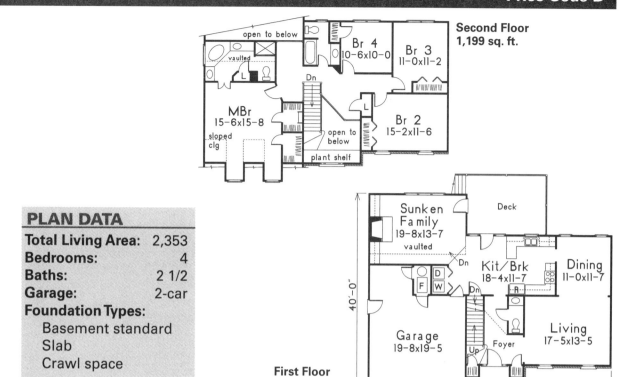

Second Floor
1,199 sq. ft.

First Floor
1,154 sq. ft.

PLAN DATA

Total Living Area: 2,353
Bedrooms: 4
Baths: 2 1/2
Garage: 2-car
Foundation Types:
  Basement standard
  Slab
  Crawl space

Second Floor
1,150 sq. ft.

First Floor
1,651 sq. ft.

PLAN DATA

Total Living Area: 2,801
Bedrooms: 5
Baths: 3
Garage: 2-car
Foundation Type:
  Slab
Features:
  9' ceilings on first
  floor

**Second Floor
1,052 sq. ft.**

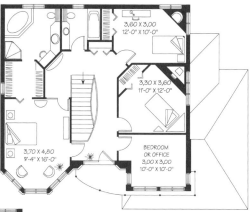

3,60 X 3,00
12'-0" X 10'-0"

3,30 X 3,60
11'-0" X 12'-0"

3,70 X 4,80
9'-4" X 16'-0"

BEDROOM
OR OFFICE
3,00 X 3,00
10'-0" X 10'-0"

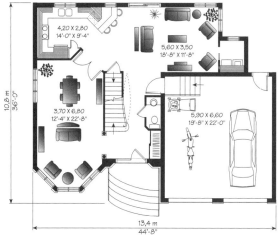

4,20 X 2,80
14'-0" X 9'-4"

5,60 X 3,50
18'-8" X 11'-8"

3,70 X 6,80
12'-4" X 22'-8"

5,90 X 6,60
19'-8" X 22'-0"

10,8 m
36'-0"

13,4 m
44'-8"

**First Floor
924 sq. ft.**

PLAN DATA

Total Living Area: 1,976
Bedrooms: 3
Baths: 2 1/2
Garage: 2-car
Foundation Type:
  Basement
Features:
- 9' ceilings on first floor
- 2" x 6" exterior walls

PLAN DATA

Total Living Area: 2,274
Bedrooms: 3
Baths: 2 1/2
Garage: 2-car
Foundation Types:
Crawl space standard
Slab

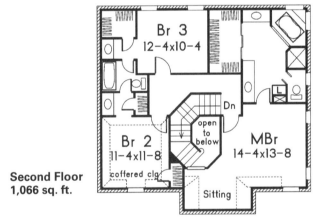

Second Floor
1,066 sq. ft.

Br 3
12-4x10-4

Dn

open to below

Br 2
11-4x11-8

coffered clg.

MBr
14-4x13-8

Sitting

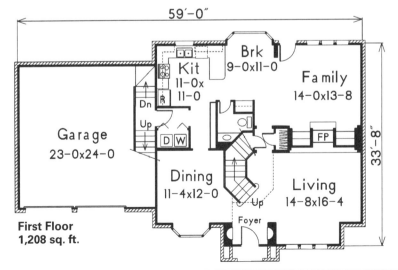

59'-0"

First Floor
1,208 sq. ft.

Garage
23-0x24-0

Kit
11-0x 11-0

Brk
9-0x11-0

Family
14-0x13-8

Dn

Up

D W

FP

Dining
11-4x12-0

Up

Living
14-8x16-4

Foyer

33'-8"

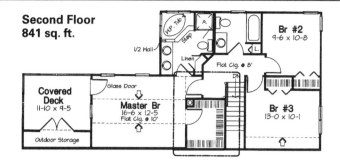

Second Floor
841 sq. ft.

1/2 Wall

H.P. Tub

Step

Linen

Flat Clg. @ 8'

Br #2
9-6 x 10-8

Covered Deck
11-10 x 9-5

Glass Door

DN

Master Br
16-6 x 12-5
Flat Clg. @ 10'

Br #3
13-0 x 10-1

Outdoor Storage

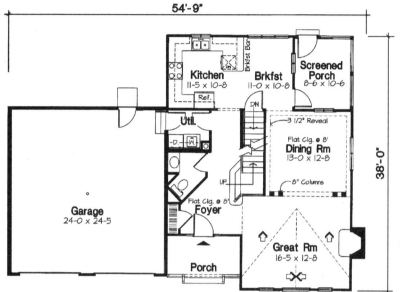

54'-9"

38'-0"

Kitchen
11-5 x 10-8

Brkfst Bar

Brkfst
11-0 x 10-8

Screened Porch
8-6 x 10-6

Util.

Ref.

DN

3 1/2" Reveal

Flat Clg. @ 8'
Dining Rm
13-0 x 12-8

D

W

UP

8" Columns

Garage
24-0 x 24-5

Flat Clg. @ 8'
Foyer

Porch

Great Rm
16-5 x 12-8

First Floor
900 sq. ft.

PLAN DATA

Total Living Area:	1,741
Bedrooms:	3
Baths:	2 1/2
Garage:	2-car

Foundation Types:
  Slab
  Basement
  Crawl space
Please specify when ordering
Features:
  Vaulted ceiling in
  great room

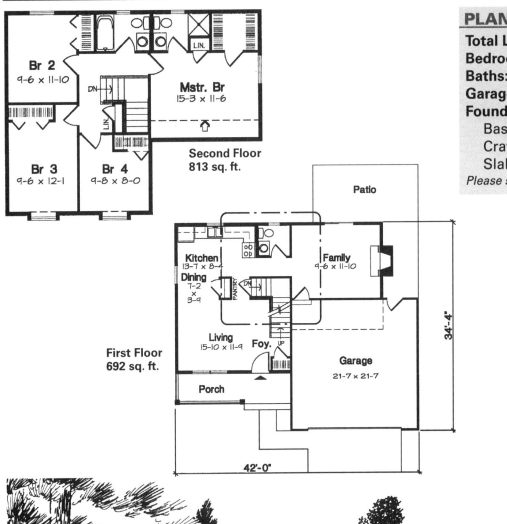

Br 2
9-6 x 11-10

DN

Mstr. Br
15-3 x 11-6

LIN.

Br 3
9-6 x 12-1

Br 4
9-8 x 8-0

Second Floor
813 sq. ft.

Patio

Kitchen
13-7 x 8-4

Dining
7-2 x 3-9

PANTRY

DN

Family
9-6 x 11-10

Living
15-10 x 11-9

Foy.

UP

Garage
21-7 x 21-7

First Floor
692 sq. ft.

Porch

34'-4"

42'-0"

PLAN DATA

Total Living Area: 1,505
Bedrooms: 4
Baths: 2 1/2
Garage: 2-car
Foundation Types:
  Basement
  Crawl space
  Slab
Please specify when ordering

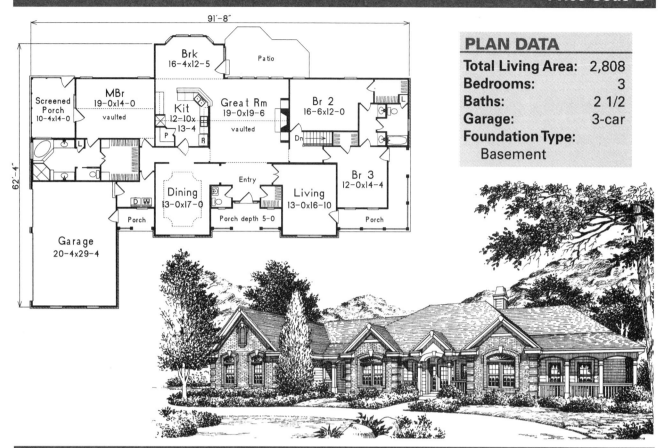

91'-8"

62'-4"

Brk
16-4x12-5

Patio

Screened Porch
10-4x14-0

MBr
19-0x14-0
vaulted

Kit
12-10x 13-4

Great Rm
19-0x19-6
vaulted

Br 2
16-6x12-0

Dn

Dining
13-0x17-0

Entry

Living
13-0x16-10

Br 3
12-0x14-4

Porch

Porch depth 5-0

Porch

Garage
20-4x29-4

PLAN DATA

Total Living Area:	2,808
Bedrooms:	3
Baths:	2 1/2
Garage:	3-car
Foundation Type:	
Basement	

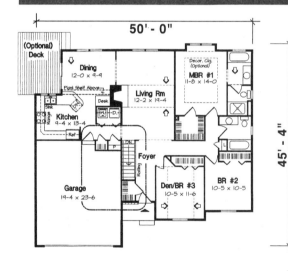

50'-0"

45'-4"

(Optional) Deck

Dining
12-0 x 9-9

Decor. Clg. (Optional)

MBR #1
11-8 x 14-0

Plant Shelf Above

Living Rm
12-2 x 19-4

Desk

Kitchen
9-4 x 13-4

Sink
Range
Ref.

DN

Foyer

Garage
19-4 x 23-6

Den/BR #3
10-5 x 11-6

BR #2
10-5 x 10-5

PLAN DATA

Total Living Area:	1,456
Bedrooms:	3
Baths:	2
Garage:	2-car

Foundation Types:
Slab
Basement
Crawl space
Please specify when ordering

Features:
2" x 6" exterior walls

Rear View

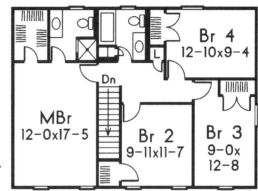

Second Floor
969 sq. ft.

Br 4
12-10x9-4

MBr
12-0x17-5

Br 2
9-11x11-7

Br 3
9-0x
12-8

Dn

L

PLAN DATA

Total Living Area: 2,032
Bedrooms: 4
Baths: 2 1/2
Foundation Type:
 Crawl space

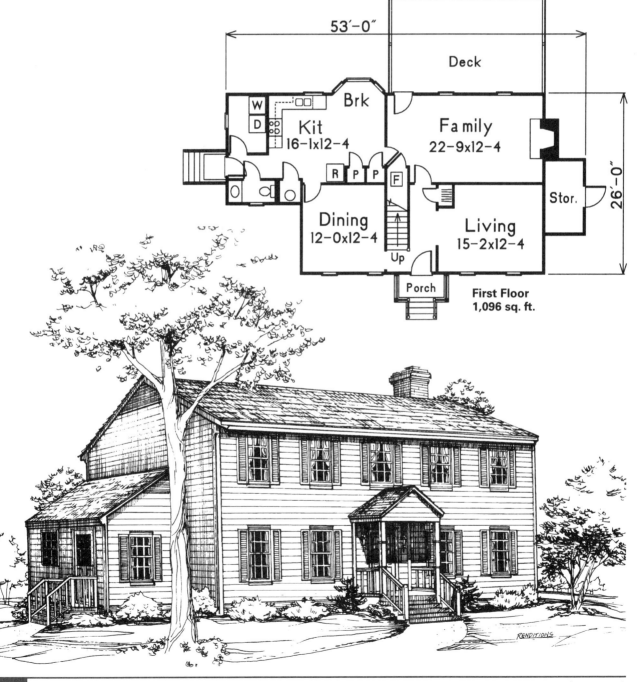

53'-0"

26'-0"

Deck

Brk

Kit
16-1x12-4

Family
22-9x12-4

W
D

R P P F

Stor.

Dining
12-0x12-4

Living
15-2x12-4

Up

Porch

First Floor
1,096 sq. ft.

Width: 65'-0"
Depth: 54'-6"

SCREENED PORCH
13/2 x 9/2

COVERED PATIO

BREAKFAST ROOM
10/10 x 13/0

MASTER
14/8 x 12/8

BDRM 2
11/0 x 12/0

TV

GREAT RM
16/4 x 20/6

EATING BAR

KIT
12/0 x 14/6

R

RAILING

DOWN

8" DIAMETER COLUMNS

PANTRY

LINEN

UTIL

ARCH

FOYER

BDRM 3
13/0 x 11/10

COVERED PORCH

DINING
12/6 x 13/8

GARAGE
21/2 x 21/8

PLAN DATA

Total Living Area:	2,148
Bedrooms:	3
Baths:	2
Garage:	2-car

Foundation Type:
Basement

Features:
- 9' ceilings on first floor
- 11' ceilings in great room, kitchen, nook and foyer

PLAN #565-0410

PLAN DATA

Total Living Area: 1,742
Bedrooms: 3
Baths: 2
Garage: 2-car
Foundation Types:
Slab standard
Crawl space

PLAN #565-NDG-521

Price Code C

First Floor
1,298 sq. ft.

Second Floor
624 sq. ft.

PLAN DATA

Total Living Area: 1,922
Bedrooms: 3
Baths: 2 1/2
Garage: 2-car
Foundation Types:
Crawl space
Slab
Please specify when ordering

PLAN DATA

Total Living Area: 1,721
Bedrooms: 3
Baths: 2
Garage: 3-car
Foundation Types:
 Walk-out basement - standard
 Slab
 Crawl space
Features:
 Vaulted ceilings in dining and great rooms

Rear View

Second Floor
719 sq. ft.

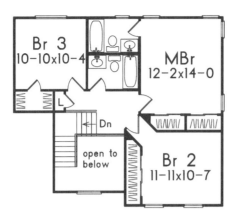

Br 3
10-10x10-4

MBr
12-2x14-0

Dn

open to below

Br 2
11-11x10-7

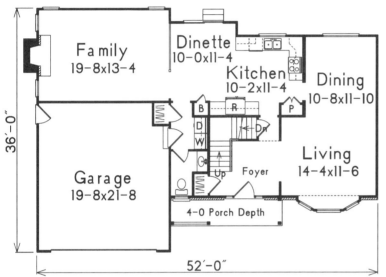

Family
19-8x13-4

Dinette
10-0x11-4

Kitchen
10-2x11-4

Dining
10-8x11-10

B R

D
W

P

Dn

Living
14-4x11-6

Up Foyer

Garage
19-8x21-8

4-0 Porch Depth

36'-0"

52'-0"

First Floor
1,094 sq. ft.

PLAN DATA

Total Living Area:	1,813
Bedrooms:	3
Baths:	2 1/2
Garage:	2-car
Foundation Type:	Basement

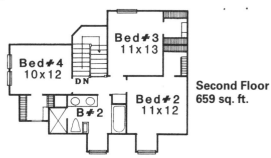

Bed #4
10 x 12

Bed #3
11 x 13

B #2

DN

Bed #2
11 x 12

Second Floor
659 sq. ft.

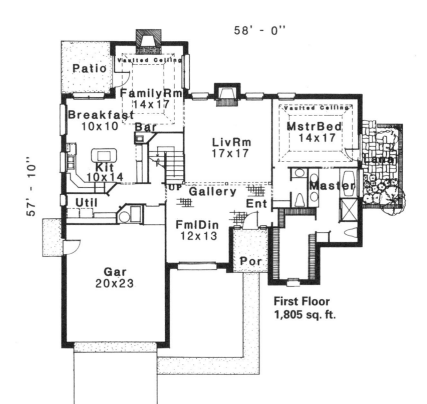

58' - 0''

57' - 10''

Patio

Vaulted Ceiling

FamilyRm
14 x 17

Breakfast
10 x 10

Bar

LivRm
17 x 17

Vaulted Ceiling

MstrBed
14 x 17

Kit
10 x 14

UP

Gallery

Ent

Master

Util

FmlDin
12 x 13

Por

Gar
20 x 23

First Floor
1,805 sq. ft.

PLAN DATA

Total Living Area: 2,464
Bedrooms: 4
Baths: 2 1/2
Garage: 2-car
Foundation Types:
   Slab
   Basement
   Crawl space
Please specify when ordering
Features:
   9' ceilings on first
   floor

35'-0"

56'-0"

MBr
17-0x13-10

Deck

Kitchen
11-4x12-0

R-P

Dn

Great Rm
13-7x18-8
Sunken

vaulted

Up

Dining
11-4x12-0

Garage
18-4x21-4

First Floor
1,114 sq. ft.

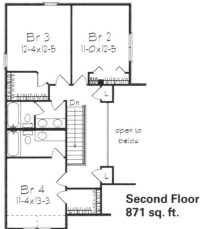

Br 3
12-4x12-5

Br 2
11-0x12-5

Dn

open to
below

L

Br 4
11-4x13-3

L

Second Floor
871 sq. ft.

PLAN DATA

Total Living Area:	1,985
Bedrooms:	4
Baths:	3 1/2
Garage:	2-car
Foundation Type:	
Basement	

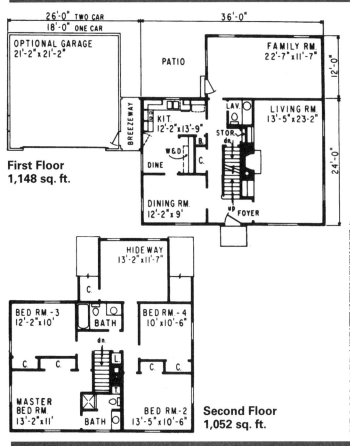

First Floor
1,148 sq. ft.

Second Floor
1,052 sq. ft.

PLAN DATA

Total Living Area: 2,200
Bedrooms: 4
Baths: 2 1/2
Garage: optional 2-car
Foundation Type:
Partial basement/
crawl space

PLAN DATA

Total Living Area: 1,699
Bedrooms: 3
Baths: 2
Garage: 2-car
Foundation Types:
Basement
Crawl space
Slab
Please specify when ordering

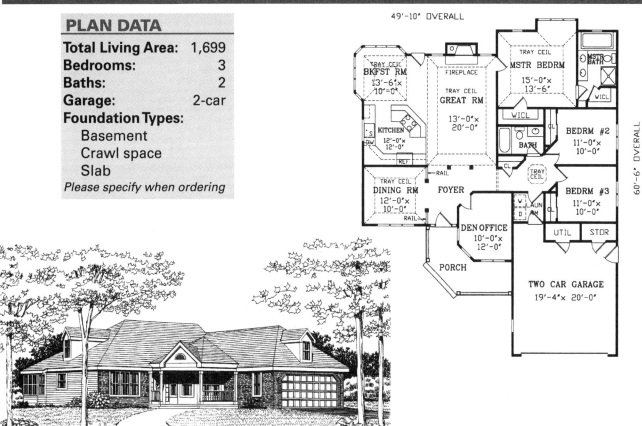

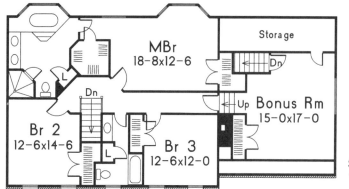

Second Floor
1,305 sq. ft.

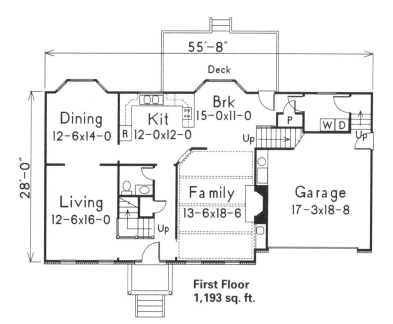

First Floor
1,193 sq. ft.

PLAN DATA

Total Living Area:	2,498
Bedrooms:	3
Baths:	2 1/2
Garage:	2-car
Foundation Type:	
Crawl space	

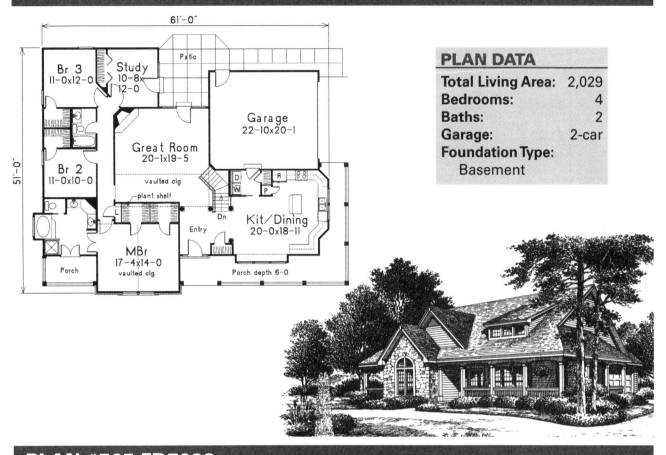

PLAN #565-0712 Floor Plan

61'-0"

51'-0"

Br 3
11-0x12-0

Study
10-8x
12-0

Patio

Garage
22-10x20-1

Great Room
20-1x19-5

vaulted clg

plant shelf

Br 2
11-0x10-0

D
W

R
P

Dn

Kit/Dining
20-0x18-11

Entry

MBr
17-4x14-0
vaulted clg

Porch

Porch depth 6-0

PLAN DATA

Total Living Area:	2,029
Bedrooms:	4
Baths:	2
Garage:	2-car
Foundation Type:	
Basement	

55' - 0"

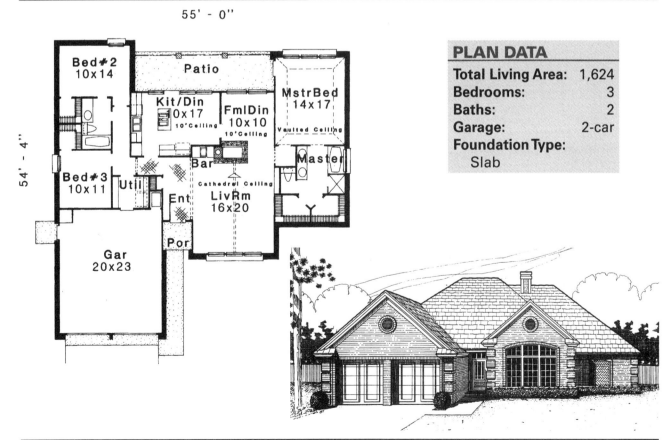

54' - 4"

Bed #2
10x14

Patio

Kit/Din
0x17
10'Ceiling

FmlDin
10x10
10'Ceiling

MstrBed
14x17
Vaulted Ceiling

Bed #3
10x11

Util

Bar

Ent

Master

Por

LivRm
16x20
Cathedral Ceiling

Gar
20x23

PLAN DATA

Total Living Area:	1,624
Bedrooms:	3
Baths:	2
Garage:	2-car
Foundation Type:	
Slab	

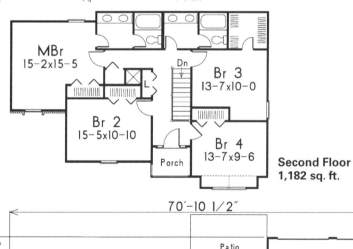

MBr
15-2x15-5

Dn

Br 3
13-7x10-0

Br 2
15-5x10-10

Br 4
13-7x9-6

Porch

Second Floor
1,182 sq. ft.

PLAN DATA

Total Living Area: 2,352
Bedrooms: 4
Baths: 2 1/2
Garage: 2-car
Foundation Types:
 Crawl space standard
 Basement
 Slab

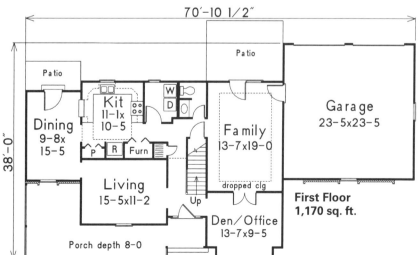

70'-10 1/2"

38'-0"

Patio

Patio

Kit
11-1x
10-5

W
D

Dining
9-8x
15-5

Garage
23-5x23-5

Family
13-7x19-0

P   R   Furn

Living
15-5x11-2

Up

dropped clg

First Floor
1,170 sq. ft.

Den/Office
13-7x9-5

Porch depth 8-0

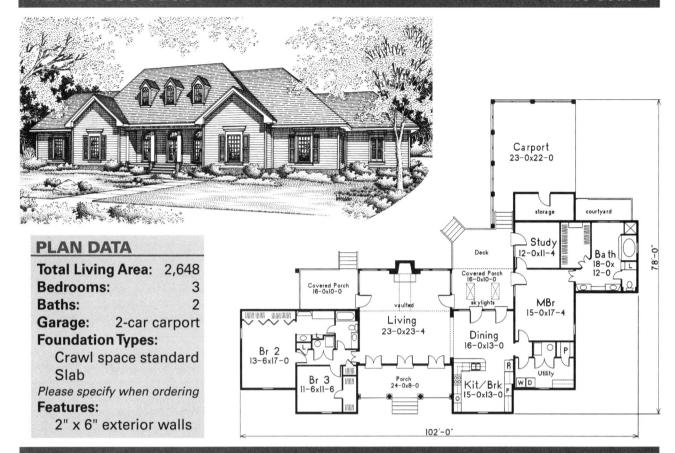

PLAN DATA

Total Living Area: 2,648
Bedrooms: 3
Baths: 2
Garage: 2-car carport
Foundation Types:
Crawl space standard
Slab
Please specify when ordering
Features:
2" x 6" exterior walls

PLAN #565-1243-1 & 2

Price Code E

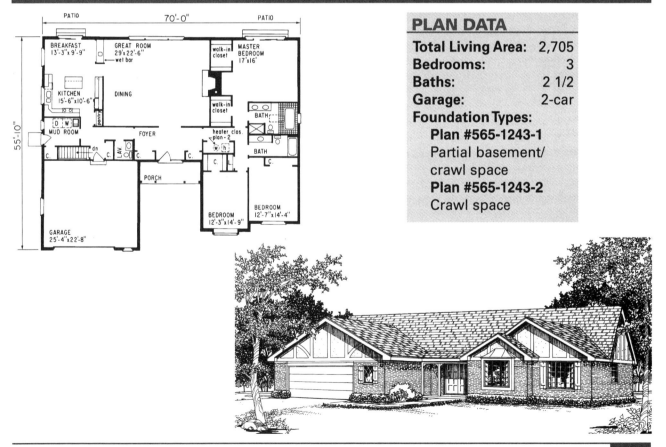

PLAN DATA

Total Living Area: 2,705
Bedrooms: 3
Baths: 2 1/2
Garage: 2-car
Foundation Types:
Plan #565-1243-1
Partial basement/
crawl space
Plan #565-1243-2
Crawl space

PLAN DATA

Total Living Area: 2,483
Bedrooms: 4
Baths: 2
Garage: 2-car
Foundation Type:
  Basement

Second Floor
1,095 sq. ft.

PLAN DATA

Total Living Area: 2,339
Bedrooms: 3
Baths: 2 1/2
Garage: 2-car
Foundation Types:
  Basement
  Crawl space
Please specify when ordering

Width: 49'-10"
Depth: 54'-0"

First Floor
1,244 sq. ft.

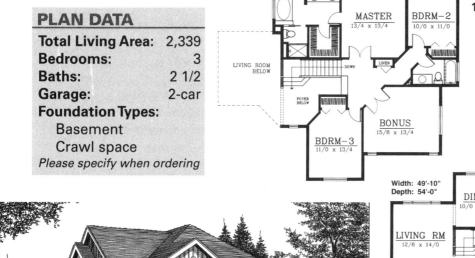

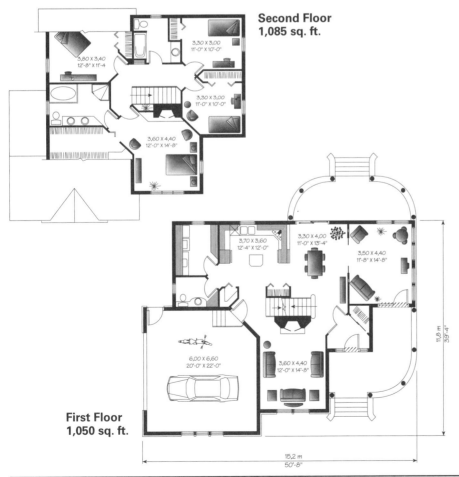

Second Floor
1,085 sq. ft.

3,80 X 3,40
12'-8" X 11'-4

3,30 X 3,00
11'-0" X 10'-0"

3,30 X 3,00
11'-0" X 10'-0"

3,60 X 4,40
12'-0" X 14'-8"

First Floor
1,050 sq. ft.

3,70 X 3,60
12'-4" X 12'-0"

3,30 X 4,00
11'-0" X 13'-4"

3,50 X 4,40
11'-8" X 14'-8"

6,00 X 6,60
20'-0" X 22'-0"

3,60 X 4,40
12'-0" X 14'-8"

11,8 m
39'-4"

15,2 m
50'-8"

PLAN DATA

Total Living Area:	2,135
Bedrooms:	4
Baths:	2 1/2
Garage:	2-car
Foundation Type:	
Basement	

Features:
- 9' ceilings on first floor
- 2" x 6" exterior walls

Second Floor
1,085 sq. ft.

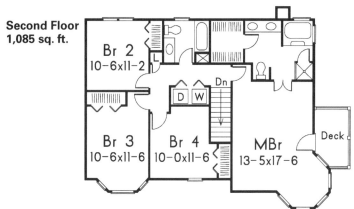

Br 2
10-6x11-2

Br 3
10-6x11-6

Br 4
10-0x11-6

MBr
13-5x17-6

Deck

D W

Dn

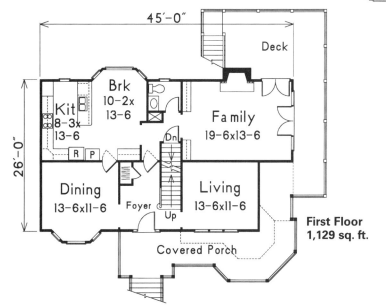

45'-0"

26'-0"

Deck

Brk
10-2x
13-6

Kit
8-3x
13-6

Family
19-6x13-6

R P

Dn

Dining
13-6x11-6

Foyer

Up

Living
13-6x11-6

First Floor
1,129 sq. ft.

Covered Porch

PLAN DATA

Total Living Area: 2,214
Bedrooms: 4
Baths: 2 1/2
Garage: 2-car
Foundation Type:
Basement
Features:
Drive-under garage

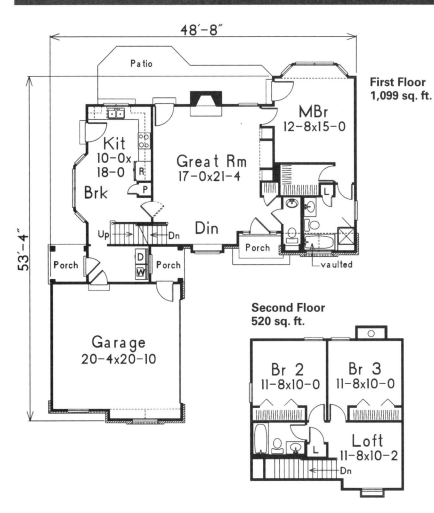

48'-8"

Patio

First Floor
1,099 sq. ft.

Kit
10-0x
18-0

Brk

Great Rm
17-0x21-4

MBr
12-8x15-0

53'-4"

Din

Up   Dn

Porch   Porch

D
W

Porch

L

vaulted

Garage
20-4x20-10

Second Floor
520 sq. ft.

Br 2
11-8x10-0

Br 3
11-8x10-0

L

Loft
11-8x10-2

Dn

PLAN DATA

Total Living Area:	1,619
Bedrooms:	3
Baths:	2 1/2
Garage:	2-car
Foundation Type:	
Basement	

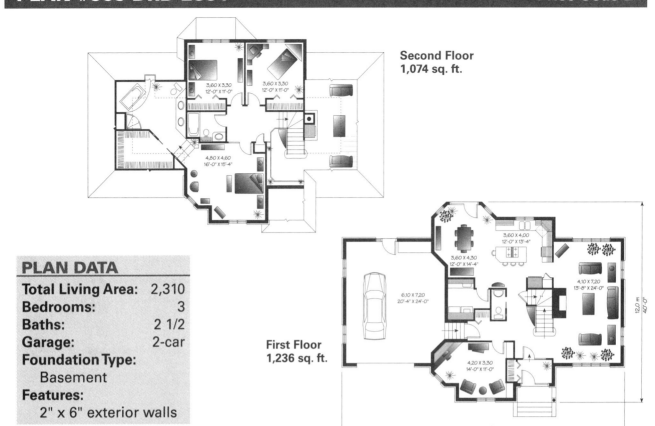

Second Floor
1,074 sq. ft.

3,60 X 3,30
12'-0" X 11'-0"

3,60 X 3,30
12'-0" X 11'-0"

4,80 X 4,60
16'-0" X 15'-4"

PLAN DATA

Total Living Area: 2,310
Bedrooms: 3
Baths: 2 1/2
Garage: 2-car
Foundation Type:
  Basement
Features:
  2" x 6" exterior walls

First Floor
1,236 sq. ft.

3,60 X 4,00
12'-0" X 13'-4"

3,60 X 4,30
12'-0" X 14'-4"

4,10 X 7,20
13'-8" X 24'-0"

6,10 X 7,20
20'-4" X 24'-0"

4,20 X 3,30
14'-0" X 11'-0"

12,0 m
40'-0"

17,4 m
58'-0"

PLAN DATA

Total Living Area:	3,808
Bedrooms:	3
Baths:	3
Garage:	2-car
Foundation Type:	
Basement	

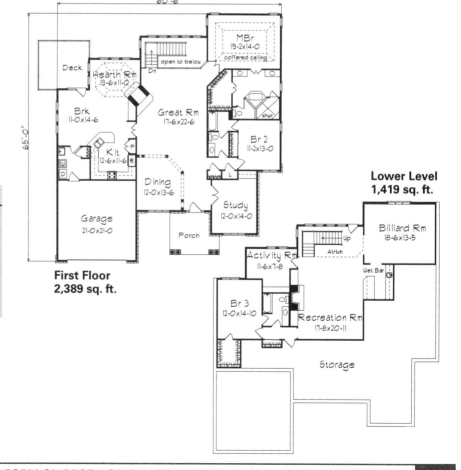

First Floor
2,389 sq. ft.

Lower Level
1,419 sq. ft.

60'-6"
65'-0"

Deck
Hearth Rm
13-6x11-0
Brk
11-0x14-6
Kit
12-6x11-6
Dining
12-0x13-6
Garage
21-0x21-0
Porch
open to below
Dn
Great Rm
17-6x22-6
MBr
19-2x14-0
coffered ceiling
Br 2
11-2x13-6
Study
12-0x14-0

Billiard Rm
18-6x13-5
Up
Atrium
Activity Rm
11-6x7-8
Wet Bar
Br 3
12-0x14-10
Recreation Rm
17-8x20-11
Storage

PLAN #565-0190

PLAN DATA

Total Living Area: 1,600
Bedrooms: 3
Baths: 2
Garage: 2-car
Foundation Types:
  Slab standard
  Crawl space
  Basement
Features:
- 16' vaulted ceiling in living room
- 2" x 6" exterior walls

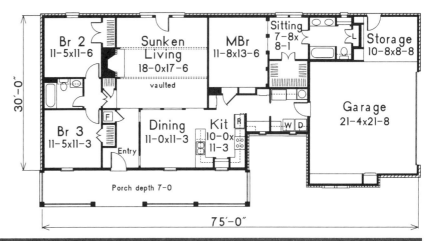

30'-0"

Br 2
11-5x11-6

Sunken Living
18-0x17-6
vaulted

MBr
11-8x13-6

Sitting
7-8x 8-1

Storage
10-8x8-8

Garage
21-4x21-8

Br 3
11-5x11-3

Entry

Dining
11-0x11-3

Kit
10-0x 11-3

Porch depth 7-0

75'-0"

PLAN #565-NDG-148

50' 0"

56' 0"

MASTER SUITE
16'-10" X 11'-6"
9' PAN CEILING

GREAT RM.
20'-0" X 15'-6"
9' BOXED CEILING

BEDROOM 3
11'-10" X 11'-0"

M.BATH
16'-0" X 10'-6"

KITCHEN
10'-0" X 10'-0"

DINING
10'-6" X 11'-10"

FOYER

BATH

STORAGE

LAU.

COVERED PORCH

BEDROOM 2
11'-10" X 11'-0"

VAULTED CEILING

GARAGE
21'-0" X 21'-0"

PLAN DATA

Total Living Area: 1,538
Bedrooms: 3
Baths: 2
Garage: 2-car
Foundation Types:
  Crawl space
  Slab
Please specify when ordering

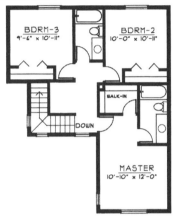

First Floor
562 sq. ft.

PLAN DATA

Total Living Area: 1,278
Bedrooms: 3
Baths: 2 1/2
Garage: 2-car
Foundation Type:
  Crawl space

Second Floor
716 sq. ft.

PLAN #565-JA-79798

Price Code B

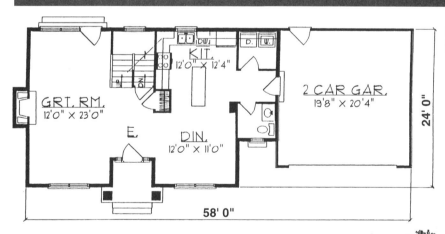

First Floor
846 sq. ft.

PLAN DATA

Total Living Area: 1,553
Bedrooms: 3
Baths: 2 1/2
Garage: 2-car
Foundation Type:
  Crawl space

Second Floor
707 sq. ft.

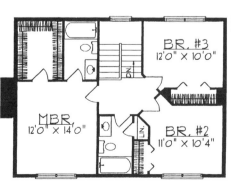

PLAN DATA

Total Living Area: 1,832
Bedrooms: 3
Baths: 2
Garage: detached 2-car
Foundation Types:
Crawl space standard
Basement
Slab

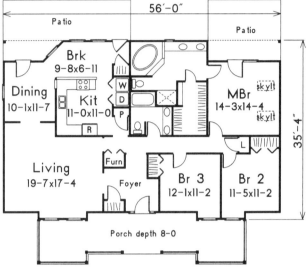

56'-0"

Patio

Patio

Brk
9-8x6-11

Dining
10-1x11-7

Kit
11-0x11-0

W
D
P
R

MBr
14-3x14-4
skylt
skylt

35'-4"

Living
19-7x17-4

Furn

Foyer

Br 3
12-1x11-2

Br 2
11-5x11-2

L

Porch depth 8-0

Bfst.
11³x11³

Kit.
13⁰x14⁰

Liv. rm.
15⁰x16⁹
11'-0" CEILING

Mbr.
15⁰x16⁰
11'-0" CEILING

TRANSOMS

WHIRLPOOL

SNACK BAR

DESK

Fam. rm.
18⁸x15³

DN.

Br.3
11¹x12⁰
OPT. SITTING

55'-4"

Din.
12⁰x14⁰
11'-0" CLG.

Den
12⁰x13²
OPT. BEDROOM
11'-0" CLG.

Br.2
12⁷x11²

Gar.
30x21⁸

COVERED PORCH

L

© design basics inc.

76'-0"

PLAN DATA

Total Living Area: 2,498
Bedrooms: 3
Baths: 2 1/2
Garage: 3-car
Foundation Type:
Basement

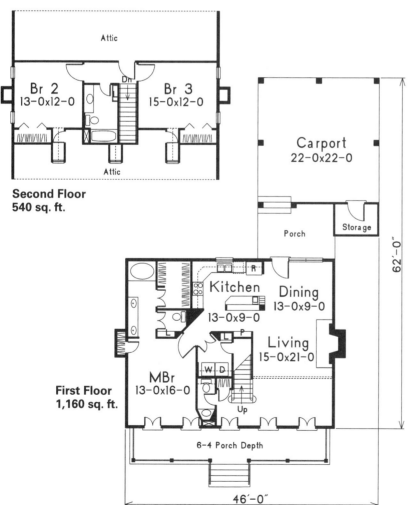

Second Floor
540 sq. ft.

Attic

Br 2
13-0x12-0

Dn

Br 3
15-0x12-0

Attic

First Floor
1,160 sq. ft.

Carport
22-0x22-0

Porch

Storage

62'-0"

Kitchen
13-0x9-0

Dining
13-0x9-0

Living
15-0x21-0

MBr
13-0x16-0

W D

Up

6-4 Porch Depth

46'-0"

PLAN DATA

Total Living Area: 1,700
Bedrooms: 3
Baths: 2 1/2
Garage: 2-car carport
Foundation Types:
   Crawl space standard
   Basement
   Slab
Features:
   2" x 6" exterior walls

PLAN DATA

Total Living Area: 1,606
Bedrooms: 3
Baths: 2
Garage: 2-car
Foundation Type:
Slab
Features:
Cathedral vaulted ceiling in great room

DINING 11' 7" x 10' 7"
GRAND ROOM 15' 7" x 21' 2"
M. BATH
MASTER BEDROOM 12' 3" x 15' 10"
KITCHEN 11' 10" x 14' 10"
W.I.C.
B#2
FOYER
2 CAR GARAGE
BEDROOM 3 11' 2" x 12' 11"
BEDROOM 2 10' 9" x 10' 1"

Width: 50'-0"
Depth: 42'-0"

58'-4"

49'-6"

STEP UP CEILING
MASTER SUITE 16'-0" x 12'-0"
NOOK 10'-0" X 11'-0"
PORCH
BED RM.2 11'-0" x 12'-0"
BATH 1
10'-0" HIGH CEILING
LIVING RM. 18'-0" x 17'-0"
WALK IN CLOSET
MARBLE TUB
WALK IN CLOSET
B.2
KITCH. 11'-0" x 11'-0"
LIN.
STORAGE
W/H
PANT.
SLOPE CLG. UP TO 10'-0"
BED RM.3 11'-6" x 11'-0"
GARAGE 19'-0" x 22'-6"
UTIL.
DINING RM. 11'-0" x 13'-0"
ENT.
SLOPE CLG. UP
SLOPE CLG. UP
P.

PLAN DATA

Total Living Area: 1,791
Bedrooms: 3
Baths: 2
Garage: 2-car
Foundation Types:
Slab
Crawl space
Please specify when ordering
Features:
10' ceiling in dining area

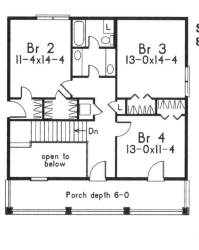

Second Floor 855 sq. ft.

Br 2
11-4x14-4

Br 3
13-0x14-4

Br 4
13-0x11-4

Dn

open to below

Porch depth 6-0

PLAN DATA

Total Living Area: 2,605
Bedrooms: 4
Baths: 2 1/2
Garage: 2-car
Foundation Types:
 Slab standard
 Basement
 Crawl space

First Floor 1,750 sq. ft.

Garage
21-4x21-8

Brk
9-4x10-0

Stor
8-2x9-4

Porch

Living
19-8x18-4

Kit
13-0x13-4

MBr
12-0x21-0

sloped clg

Up

Foyer

Dining
13-0x11-4

Porch depth 6-0

52'-0"

77'-0"

© Michael E. Nelson
NELSON DESIGN GROUP, LLC

First Floor
1,843 sq. ft.

58' 8"

61' 9"

© 2001 NELSON DESIGN GROUP, LLC.

GARAGE
25'-0" X 21'-0"

WHP TUB

M. BATH
15'-8" X 11'-6"

KNEE SPACE

MASTER SUITE
15'-8" X 14'-6"
10' BOXED CEILING

LIN

D
W
LAU

UP

REF
KIT.
10'-8" X 8'-0"

RG

DW

BREAKFAST ROOM
10'-8" X 8'-6"

DINING ROOM
10' CEILING
10'-6" X 12'-6"

GRILLING PORCH
16'-10" X 10'-0"

FRENCH DOOR   FRENCH DOOR

GREAT ROOM
10' CEILING
16'-10" X 16'-6"

FOYER
10' CEIL.
6'-0" X 10'-0"

PRCH

BEDROOM 4
12'-0" X 10'-6"

LIN

BATH

BEDROOM 3
11'-0" X 10'-0"

BEDROOM 2
11'-0" X 10'-0"

PLAN DATA

Total Living Area: 1,863
Bedrooms: 4
Baths: 2
Garage: 2-car
Foundation Types:
  Slab
  Crawl space
Please specify when ordering
Features:
  10' ceilings in dining room and master bedroom

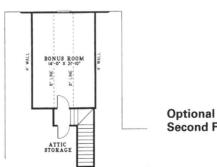

BONUS ROOM
14'-0" X 21'-10"

4' WALL

4' WALL

8' LINE

8' LINE

ATTIC STORAGE

Optional
Second Floor

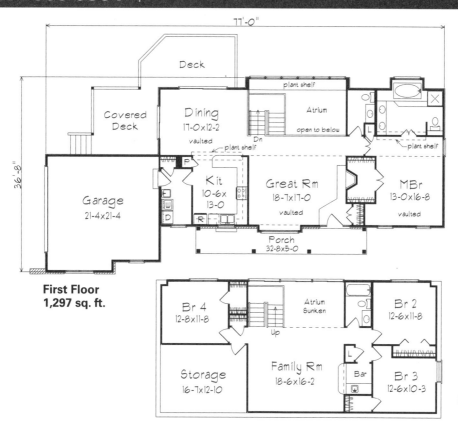

First Floor
1,297 sq. ft.

77'-0"

36'-8"

Deck

Covered Deck

Dining
17-0x12-2
vaulted

plant shelf

Atrium
open to below

plant shelf

Garage
21-4x21-4

Kit
10-6x
13-0

Great Rm
18-7x17-0
vaulted

MBr
13-0x16-8
vaulted

Porch
32-8x5-0

Lower Level
1,234 sq. ft.

Br 4
12-8x11-8

Atrium
Sunken

Br 2
12-6x11-8

Storage
16-7x12-10

Family Rm
18-6x16-2

Bar

Br 3
12-6x10-3

Rear View

PLAN DATA

Total Living Area:	2,531
Bedrooms:	4
Baths:	2 1/2
Garage:	2-car
Foundation Type:	
	Walk-out basement

PLAN DATA

Total Living Area: 2,050
Bedrooms: 3
Baths: 2
Garage: 2-car
Foundation Types:
Crawl space
Slab
Please specify when ordering

PLAN DATA

Total Living Area: 1,785
Bedrooms: 3
Baths: 1 1/2
Garage: 2-car
Foundation Types:
Slab standard
Basement
Crawl space
Please specify when ordering
Features:
2" x 6" exterior walls

Second Floor
894 sq. ft.

Rear View

First Floor
891 sq. ft.

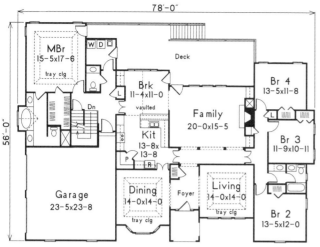

PLAN DATA

Total Living Area: 2,178
Bedrooms: 4
Baths: 2 1/2
Garage: 2-car
Foundation Type:
Basement
Features:
12' ceiling in family room

PLAN DATA

Total Living Area: 1,200
Bedrooms: 3
Baths: 1
Garage: optional 2-car
Foundation Types:
Plan #565-1199-1
Basement
Plan #565-1199-2
Crawl space & slab

PLAN DATA

Total Living Area: 2,730
Bedrooms: 3
Baths: 2 1/2
Garage: 2-car
Foundation Type:
  Crawl space

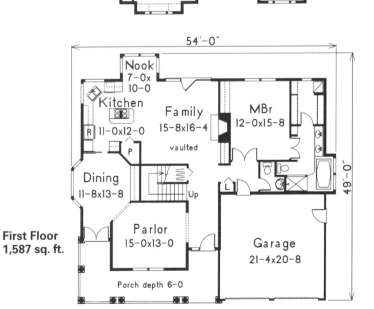

Br 3
10-0x
13-4

Br 2
12-8x15-0

open to below

W D

skylt

Bonus
21-0x20-0

vaulted

Dn

open to below

Second Floor
1,143 sq. ft.

Nook
7-0x
10-0

Kitchen
11-0x12-0

Family
15-8x16-4
vaulted

MBr
12-0x15-8

Dining
11-8x13-8

Parlor
15-0x13-0

Garage
21-4x20-8

Up

54'-0"

49'-0"

Porch depth 6-0

First Floor
1,587 sq. ft.

Second Floor
968 sq. ft.

First Floor
1,530 sq. ft.

PLAN DATA

Total Living Area: 2,498
Bedrooms: 3
Baths: 2 1/2
Garage: 2-car
Foundation Types:
   Crawl space standard
   Slab
   Basement
Features:
 - 10' ceilings on first
   floor
 - 9' ceilings on second
   floor

Interior View

Second Floor
833 sq. ft.

MASTER BEDRM
13'-6" x 18'

dress

ROOF

5' high wall
slope ceiling

dn

BATH

C

BEDROOM
10' x 10'-8"

BEDROOM
10' x 13'-2"

C

dn
slope ceiling
5' high wall

STUDIO
13'-8" x 23'-3"

PLAN DATA

Total Living Area: 2,155
Bedrooms: 4
Baths: 3
Garage: 2-car
Foundation Types:
   Plan #565-1128-1
   Partial basement/
   crawl space
   Plan #565-1128-2
   Crawl space & slab

First Floor
1,322 sq. ft.

66'-0"

PATIO

GARAGE
23'-4" x 23'-4"

FAMILY ROOM
16' x 14'-3"

KITCHEN
13' x 15'

DINING RM
OR DEN
12' x 11'-9"

C

L'DRY

w   d

FOYER

up

PORCH

up

dn

BATH

C

40'-5"

LIVING ROOM
13' x 16'-7"

BEDROOM
12' x 13'

PLAN #565-0315

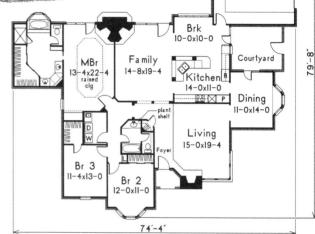

PLAN DATA

Total Living Area: 2,481
Bedrooms: 3
Baths: 2
Garage: 3-car
Foundation Type:
  Slab
Features:
  Varied ceiling heights
  throughout

PLAN #565-DRD-1478

Price Code AA

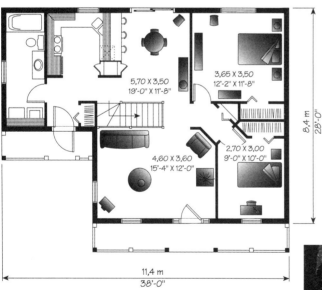

PLAN DATA

Total Living Area: 920
Bedrooms: 2
Baths: 1
Foundation Type:
  Basement
Features:
  2" x 6" exterior walls

PLAN DATA

Total Living Area: 2,255
Bedrooms: 3
Baths: 2
Garage: 2-car
Foundation Types:
    Crawl space standard
    Slab
    Basement
Features:
    2" x 6" exterior walls

Second Floor 96 sq. ft.

Attic Space

open to below

Attic Space

Dn   balcony

Attic Space

storage

Garage
23-4x25-8

Dn

MBr
12-6x18-4

Eating
12-0x10-6

Covered Porch

Br 2
11-0x13-4

Kit
20-0x
11-0

Family
19-4x16-10

Up

86'-0"

balcony above

Dining
15-4x11-4

Br 3
12-10x11-4

First Floor 2,159 sq. ft.

8-0 Porch Depth

56'-0"

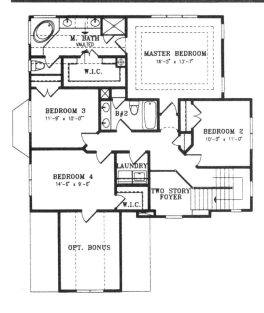

Second Floor
1,266 sq. ft.

MASTER BEDROOM
16'-5" x 13'-7"

M. BATH
VAULTED

W.I.C.

BEDROOM 3
11'-9" x 10'-0"

B#2

BEDROOM 2
10'-0" x 11'-0"

BEDROOM 4
14'-6" x 9'-6"

LAUNDRY

TWO STORY
FOYER

W.I.C.

OPT. BONUS

PLAN DATA

Total Living Area: 2,379
Bedrooms: 4
Baths: 2 1/2
Garage: 2-car
Foundation Type:
Basement

First Floor
1,113 sq. ft.

FAMILY ROOM/
KEEPING
14'-0" x 13'-9"

GRAND ROOM
17'-2" x 13'-7"

BRKFST

KITCHEN

POWDER

GALLERY

DINING
12'-0" x 11'-4"

TWO STORY
FOYER

TWO CAR GARAGE

Width: 42'-0"
Depth: 46'-6"

storage

Dn

Bonus Rm
23-6x15-4

sloped clg

Second Floor
838 sq. ft.

First Floor
1,798 sq. ft.

Br 4
11-4x9-10

Br 2
11-6x14-0

Br 3
11-6x14-0

Dn

open to below

sloped clg

Garage
27-8x23-4

Up

D
W

P

Deck

R

Living
25-6x13-6

Kitchen

vaulted

L

13-8x11-0
vaulted

Sitting
10-0x11-6
vaulted

MBr
11-6x17-6

Foyer

Up

Dn

Dining
11-6x13-5

Brk
13-8x9-0

Porch depth 8-0

64'-0"

76'-0"

PLAN DATA

Total Living Area: 3,025
Bedrooms: 4
Baths: 3 1/2
Garage: 2-car
Foundation Type:
   Basement
Features:
   Plan also includes a
   1-car drive-under
   garage

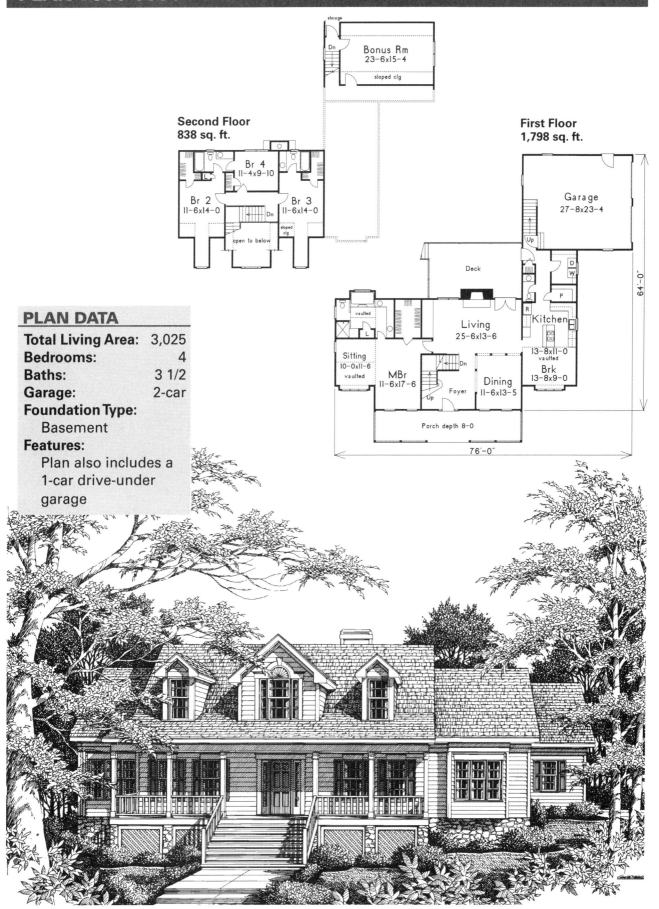

PLAN DATA

Total Living Area: 3,035
Bedrooms: 4
Baths: 3 1/2
Garage: 2-car
Foundation Types:
　Crawl space standard
　Slab
　Basement
Features:
　2" x 6" exterior walls

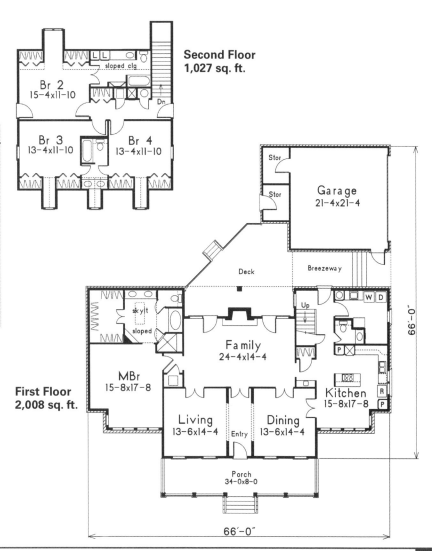

Second Floor
1,027 sq. ft.

Br 2
15-4x11-10

sloped clg

Dn

Br 3
13-4x11-10

Br 4
13-4x11-10

First Floor
2,008 sq. ft.

Stor

Stor

Garage
21-4x21-4

Deck

Breezeway

skylt

sloped

Family
24-4x14-4

Up

W D

P

P

R

P

MBr
15-8x17-8

Kitchen
15-8x17-8

Living
13-6x14-4

Entry

Dining
13-6x14-4

Porch
34-0x8-0

66'-0"

66'-0"

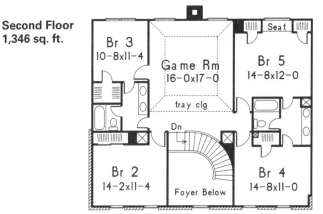

Second Floor
1,346 sq. ft.

Br 3
10-8x11-4

Game Rm
16-0x17-0
tray clg

Seat

Br 5
14-8x12-0

Dn

Br 2
14-2x11-4

Foyer Below

Br 4
14-8x11-0

PLAN DATA

Total Living Area: 3,503
Bedrooms: 5
Baths: 3 1/2
Foundation Type:
   Slab
Features:
   14' ceiling in family
   room

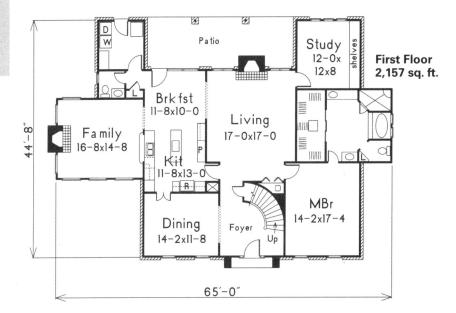

D
W

Patio

Study
12-0x
12x8

shelves

Brkfst
11-8x10-0

Living
17-0x17-0

Family
16-8x14-8

Kit
11-8x13-0

P

R

MBr
14-2x17-4

Dining
14-2x11-8

Foyer

Up

First Floor
2,157 sq. ft.

44'-8"

65'-0"

Second Floor
661 sq. ft.

- OPTIONAL BALCONY
- WOOD RAIL
- BED RM.4 — 11'-0" X 11'-0"
- B.3
- LINEN STOR.
- STAIRS DOWN
- WOOD RAIL
- WALK IN CLOSET
- WALK IN CLOSET
- BED RM.2 — 11'-0" X 12'-0"
- SHELVES
- BED RM.3 — 11'-0" X 11'-0"

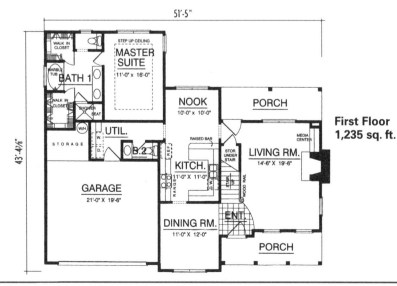

First Floor
1,235 sq. ft.

- 51'-5"
- 43'-4⅞"
- WALK IN CLOSET
- MARBLE TUB
- BATH 1
- WALK IN CLOSET
- SHOWER SEAT
- W/H
- UTIL.
- W.
- D.
- STORAGE
- B.2
- REF.
- STEP UP CEILING
- MASTER SUITE — 11'-0" x 16'-0"
- NOOK — 10'-0" x 10'-0"
- PORCH
- RAISED BAR
- MEDIA CENTER
- KITCH. — 11'-0" X 11'-0"
- RANGE
- D.W.
- STOR. UNDER STAIR
- STAIRS UP
- LIVING RM. — 14'-6" X 19'-6"
- WOOD RAIL
- GARAGE — 21'-0" X 19'-6"
- DINING RM. — 11'-0" X 12'-0"
- ENT
- PORCH

PLAN DATA

Total Living Area:	1,896
Bedrooms:	4
Baths:	2 1/2
Garage:	2-car

Foundation Types:
   Basement
   Crawl space
   Slab
Please specify when ordering

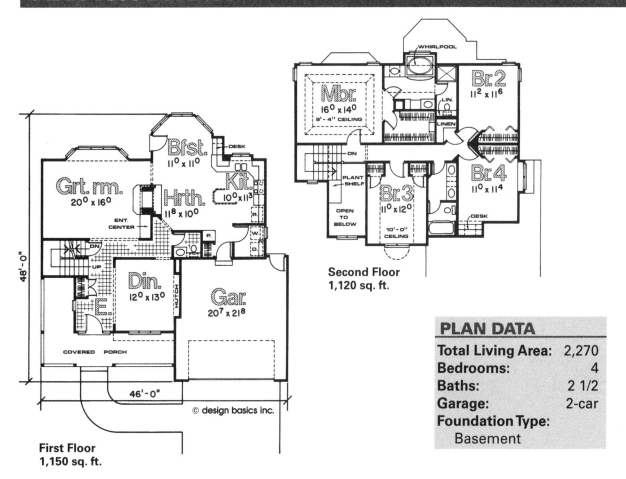

First Floor
1,150 sq. ft.

Second Floor
1,120 sq. ft.

© design basics inc.

PLAN DATA

Total Living Area:	2,270
Bedrooms:	4
Baths:	2 1/2
Garage:	2-car
Foundation Type:	
Basement	

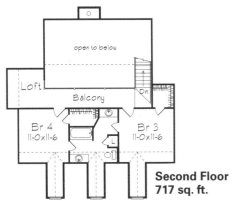

Second Floor 717 sq. ft.

open to below

Loft

Balcony

Dn

Br 4
11-0x11-6

Br 3
11-0x11-6

PLAN DATA

Total Living Area: 2,869
Bedrooms: 4
Baths: 3
Garage: 2-car
Foundation Types:
   Slab standard
   Crawl space
Features:
   - 10' ceilings on first floor
   - 9' ceilings on second floor

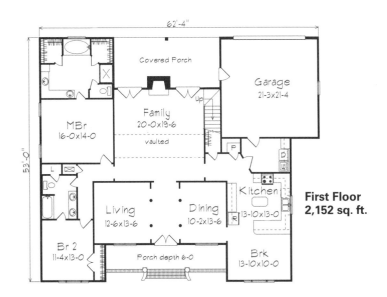

62'-4"

53'-0"

Covered Porch

Garage
21-3x21-4

up

Family
20-0x19-6
vaulted

MBr
16-0x14-0

P

Kitchen
13-10x13-0

First Floor 2,152 sq. ft.

Living
12-6x13-6

Dining
10-2x13-6

R

Br 2
11-4x13-0

Porch depth 6-0

Brk
13-10x10-0

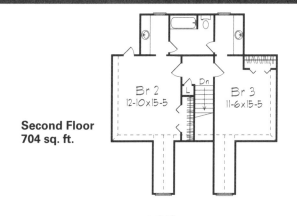

**Second Floor
704 sq. ft.**

Br 2
12-10x15-5

Dn

Br 3
11-6x15-5

PLAN DATA

Total Living Area: 2,824
Bedrooms: 4
Baths: 3
Garage: 2-car
Foundation Types:
 Slab standard
 Crawl space
Features:
 9' ceilings on first
 floor

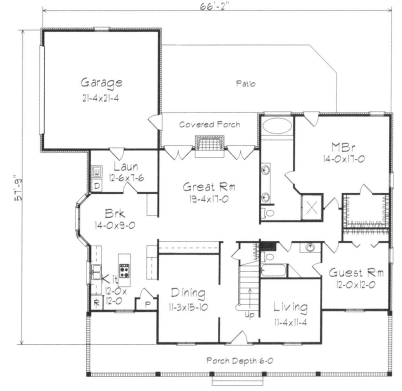

66'-2"

57'-9"

Garage
21-4x21-4

Patio

Covered Porch

**First Floor
2,120 sq. ft.**

Laun
12-6x7-6

MBr
14-0x17-0

Great Rm
19-4x17-0

Brk
14-0x9-0

Kit
12-0x
12-0

Guest Rm
12-0x12-0

Dining
11-3x15-10

Living
11-4x11-4

Up

Porch Depth 6-0

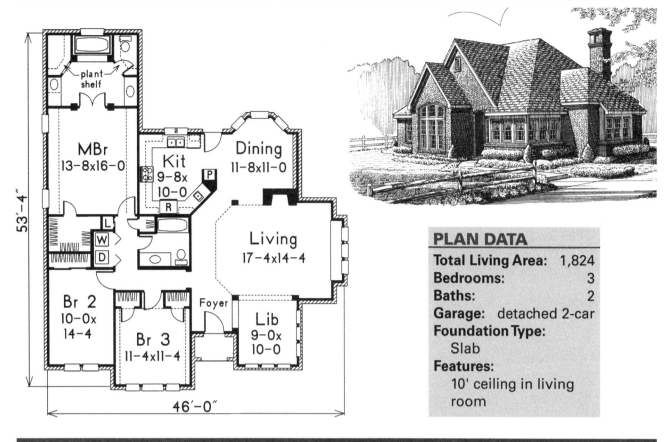

53'-4"

plant shelf

MBr
13-8x16-0

Kit
9-8x
10-0

P

R

Dining
11-8x11-0

L

W
D

Living
17-4x14-4

Br 2
10-0x
14-4

Br 3
11-4x11-4

Foyer

Lib
9-0x
10-0

46'-0"

PLAN DATA

Total Living Area: 1,824
Bedrooms: 3
Baths: 2
Garage: detached 2-car
Foundation Type:
 Slab
Features:
 10' ceiling in living
 room

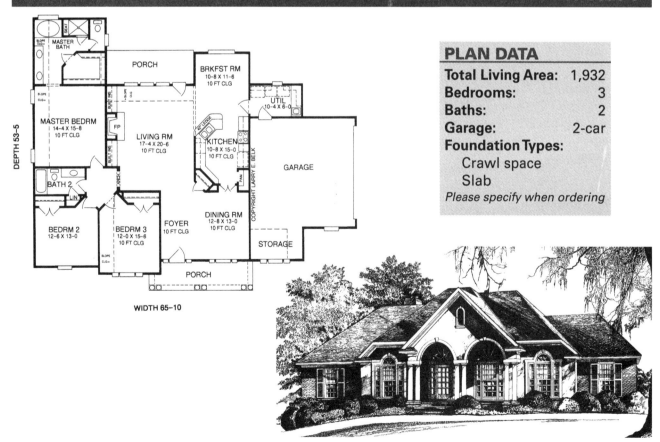

DEPTH 53-5

MASTER BATH

PORCH

BRKFST RM
10-8 X 11-6
10 FT CLG

UTIL
10-4 X 6-0

MASTER BEDRM
14-4 X 15-8
10 FT CLG

FP

LIVING RM
17-4 X 20-6
10 FT CLG

KITCHEN
10-8 X 15-0
10 FT CLG

GARAGE

COPYRIGHT LARRY E. BELK

BATH 2

LIN

BEDRM 2
12-6 X 13-0

BEDRM 3
12-0 X 15-6
10 FT CLG

FOYER
10 FT CLG

DINING RM
12-8 X 13-0
10 FT CLG

STORAGE

PORCH

WIDTH 65-10

PLAN DATA

Total Living Area: 1,932
Bedrooms: 3
Baths: 2
Garage: 2-car
Foundation Types:
 Crawl space
 Slab
Please specify when ordering

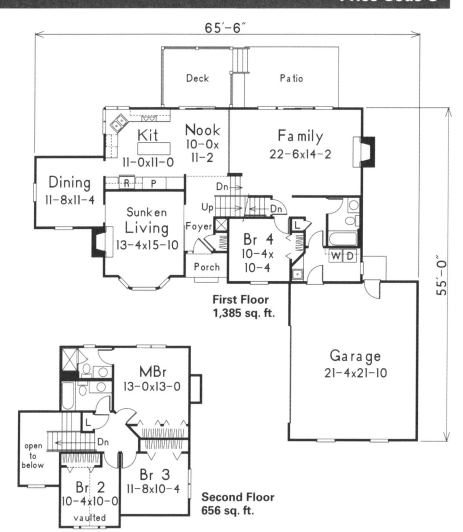

65'-6"

Deck   Patio

Kit
11-0x11-0

Nook
10-0x
11-2

Family
22-6x14-2

Dining
11-8x11-4

Sunken
Living
13-4x15-10

R   P

Dn

Up   Dn

Foyer

Br 4
10-4x
10-4

L

W D

Porch

**First Floor
1,385 sq. ft.**

55'-0"

Garage
21-4x21-10

MBr
13-0x13-0

open
to
below

Dn   L

Br 2
10-4x10-0
vaulted

Br 3
11-8x10-4

**Second Floor
656 sq. ft.**

PLAN DATA

Total Living Area: 2,041
Bedrooms: 4
Baths: 3
Garage: 2-car
Foundation Type:
  Partial basement/slab
Features:
  Vaulted living room

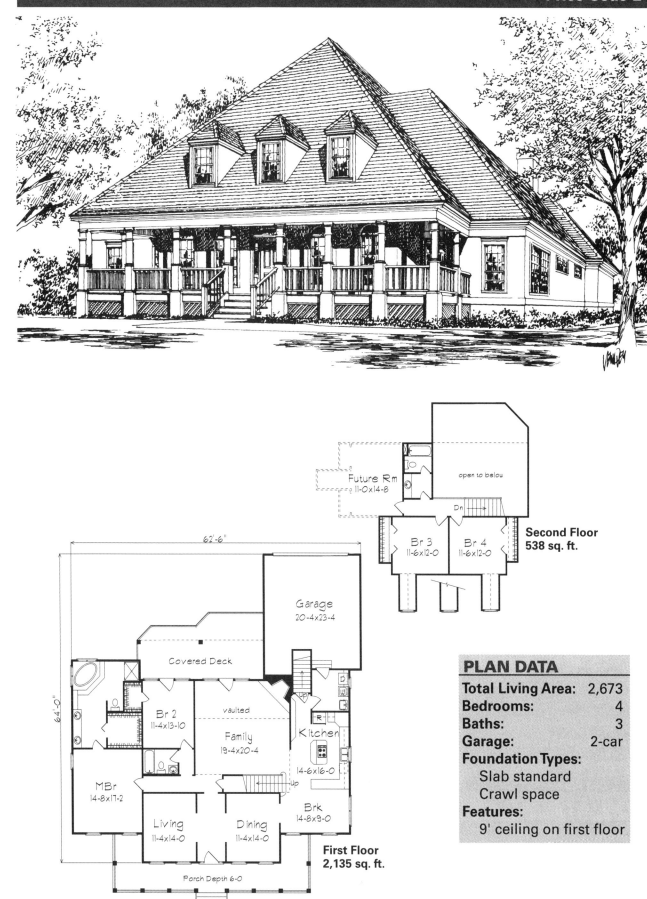

Second Floor 538 sq. ft.

Future Rm
11-0x14-8

open to below

Dn

Br 3
11-6x12-0

Br 4
11-6x12-0

62'-6"

64'-0"

Garage
20-4x23-4

Covered Deck

Up

Br 2
11-4x13-10

vaulted

Family
19-4x20-4

Kitchen
14-6x16-0

R

MBr
14-8x17-2

Up

Brk
14-8x9-0

Living
11-4x14-0

Dining
11-4x14-0

First Floor 2,135 sq. ft.

Porch Depth 6-0

PLAN DATA

Total Living Area:	2,673
Bedrooms:	4
Baths:	3
Garage:	2-car

Foundation Types:
   Slab standard
   Crawl space

Features:
   9' ceiling on first floor

Second Floor
952 sq. ft.

BEDROOM 4
13' 0" × 16' 0"

TWO STORY
GRAND ROOM

ENT. LOFT
13' 4" × 14' 6"

W.I.C.

TWO STORY
FOYER

BEDROOM 3
12' 0" × 11' 7"

B/3

BEDROOM 5
15' 0" × 13' 0"

UNFINISHED
BONUS

MASTER
BEDROOM
13' 10" × 19' 6"
tray ceiling

TWO STORY
GRAND ROOM
15' 9" × 20' 0"

BREAKFAST
13' 0" × 11' 0"

GUEST
BEDROOM
11' 0" × 11' 1"

KITCHEN

W.I.C.

M. BATH
13' 10" × 13' 0"

13' 0" × 16' 0"

B/2

W.I.C.

LAUNDRY

W.I.C.

LIVING ROOM
13' 6" × 11' 6"

TWO STORY
FOYER

DINING ROOM
12'7" × 13' 11"
tray ceiling

TWO CAR GARAGE
20 4" × 22' 6"

Width: 61'-0"
Depth: 57'-8"

First Floor
2,352 sq. ft.

PLAN DATA

Total Living Area:	3,304
Bedrooms:	5
Baths:	4
Garage:	2-car
Foundation Type:	
Basement	

PLAN #565-0127

PLAN DATA

Total Living Area: 1,996
Bedrooms: 3
Baths: 2
Garage: 2-car
Foundation Types:
  Slab standard
  Crawl space

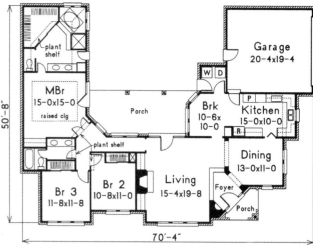

PLAN #565-BF-1314

PLAN DATA

Total Living Area: 1,375
Bedrooms: 3
Baths: 2
Garage: 2-car carport
Foundation Type:
  Slab

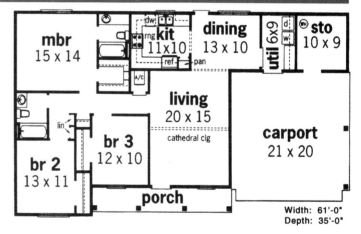

Width: 61'-0"
Depth: 35'-0"

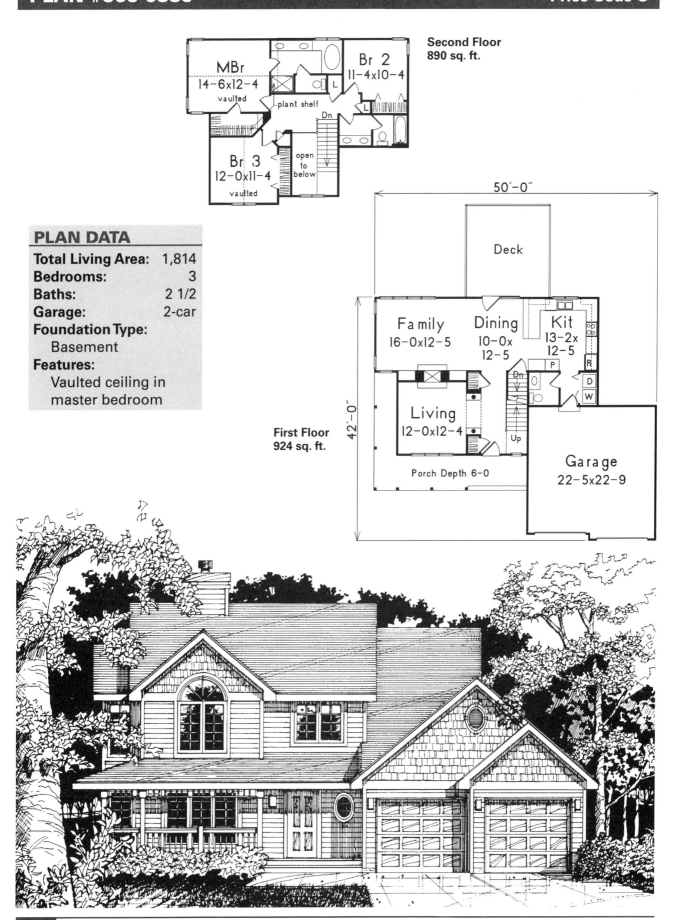

Second Floor
890 sq. ft.

MBr
14-6x12-4
vaulted

plant shelf

Br 2
11-4x10-4

Dn

Br 3
12-0x11-4

open
to
below

vaulted

PLAN DATA

Total Living Area: 1,814
Bedrooms: 3
Baths: 2 1/2
Garage: 2-car
Foundation Type:
  Basement
Features:
  Vaulted ceiling in
  master bedroom

50'-0"

Deck

Family
16-0x12-5

Dining
10-0x
12-5

Kit
13-2x
12-5

42'-0"

Living
12-0x12-4

Dn

Up

P

R

D

W

First Floor
924 sq. ft.

Porch Depth 6-0

Garage
22-5x22-9

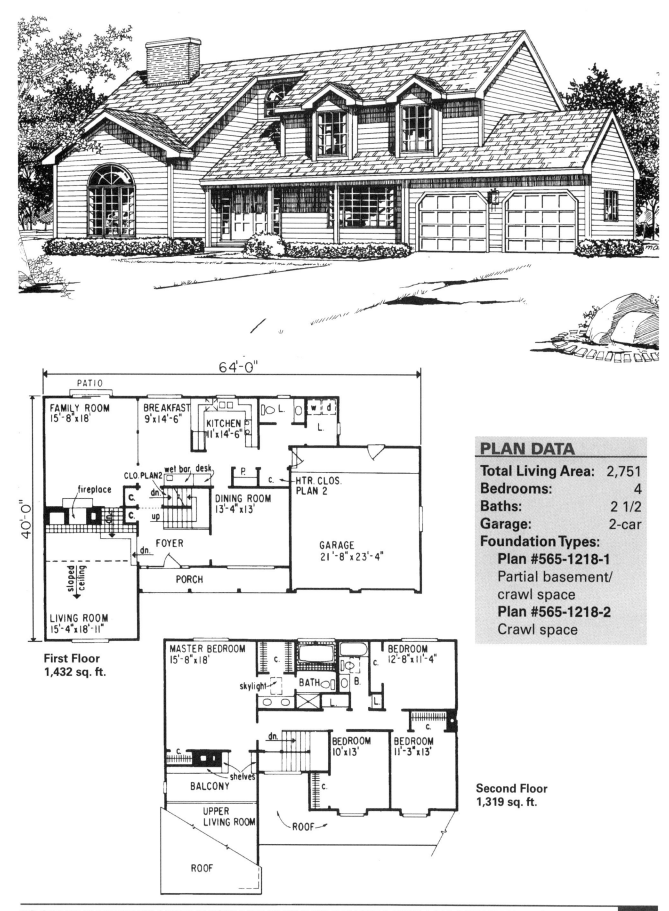

64'-0"

PATIO

FAMILY ROOM
15'-8"x18'

BREAKFAST
9'x14'-6"

KITCHEN
11'x14'-6"

w d

L.

CLO.PLAN2 wet bar desk

fireplace

dn.

up

c.

c.

P.

c.

HTR. CLOS.
PLAN 2

DINING ROOM
13'-4"x13'

40'-0"

FOYER

dn.

PORCH

GARAGE
21'-8" x 23'-4"

sloped
ceiling

LIVING ROOM
15'-4"x18'-11"

First Floor
1,432 sq. ft.

MASTER BEDROOM
15'-8"x18'

c.

BEDROOM
12'-8"x11'-4"

skylight

BATH

B.

c.

L.

L.

c.

dn.

BEDROOM
10'x13'

BEDROOM
11'-3"x13'

c.

shelves

BALCONY

UPPER
LIVING ROOM

ROOF

ROOF

Second Floor
1,319 sq. ft.

PLAN DATA

Total Living Area: 2,751
Bedrooms: 4
Baths: 2 1/2
Garage: 2-car
Foundation Types:
   Plan #565-1218-1
   Partial basement/
   crawl space
   Plan #565-1218-2
   Crawl space

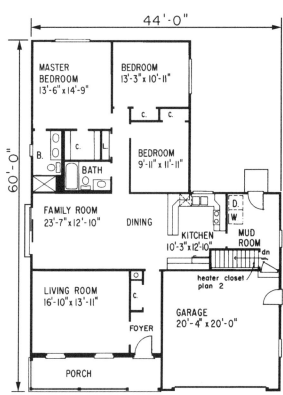

44'-0"

60'-0"

MASTER BEDROOM
13'-6" x 14'-9"

BEDROOM
13'-3" x 10'-11"

c.   c.

BEDROOM
9'-11" x 11'-11"

B.   c.

BATH

FAMILY ROOM
23'-7" x 12'-10"

DINING

KITCHEN
10'-3" x 12'-10"

D. / W.

MUD ROOM

dn

heater closet plan 2

LIVING ROOM
16'-10" x 13'-11"

c.

GARAGE
20'-4" x 20'-0"

FOYER

PORCH

PLAN DATA

Total Living Area:	1,668
Bedrooms:	3
Baths:	2
Garage:	2-car

Foundation Types:

Plan #565-1216-1
Partial basement/
crawl space

Plan #565-1216-2
Crawl space & slab

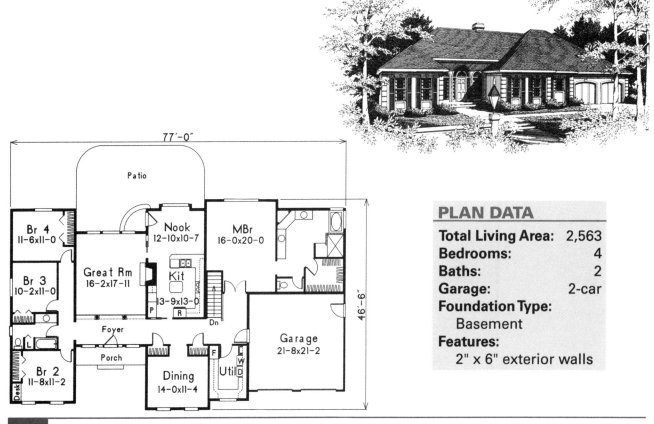

77'-0"

46'-6"

Patio

Br 4
11-6x11-0

Nook
12-10x10-7

MBr
16-0x20-0

Great Rm
16-2x17-11

Kit
13-9x13-0

Br 3
10-2x11-0

P
R

Dn

Foyer

Br 2
11-8x11-2

Porch

Garage
21-8x21-2

Desk

L

Dining
14-0x11-4

Util
W D

F

PLAN DATA

Total Living Area:	2,563
Bedrooms:	4
Baths:	2
Garage:	2-car

Foundation Type:
Basement

Features:
2" x 6" exterior walls

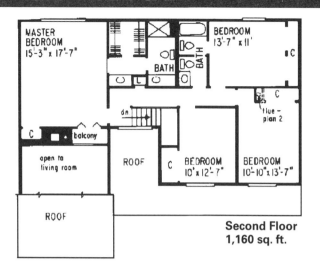

MASTER
BEDROOM
15'-3" x 17'-7"

BEDROOM
13'-7" x 11'

BATH

BATH

C

dn

flue –
plan 2

balcony

C

open to
living room

ROOF

C

BEDROOM
10' x 12'-7"

BEDROOM
10'-10" x 13'-7"

ROOF

**Second Floor
1,160 sq. ft.**

PLAN DATA

Total Living Area:	2,528
Bedrooms:	4
Baths:	2 1/2
Garage:	2-car
Foundation Types:	

Plan #565-1162-1
Partial basement
Plan #565-1162-2
Crawl space & slab

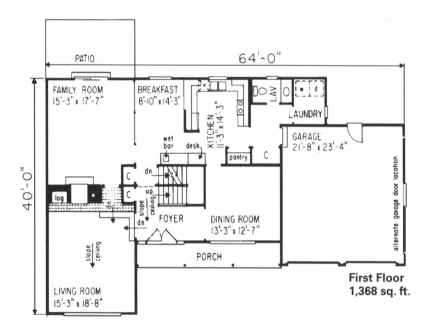

PATIO

64'-0"

40'-0"

FAMILY ROOM
15'-3" x 17'-7"

BREAKFAST
8'-10" x 14'-3"

LAV

w d

LAUNDRY

wet
bar

desk

KITCHEN
11'-3" x 14'-3"

pantry

C

GARAGE
21'-8" x 23'-4"

alternate garage door location

C

dn

C

up

slope ceiling

FOYER

DINING ROOM
13'-3" x 12'-7"

log

dn

slope ceiling

PORCH

LIVING ROOM
15'-3" x 18'-8"

**First Floor
1,368 sq. ft.**

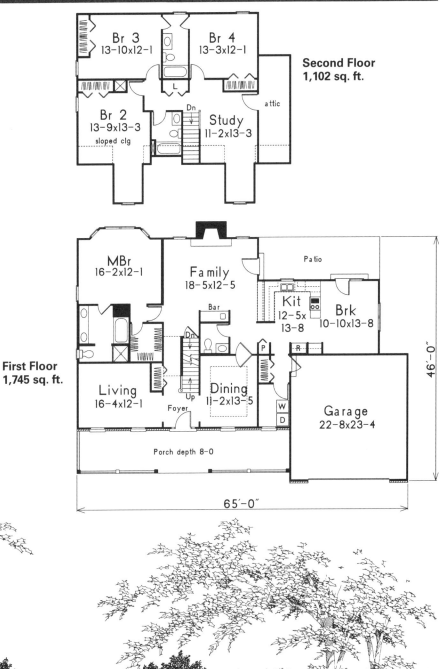

Second Floor
1,102 sq. ft.

Br 3
13-10x12-1

Br 4
13-3x12-1

L

Br 2
13-9x13-3
sloped clg

Dn

Study
11-2x13-3

attic

PLAN DATA

Total Living Area:	2,847
Bedrooms:	4
Baths:	3 1/2
Garage:	2-car
Foundation Types:	

Basement standard
Slab
Crawl space

First Floor
1,745 sq. ft.

MBr
16-2x12-1

Family
18-5x12-5

Patio

Kit
12-5x
13-8

Brk
10-10x13-8

Bar

Dn

P

R

Living
16-4x12-1

Up

Dining
11-2x13-5

Foyer

W
D

Garage
22-8x23-4

46'-0"

Porch depth 8-0

65'-0"

J.N. HANSEN S.D.G.

PLAN DATA

Total Living Area: 1,492
Bedrooms: 3
Baths: 2 1/2
Garage: 2-car
Foundation Type:
  Basement

35'-0"

41'-8"

Deck

Kit
Brk
9-0x
11-0
Dining
12-0x9-4

10-9x14-6

Dn

Living
15-8x14-0

Up

Porch

Garage
19-4x21-4

First Floor
760 sq. ft.

Second Floor
732 sq. ft.

MBr
11-0x14-8

Br 2
12-0x11-0

Dn

Br 3
12-0x9-9

raised ceiling

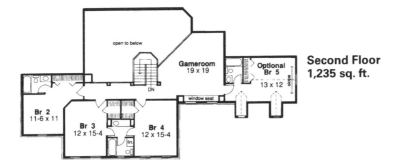

**Second Floor
1,235 sq. ft.**

- open to below
- Gameroom 19 x 19
- Optional Br 5 13 x 12
- slope
- DN
- window seat
- Br 2 11-6 x 11
- Br 3 12 x 15-4
- Br 4 12 x 15-4
- lin

PLAN DATA

Total Living Area: 3,658
Bedrooms: 5
Baths: 4 1/2
Garage: 2-car
Foundation Types:
　　Slab
　　Basement
　　Crawl space
Please specify when ordering
Features:
　　2" x 6" exterior walls

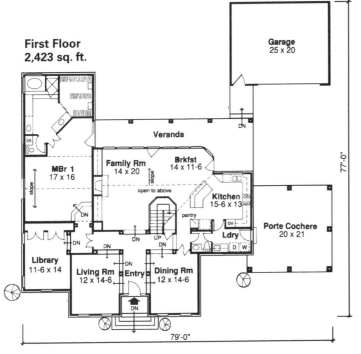

**First Floor
2,423 sq. ft.**

- Garage 25 x 20
- Veranda
- MBr 1 17 x 16
- slope
- Family Rm 14 x 20
- Brkfst 14 x 11-6
- open to above
- Kitchen 15-6 x 13
- pantry
- ov
- Ldry
- D W
- Porte Cochere 20 x 21
- Library 11-6 x 14
- Living Rm 12 x 14-6
- Entry
- Dining Rm 12 x 14-6
- DN
- UP
- DN
- 77'-0"
- 79'-0"

PLAN DATA

Total Living Area: 1,922
Bedrooms: 3
Baths: 2 1/2
Garage: 2-car
Foundation Type:
  Partial basement/
  crawl space
Features:
  - 9' ceilings
  - 2" x 6" exterior
    walls

**Second Floor
629 sq. ft.**

**First Floor
1,293 sq. ft.**

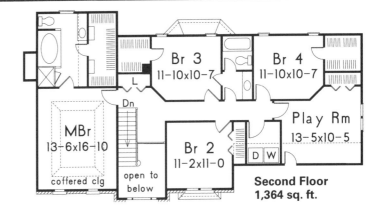

Second Floor
1,364 sq. ft.

Br 3
11-10x10-7

Br 4
11-10x10-7

Play Rm
13-5x10-5

MBr
13-6x16-10

coffered clg

Dn

open to below

Br 2
11-2x11-0

D W

L

PLAN DATA

Total Living Area:	2,336
Bedrooms:	4
Baths:	2 1/2
Garage:	2-car
Foundation Type:	
Basement	

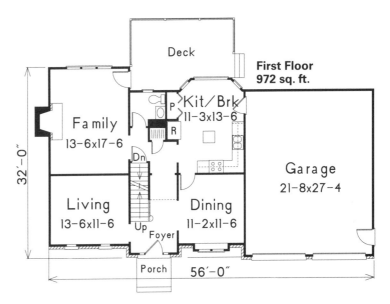

First Floor
972 sq. ft.

Deck

Family
13-6x17-6

Kit/Brk
11-3x13-6

Garage
21-8x27-4

Living
13-6x11-6

Dining
11-2x11-6

Dn

Up

Foyer

Porch

32'-0"

56'-0"

PLAN DATA

Total Living Area: 2,715
Bedrooms: 4
Baths: 2 1/2
Garage: 2-car
Foundation Type:
    Crawl space
Features:
    9' ceilings on first
    floor

Second Floor
1,407 sq. ft.

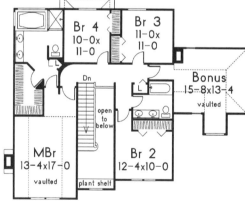

Br 4
10-0x
11-0

Br 3
11-0x
11-0

Bonus
15-8x13-4
vaulted

Dn

open to below

MBr
13-4x17-0
vaulted

plant shelf

Br 2
12-4x10-0

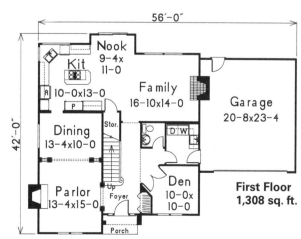

56'-0"

Nook
9-4x
11-0

Kit
10-0x13-0

Family
16-10x14-0

Garage
20-8x23-4

42'-0"

Dining
13-4x10-0

Stor.

D W

Parlor
13-4x15-0

Up
Foyer

Den
10-0x
10-0

Porch

First Floor
1,308 sq. ft.

PLAN DATA

Total Living Area: 2,414
Bedrooms: 4
Baths: 2 1/2
Garage: 2-car
Foundation Types:
  Plan #565-1211-1
  Partial basement/
  crawl space
  Plan #565-1211-2
  Crawl space & slab

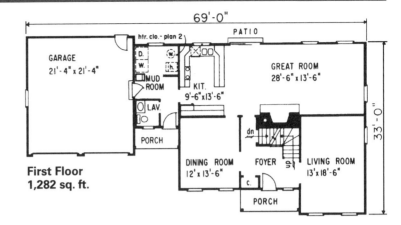

First Floor
1,282 sq. ft.

Second Floor
1,132 sq. ft.

Second Floor
882 sq. ft.

PLAN DATA

Total Living Area: 1,994
Bedrooms: 3
Baths: 2 1/2
Garage: 2-car
Foundation Type:
  Crawl space

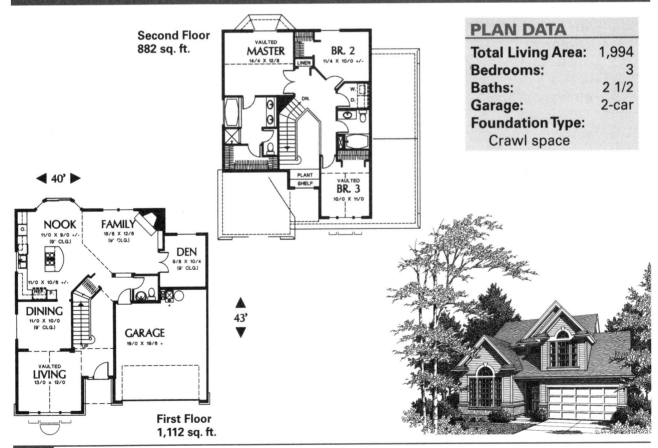

First Floor
1,112 sq. ft.

PLAN DATA

Total Living Area:	2,485
Bedrooms:	4
Baths:	3
Garage:	2-car

Foundation Types:
- Basement
- Crawl space
- Slab

Please specify when ordering

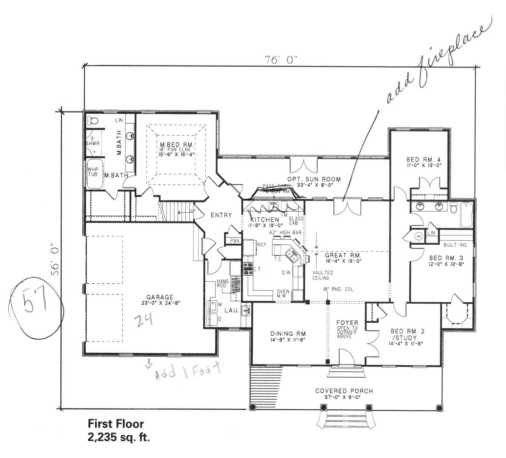

76' 0"

56' 0"

add fireplace

(57)

M.BATH
5' SHWR
WHP TUB
M.BATH
LIN

M.BED RM.
10' PAN CLNG.
16'-6" X 16'-4"

ENTRY

KITCHEN
11'-8" X 19'-0"
42" HIGH BAR
PAN
REF.
T.C.
C.T
D.W.
OVEN
M.W

OPT. SUN ROOM
33'-4" X 8'-0"
PASS THRU
GLASS CAB

GREAT RM.
16'-4" X 19'-0"
VAULTED CEILING
10" RND COL.

BED RM. 4
11'-0" X 13'-0"

LIN
BUILT-INS

BED RM. 3
12'-0" X 13'-8"

GARAGE
23'-0" X 24'-8"
24

HANG ROD
W D
LAU.

DINING RM.
14'-8" X 11'-8"

FOYER
OPEN TO DORMER ABOVE

BED RM. 2 /STUDY
14'-4" X 11'-8"

Add 1 Foot

COVERED PORCH
37'-0" X 8'-0"

First Floor
2,235 sq. ft.

Second Floor
399 sq. ft.

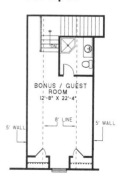

BONUS / GUEST ROOM
12'-8" X 22'-4"

5' WALL   8' LINE   5' WALL

DN

Holzhauer INK.

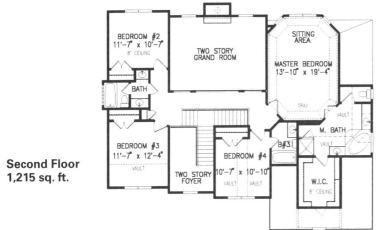

BEDROOM #2
11'-7" x 10'-7"
8' CEILING

TWO STORY
GRAND ROOM

SITTING
AREA

MASTER BEDROOM
13'-10" x 19'-4"

TRAY

BATH

VAULT

BEDROOM #3
11'-7" x 12'-4"
VAULT

TWO STORY
FOYER

BEDROOM #4
10'-7" x 10'-10"
VAULT   VAULT

B#3

M. BATH
VAULT

W.I.C.
8' CEILING

**Second Floor
1,215 sq. ft.**

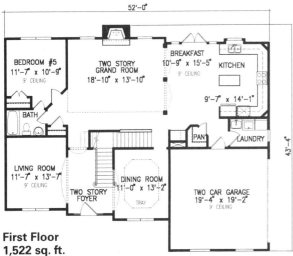

52'-0"

BEDROOM #5
11'-7" x 10'-9"
9' CEILING

TWO STORY
GRAND ROOM
18'-10" x 13'-10"

BREAKFAST
10'-9" x 15'-5"
9' CEILING

KITCHEN

9'-7" x 14'-1"

BATH

PAN

LAUNDRY

43'-4"

LIVING ROOM
11'-7" x 13'-7"
9' CEILING

TWO STORY
FOYER

DINING ROOM
11'-0" x 13'-2"
TRAY

TWO CAR GARAGE
19'-4" x 19'-2"
9' CEILING

**First Floor
1,522 sq. ft.**

PLAN DATA
Total Living Area: 2,737
Bedrooms: 5
Baths: 4
Garage: 2-car
Foundation Type:
  Basement

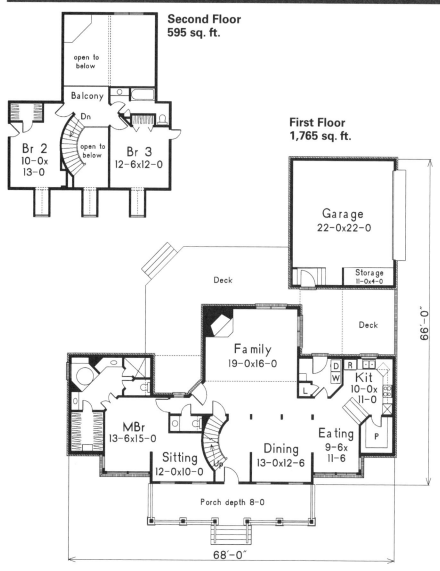

Second Floor
595 sq. ft.

open to below

Balcony

Dn

open to below

Br 2
10-0x 13-0

Br 3
12-6x12-0

First Floor
1,765 sq. ft.

Garage
22-0x22-0

Storage
11-0x4-0

Deck

Deck

Family
19-0x16-0

Kit
10-0x 11-0

D R
W

L

MBr
13-6x15-0

Sitting
12-0x10-0

Up

Dining
13-0x12-6

Eating
9-6x 11-6

P

Porch depth 8-0

68'-0"

66'-0"

PLAN DATA

Total Living Area: 2,360
Bedrooms: 3
Baths: 2 1/2
Garage: 2-car
Foundation Types:
  Crawl space standard
  Slab
  Basement
Features:
  Sloped ceiling in
  family room

PLAN DATA

Total Living Area: 2,563
Bedrooms: 3
Baths: 2
Garage: 2-car
Foundation Type:
  Basement
Features:
  13' ceilings in entry
  and living room

Interior View - Dining Room

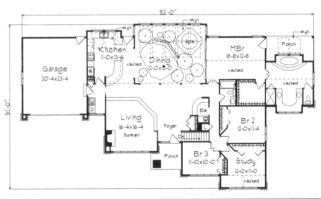

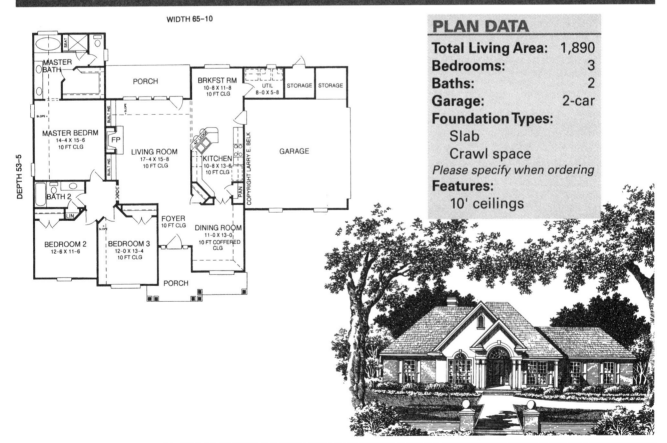

PLAN DATA

Total Living Area: 1,890
Bedrooms: 3
Baths: 2
Garage: 2-car
Foundation Types:
  Slab
  Crawl space
Please specify when ordering
Features:
  10' ceilings

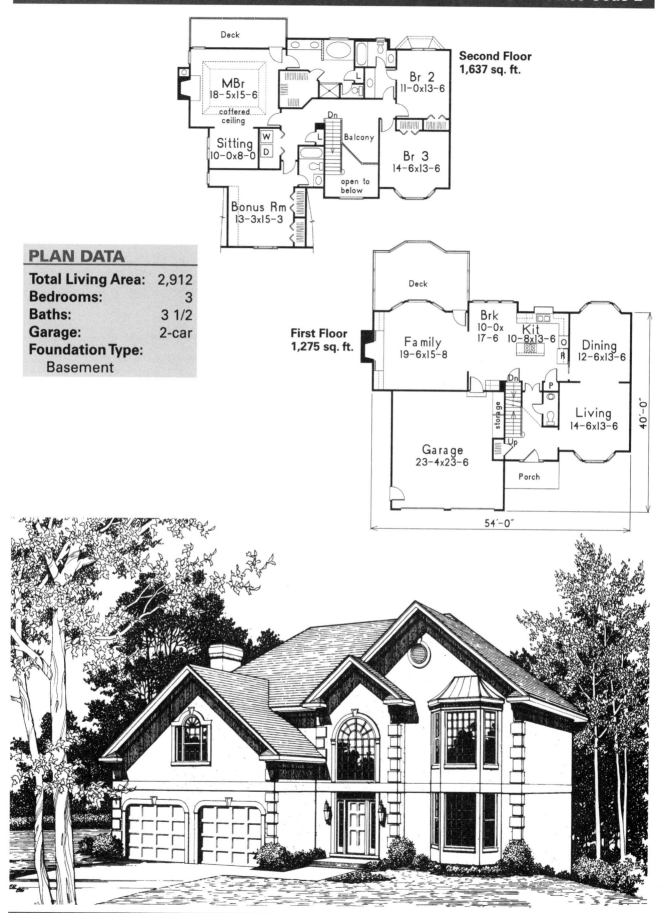

Deck

MBr
18-5x15-6

coffered
ceiling

Second Floor
1,637 sq. ft.

Br 2
11-0x13-6

Dn

L

Balcony

Sitting
10-0x8-0

W
D

Br 3
14-6x13-6

open to
below

Bonus Rm
13-3x15-3

PLAN DATA

Total Living Area:	2,912
Bedrooms:	3
Baths:	3 1/2
Garage:	2-car
Foundation Type:	
Basement	

Deck

Brk
10-0x
17-6

Kit
10-8x13-6

First Floor
1,275 sq. ft.

Family
19-6x15-8

Dining
12-6x13-6

Dn

storage

P

Living
14-6x13-6

40'-0"

Garage
23-4x23-6

Up

Porch

54'-0"

PLAN DATA

Total Living Area: 1,546
Bedrooms: 3
Baths: 2
Garage: 2-car
Foundation Type:
Basement

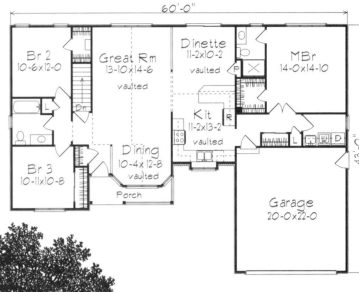

PLAN #565-GSD-1260

Price Code E

PLAN DATA

Total Living Area: 2,788
Bedrooms: 3
Baths: 2 1/2
Garage: 3-car
Foundation Type:
Crawl space

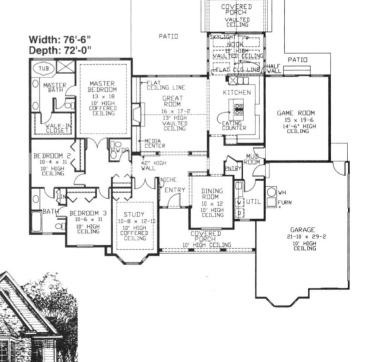

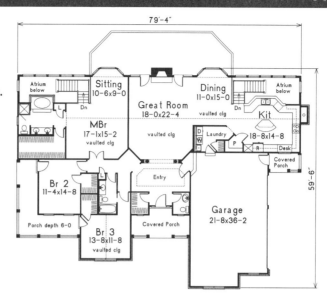

First Floor
2,349 sq. ft.

79'-4"

Atrium below

Sitting
10-6x9-0

Dining
11-0x15-0

Atrium below

Great Room
18-0x22-4
vaulted clg

Kit
18-8x14-8

MBr
17-1x15-2
vaulted clg

Laundry

Covered Porch

Br 2
11-4x14-8

Entry

Garage
21-8x36-2

Porch depth 6-0

Covered Porch

Br 3
13-8x11-8
vaulted clg

59'-6"

PLAN DATA

Total Living Area:	3,199
Bedrooms:	3
Baths:	2 1/2
Garage:	3-car
Foundation Type:	
Walk-out basement	
Features:	
Double atrium	

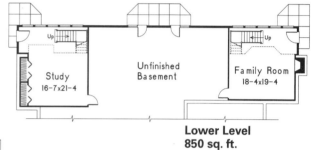

Up

Study
16-7x21-4

Unfinished Basement

Family Room
18-4x19-4

Up

Lower Level
850 sq. ft.

Rear View

PLAN DATA

Total Living Area: 2,024
Bedrooms: 3
Baths: 2 1/2
Garage: 2-car
Foundation Types:
Crawl space standard
Slab
Basement

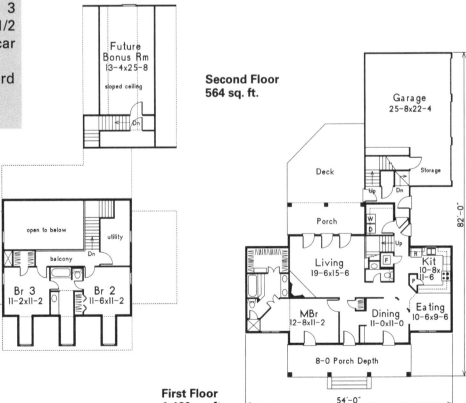

Future
Bonus Rm
13-4x25-8

sloped ceiling

Dn

Second Floor
564 sq. ft.

Garage
25-8x22-4

Deck

Storage

Porch

Up   Dn

open to below

utility

W
D

Up

balcony   Dn

Living
19-6x15-6

F

Kit
10-8x
11-6

R

Br 3
11-2x11-2

Br 2
11-6x11-2

MBr
12-8x11-2

Dining
11-0x11-0

Eating
10-6x9-6

8-0 Porch Depth

82'-0"

54'-0"

First Floor
1,460 sq. ft.

PLAN #565-0541

PLAN DATA

Total Living Area: 2,080
Bedrooms: 4
Baths: 2
Garage: 2-car
Foundation Types:
  Crawl space standard
  Basement
  Slab

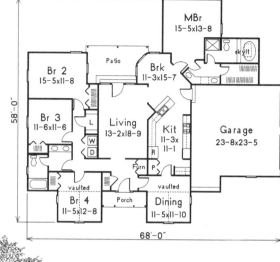

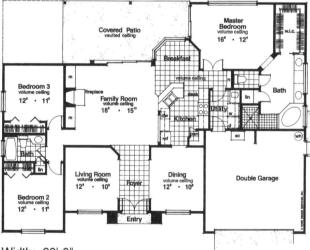

PLAN #565-HDS-1758

PLAN DATA

Total Living Area: 1,783
Bedrooms: 3
Baths: 2
Garage: 2-car
Foundation Type:
  Slab

Width: 60'-0"
Depth: 45'-0"

**Second Floor
1,059 sq. ft.**

Br 4 / Sitting
9-10x11-5

Br 2
13-6x11-0

W
D

MBr
17-7x13-7
sloped clg

Dn

Br 3
13-6x10-0

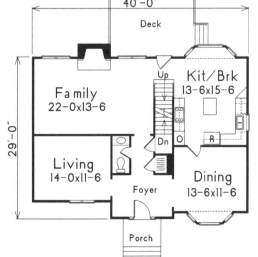

40'-0"

Deck

29'-0"

Family
22-0x13-6

Up

Kit/Brk
13-6x15-6

Dn

R

Living
14-0x11-6

Dn

Dining
13-6x11-6

Foyer

Porch

**First Floor
1,136 sq. ft.**

PLAN DATA

Total Living Area: 2,195
Bedrooms: 4
Baths: 2 1/2
Garage: 2-car
Foundation Type:
  Basement
Features:
  Drive-under garage

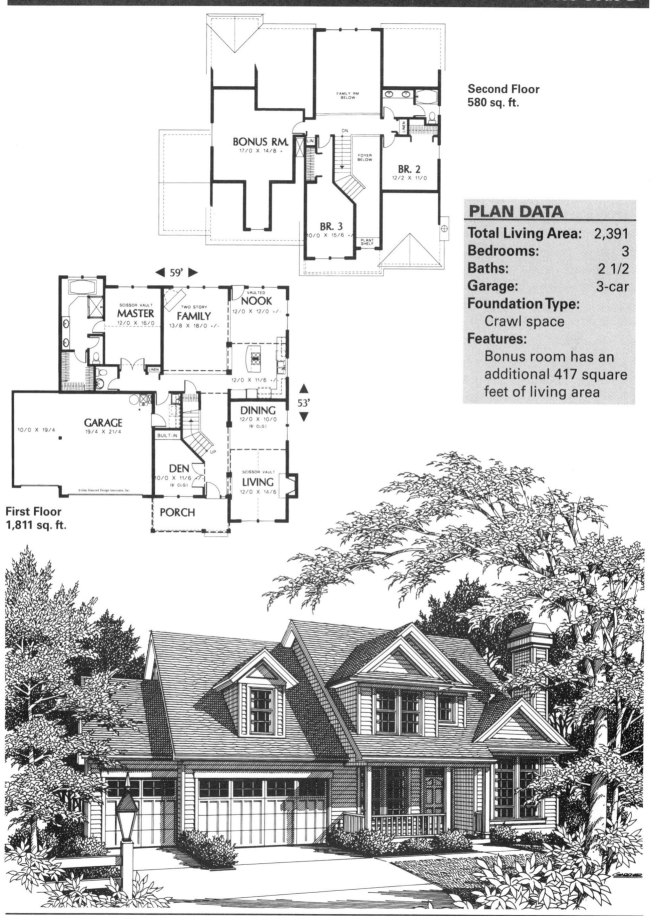

Second Floor
580 sq. ft.

BONUS RM.
17/0 X 14/8 +

FAMILY RM
BELOW

DN

FOYER
BELOW

BR. 2
12/2 X 11/0

BR. 3
10/0 X 15/6

PLANT
SHELF

PLAN DATA

Total Living Area:	2,391
Bedrooms:	3
Baths:	2 1/2
Garage:	3-car

Foundation Type:
Crawl space

Features:
Bonus room has an additional 417 square feet of living area

◄ 59' ►

SCISSOR VAULT
MASTER
12/0 X 16/0

TWO STORY
FAMILY
13/8 X 18/0 +/-

VAULTED
NOOK
12/0 X 12/0 +/-

LINEN

12/0 X 11/6

53'

DINING
12/0 X 10/0
(9' CLG.)

GARAGE
19/4 X 21/4

10/0 X 19/4

BUILT-IN

UP

DEN
10/0 X 11/6
(9' CLG.)

SCISSOR VAULT
LIVING
12/0 X 14/6

©Alan Mascord Design Associates, Inc.

PORCH

First Floor
1,811 sq. ft.

**First Floor
3,050 sq. ft.**

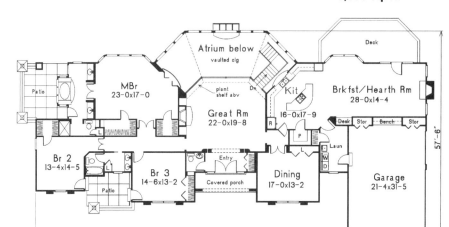

PLAN DATA

Total Living Area:	4,826
Bedrooms:	4
Baths:	3 1/2
Garage:	3-car
Foundation Type:	
Walk-out basement	

**Lower Level
1,776 sq. ft.**

**Great Room/Atrium
Interior View**

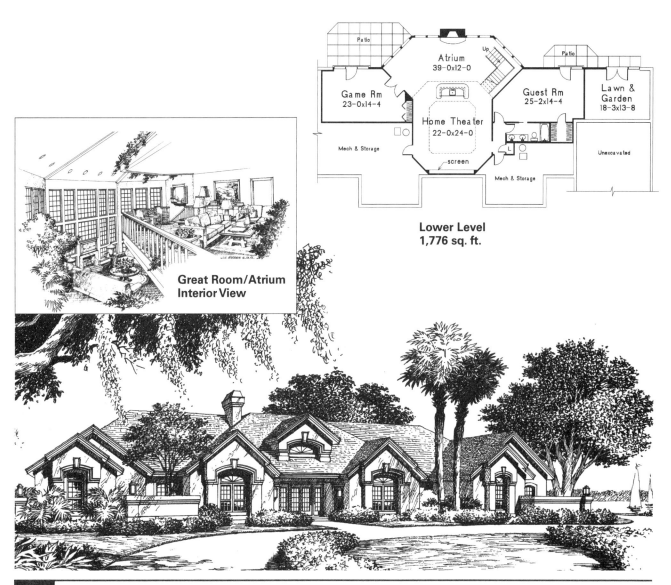

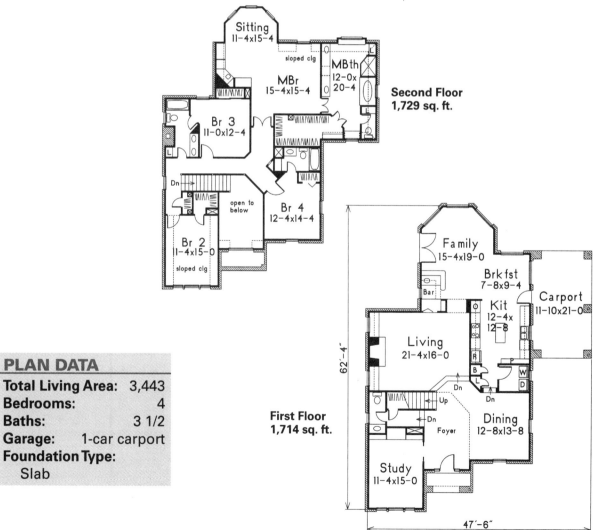

Sitting
11-4x15-4

sloped clg

MBr
15-4x15-4

MBth
12-0x
20-4

**Second Floor
1,729 sq. ft.**

Br 3
11-0x12-4

Dn

open to
below

Br 4
12-4x14-4

Br 2
11-4x15-0

sloped clg

Family
15-4x19-0

Brkfst
7-8x9-4

Carport
11-10x21-0

Kit
12-4x
12-8

Bar

Living
21-4x16-0

Dn

Up

Dn

W
D

62'-4"

**First Floor
1,714 sq. ft.**

Dining
12-8x13-8

Foyer

Study
11-4x15-0

47'-6"

PLAN DATA

Total Living Area: 3,443
Bedrooms: 4
Baths: 3 1/2
Garage: 1-car carport
Foundation Type:
  Slab

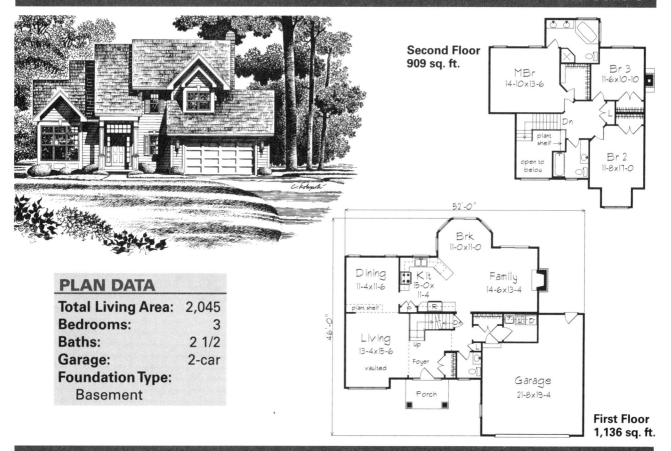

Second Floor 909 sq. ft.

MBr 14-10x13-6

Br 3 11-6x10-10

Dn

plant shelf

open to below

Br 2 11-8x17-0

52'-0"

46'-0"

Brk 11-0x11-0

Dining 11-4x11-6

Kit 15-0x 11-4

Family 14-6x13-4

plant shelf

Living 13-4x15-6 vaulted

up

Foyer

Porch

Garage 21-8x19-4

First Floor 1,136 sq. ft.

PLAN DATA

Total Living Area:	2,045
Bedrooms:	3
Baths:	2 1/2
Garage:	2-car
Foundation Type:	Basement

PLAN #565-0717

Price Code A

PLAN DATA

Total Living Area:	1,268
Bedrooms:	3
Baths:	2
Garage:	2-car
Foundation Type:	Basement

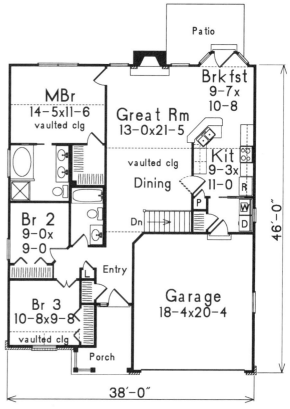

Patio

Brkfst 9-7x 10-8

MBr 14-5x11-6 vaulted clg

Great Rm 13-0x21-5

vaulted clg

Kit 9-3x 11-0

Dining

Br 2 9-0x 9-0

Dn

46'-0"

Br 3 10-8x9-8 vaulted clg

Entry

Garage 18-4x20-4

Porch

38'-0"

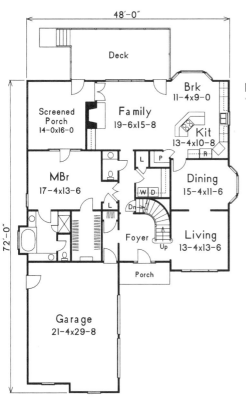

First Floor
1,852 sq. ft.

48'-0"

Deck

Screened Porch
14-0x16-0

Family
19-6x15-8

Brk
11-4x9-0

Kit
13-4x10-8

MBr
17-4x13-6

Dining
15-4x11-6

W D

Foyer

Living
13-4x13-6

Porch

Garage
21-4x29-8

72'-0"

Br 3
16-4x11-10

Br 2
13-4x11-2

Dn

open to below

Unfinished Storage
13-4x34-10

Second Floor
659 sq. ft.

PLAN DATA

Total Living Area: 2,511
Bedrooms: 3
Baths: 2 1/2
Garage: 2-car
Foundation Types:
   Basement standard
   Slab
   Crawl space
Features:
   Vaulted ceilings in
   family and kitchen
   area

PLAN DATA

Total Living Area: 1,818
Bedrooms: 3
Baths: 2 1/2
Garage: 1-car carport
Foundation Types:
  Crawl space standard
  Basement
  Slab
Features:
  Extra storage in carport

Second Floor
890 sq. ft.

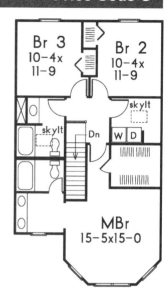

Br 3
10-4x
11-9

Br 2
10-4x
11-9

skylt

skylt

Dn

W | D

MBr
15-5x15-0

Patio

Living
23-5x15-8
raised ceiling

Storage

L

Furn

Kit
12-3x
12-2

Carport

R

Foyer

Up

Dining
15-5x13-0

First Floor
928 sq. ft.

Porch depth 6-0

42'-0"

36'-0"

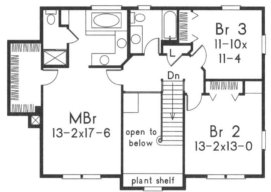

Second Floor
994 sq. ft.

Br 3
11-10x
11-4

Dn

MBr
13-2x17-6

open to
below

Br 2
13-2x13-0

plant shelf

PLAN DATA

Total Living Area: 2,106
Bedrooms: 3
Baths: 2 1/2
Garage: 2-car
Foundation Type:
  Basement
Features:
  9' ceilings

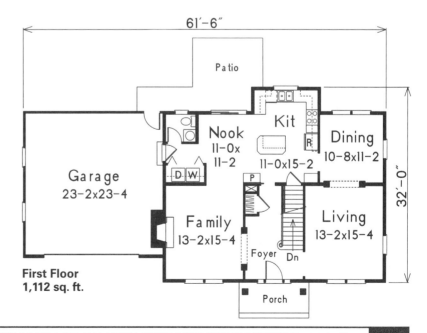

61'-6"

Patio

Nook
11-0x
11-2

Kit

Dining
10-8x11-2

32'-0"

Garage
23-2x23-4

D W

P

R

Family
13-2x15-4

Living
13-2x15-4

Foyer

Dn

First Floor
1,112 sq. ft.

Porch

PLAN DATA

Total Living Area:	1,189
Bedrooms:	3
Baths:	2 1/2
Garage:	2-car
Foundation Type:	
Basement	

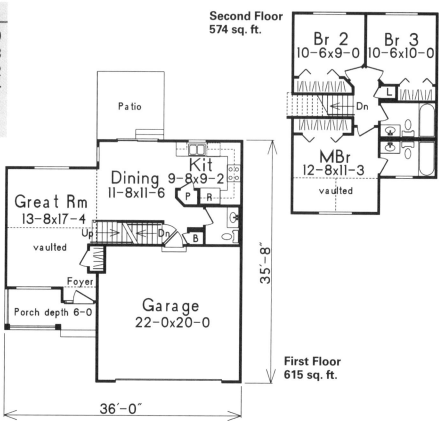

Second Floor
574 sq. ft.

Br 2
10-6x9-0

Br 3
10-6x10-0

Dn

L

MBr
12-8x11-3

vaulted

Patio

Dining 9-8x9-2
11-8x11-6

Kit

P

R

Great Rm
13-8x17-4

vaulted

Up

Dn

B

Foyer

Porch depth 6-0

Garage
22-0x20-0

35'-8"

First Floor
615 sq. ft.

36'-0"

**Second Floor
1,339 sq. ft.**

Br 3
10-0x
15-4

Br 4
10-6x11-6

Br 5
10-0x11-6

skylt

Dn

Br 2
12-8x13-0

open to below

MBr
13-0x17-8
raised clg

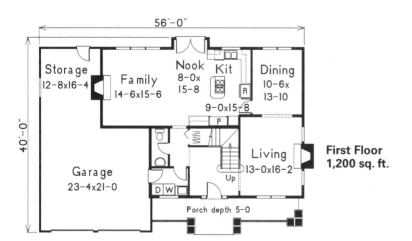

56'-0"

40'-0"

Storage
12-8x16-4

Family
14-6x15-6

Nook
8-0x
15-8

Kit

Dining
10-6x
13-10

9-0x15-8

P

Garage
23-4x21-0

Living
13-0x16-2

Up

D W

Porch depth 5-0

**First Floor
1,200 sq. ft.**

PLAN DATA

Total Living Area:	2,539
Bedrooms:	5
Baths:	2 1/2
Garage:	2-car
Foundation Type:	
Crawl space	

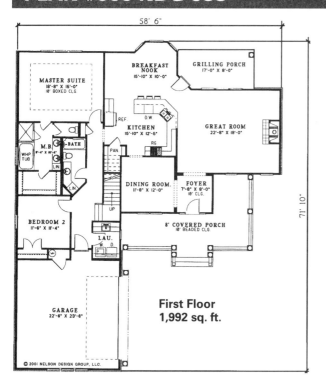

58' 6"

71' 10"

MASTER SUITE
18'-8" X 16'-0"
10' BOXED CLG.

BREAKFAST NOOK
15'-10" X 10'-0"

GRILLING PORCH
17'-0" X 8'-0"

REF.

M.B.

BATH

WHP TUB

LIN

LIN

GREAT ROOM
22'-8" X 18'-0"

KITCHEN
15'-10" X 12'-6"

PAN.

RG

DINING ROOM
11'-8" X 12'-0"

FOYER
7'-8" X 8'-0"
10' CLG.

BEDROOM 2
11'-6" X 11'-4"

UP

LAU.
W D

8' COVERED PORCH
10' BEADED CLG.

GARAGE
22'-8" X 23'-8"

First Floor
1,992 sq. ft.

© 2001 NELSON DESIGN GROUP, LLC.

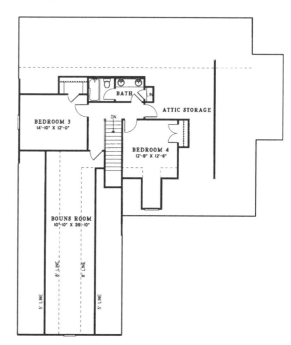

Second Floor
643 sq. ft.

BATH
LIN

BEDROOM 3
14'-10" X 12'-0"

ATTIC STORAGE

DN.

BEDROOM 4
12'-8" X 12'-6"

BONUS ROOM
10'-10" X 39'-10"

5' LINE 8' LINE 8' LINE 5' LINE

PLAN DATA

Total Living Area:	2,635
Bedrooms:	4
Baths:	3
Garage:	2-car

Foundation Types:
  Crawl space
  Slab
Please specify when ordering

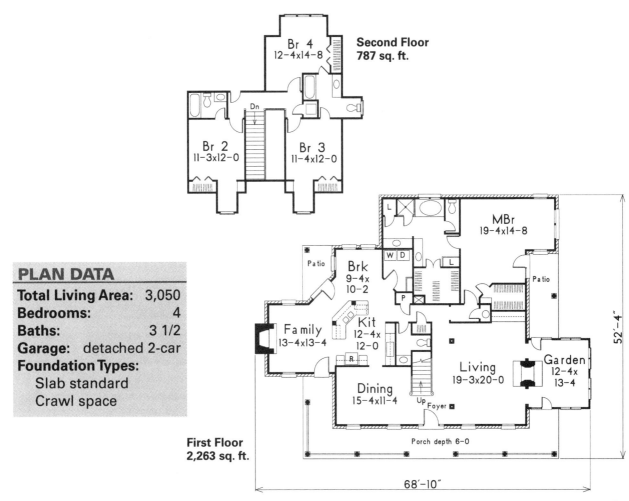

**Second Floor
787 sq. ft.**

Br 4
12-4x14-8

Br 2
11-3x12-0

Dn

Br 3
11-4x12-0

MBr
19-4x14-8

Patio

Brk
9-4x
10-2

W D

L

P

Patio

Family
13-4x13-4

Kit
12-4x
12-0

R

Dining
15-4x11-4

Up Foyer

Living
19-3x20-0

Garden
12-4x
13-4

Porch depth 6-0

52'-4"

68'-10"

PLAN DATA

Total Living Area: 3,050
Bedrooms: 4
Baths: 3 1/2
Garage: detached 2-car
Foundation Types:
  Slab standard
  Crawl space

**First Floor
2,263 sq. ft.**

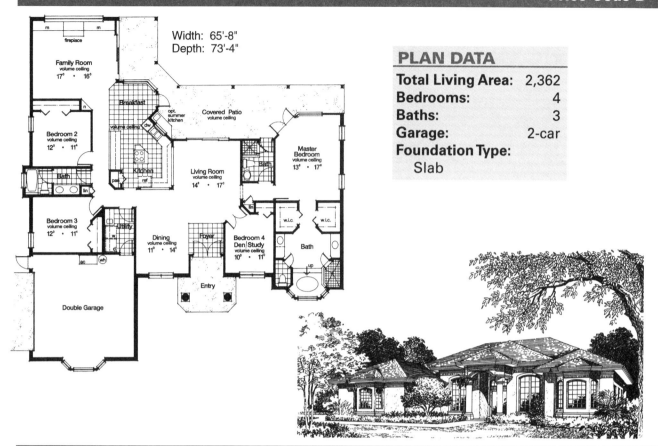

Width: 65'-8"
Depth: 73'-4"

PLAN DATA

Total Living Area: 2,362
Bedrooms: 4
Baths: 3
Garage: 2-car
Foundation Type:
  Slab

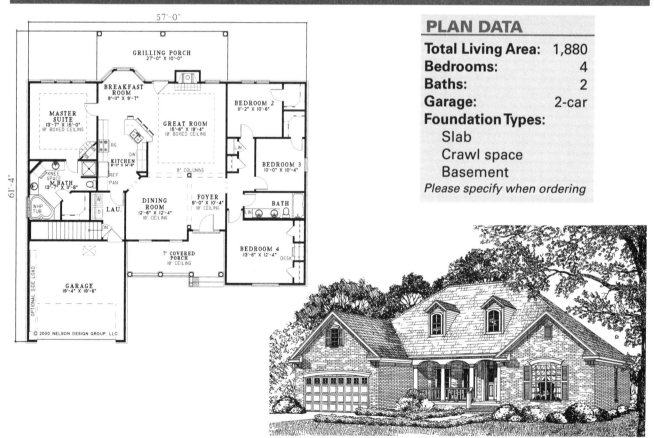

PLAN DATA

Total Living Area: 1,880
Bedrooms: 4
Baths: 2
Garage: 2-car
Foundation Types:
  Slab
  Crawl space
  Basement
Please specify when ordering

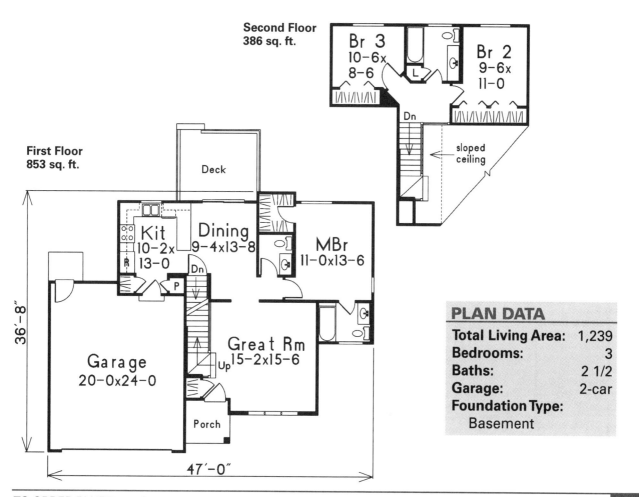

Second Floor 386 sq. ft.

Br 3
10-6x
8-6

Br 2
9-6x
11-0

L

Dn

sloped ceiling

First Floor 853 sq. ft.

Deck

36'-8"

Kit
10-2x
13-0

Dining
9-4x13-8

MBr
11-0x13-6

Dn

P

Garage
20-0x24-0

Great Rm
15-2x15-6

Up

Porch

47'-0"

PLAN DATA

Total Living Area: 1,239
Bedrooms: 3
Baths: 2 1/2
Garage: 2-car
Foundation Type:
  Basement

First Floor 768 sq. ft.

24'-0"

DINE
opt. fireplace
bar
GREAT RM. 23'-3" x 12'-10"
ONE CAR 13'-8"
TWO CAR 21'-8"
GARAGE 13'-4"x21'-4"
LIVING RM. 11'-6" x 15'
dn up
storage
LAV.
FOYER
32'-0"
4'-0"

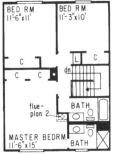

BED RM 11'-6"x11'
BED RM 11'-3"x10'
C. C. C.
dn
BATH
flue-plan 2
MASTER BEDRM 11'-6"x15'
BATH

Second Floor 768 sq. ft.

PLAN DATA

Total Living Area: 1,536
Bedrooms: 3
Baths: 2 1/2
Garage: 1-car
Foundation Types:
   Plan #565-1197-1
   Basement
   Plan #565-1197-2
   Crawl space & slab
Features:
   Optional 2-car garage

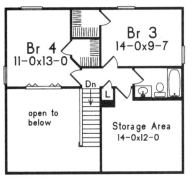

Second Floor 446 sq. ft.

Br 4 11-0x13-0
Br 3 14-0x9-7
Dn L
open to below
Storage Area 14-0x12-0

PLAN DATA

Total Living Area: 1,330
Bedrooms: 4
Baths: 2
Garage: 1-car
Foundation Type:
   Basement

First Floor 884 sq. ft.

Patio
Dining 10-7x9-10
Kit 9-9x 9-7
Br 2 11-8x9-7
Dn L
Garage 12-4x20-4
Living 12-8x17-5 vaulted
Entry
Br 1 11-8x12-0
Porch depth 5-0
33'-0"
43'-8"

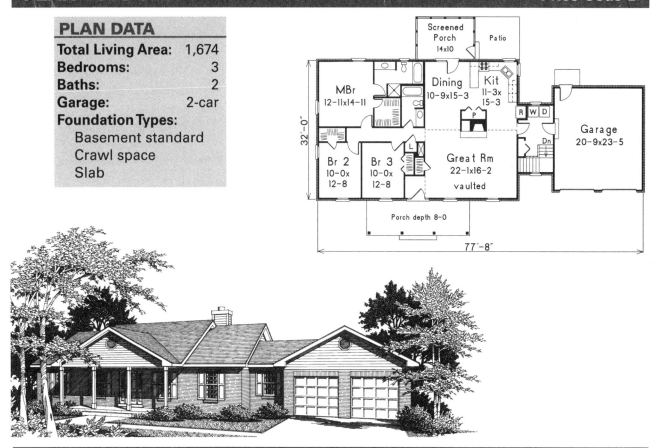

PLAN DATA

Total Living Area:	1,674
Bedrooms:	3
Baths:	2
Garage:	2-car

Foundation Types:
- Basement standard
- Crawl space
- Slab

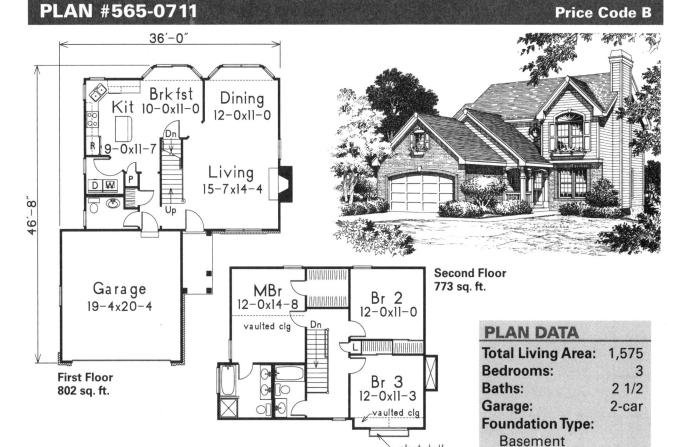

First Floor
802 sq. ft.

Second Floor
773 sq. ft.

PLAN DATA

Total Living Area:	1,575
Bedrooms:	3
Baths:	2 1/2
Garage:	2-car

Foundation Type:
- Basement

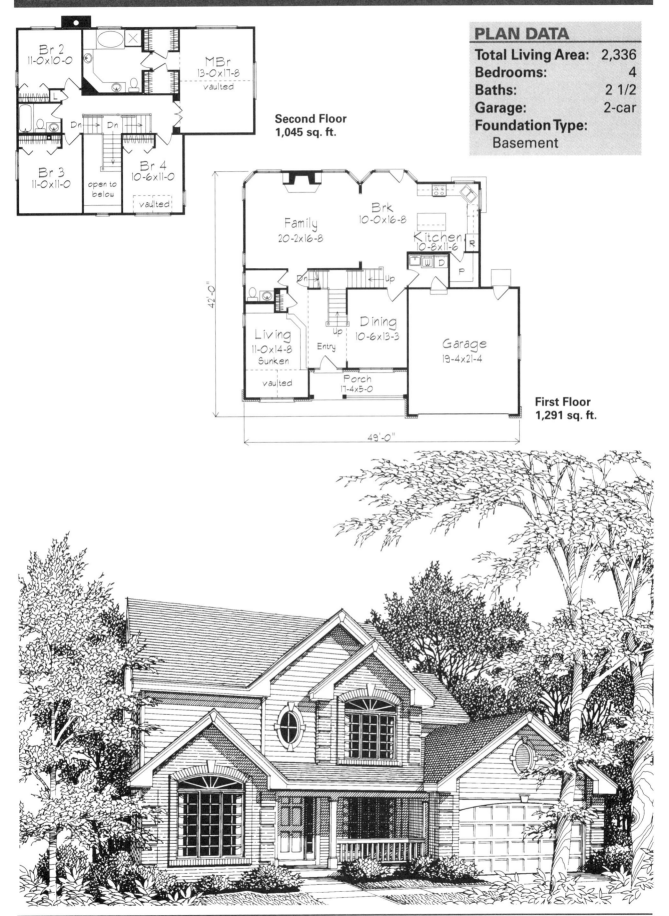

PLAN DATA

Total Living Area: 2,336
Bedrooms: 4
Baths: 2 1/2
Garage: 2-car
Foundation Type:
Basement

Br 2
11-0x10-0

MBr
13-0x17-8
vaulted

Br 3
11-0x11-0

open to below

Br 4
10-6x11-0
vaulted

Dn   Dn

Second Floor
1,045 sq. ft.

Family
20-2x16-8

Brk
10-0x16-8

Kitchen
10-8x11-6

Dn   Up

Living
11-0x14-8
Sunken

Dining
10-6x13-3

Garage
19-4x21-4

Up

Entry

vaulted

Porch
17-4x5-0

42'-0"

49'-0"

First Floor
1,291 sq. ft.

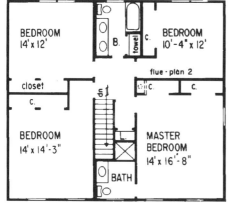

BEDROOM
14' x 12'

BEDROOM
10'-4" x 12'

B.

towel

c.

flue - plan 2

closet

c.

c.

c.

c.

dn

BEDROOM
14' x 14'-3"

MASTER
BEDROOM
14' x 16'-8"

BATH

Second Floor
1,152 sq. ft.

PLAN DATA

Total Living Area: 2,304
Bedrooms: 4
Baths: 2 1/2
Garage: 2-car
Foundation Types:
 Plan #565-1209-1
 Basement
 Plan #565-1209-2
 Crawl space & slab

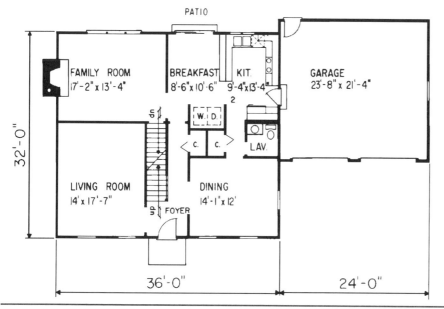

PATIO

FAMILY ROOM
17'-2" x 13'-4"

BREAKFAST
8'-6" x 10'-6"

KIT.
9'-4" x 13'-4"

GARAGE
23'-8" x 21'-4"

dn

W.D.

c.

c.

LAV.

LIVING ROOM
14' x 17'-7"

DINING
14'-1" x 12'

up

FOYER

32'-0"

36'-0"

24'-0"

First Floor
1,152 sq. ft.

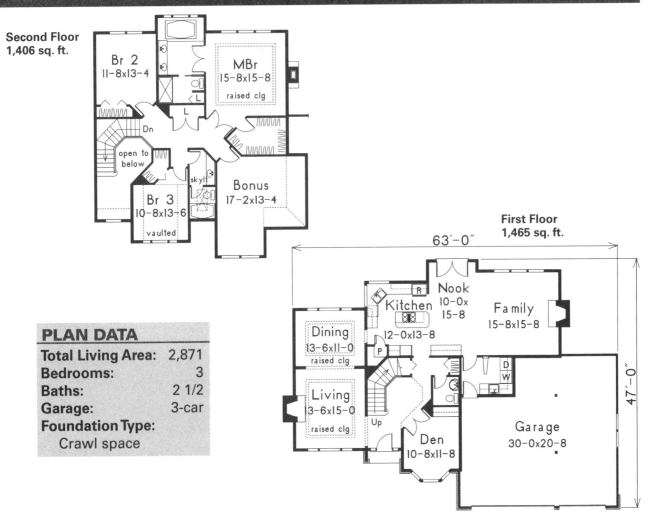

Second Floor
1,406 sq. ft.

Br 2
11-8x13-4

MBr
15-8x15-8
raised clg

L

L

Dn

open to
below

skylt

Br 3
10-8x13-6
vaulted

Bonus
17-2x13-4

First Floor
1,465 sq. ft.

63'-0"

Nook
10-0x
15-8

Kitchen
12-0x13-8

Family
15-8x15-8

Dining
13-6x11-0
raised clg

R

P

D
W

47'-0"

Living
13-6x15-0
raised clg

Up

Den
10-8x11-8

Garage
30-0x20-8

PLAN DATA

Total Living Area:	2,871
Bedrooms:	3
Baths:	2 1/2
Garage:	3-car
Foundation Type:	
Crawl space	

Second Floor
894 sq. ft.

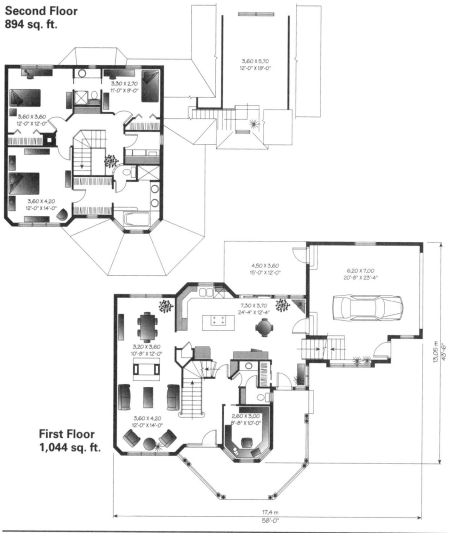

3,60 X 5,70
12'-0" X 19'-0"

3,30 X 2,70
11'-0" X 9'-0"

3,60 X 3,60
12'-0" X 12'-0"

3,60 X 4,20
12'-0" X 14'-0"

4,50 X 3,60
15'-0" X 12'-0"

6,20 X 7,00
20'-8" X 23'-4"

7,30 X 3,70
24'-4" X 12'-4"

3,20 X 3,60
10'-8" X 12'-0"

3,60 X 4,20
12'-0" X 14'-0"

2,60 X 3,00
8'-8" X 10'-0"

13,05 m
43'-6"

17,4 m
58'-0"

First Floor
1,044 sq. ft.

PLAN DATA

Total Living Area:	1,938
Bedrooms:	3
Baths:	2 1/2
Garage:	2-car

Foundation Type:
  Basement

Features:
  - 9' ceilings on first
    floor
  - 2" x 6" exterior
    walls

PLAN DATA

Total Living Area: 2,523
Bedrooms: 3
Baths: 2
Garage: 3-car
Foundation Type:
Basement
Features:
Vaulted ceiling in master bedroom

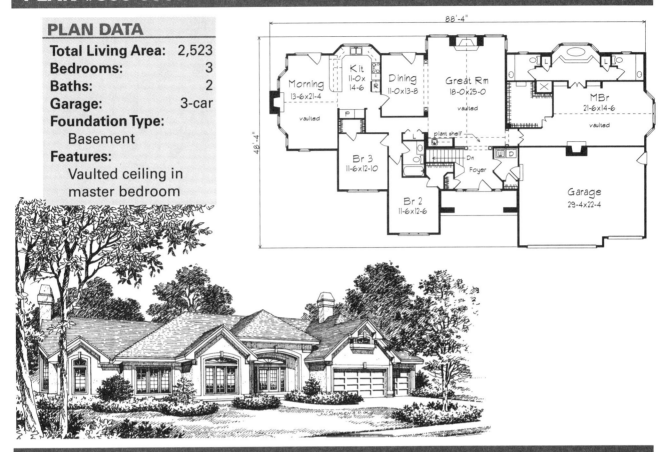

PLAN DATA

Total Living Area: 1,440
Bedrooms: 3
Baths: 2
Garage: 2-car
Foundation Types:
Basement standard
Slab
Crawl space

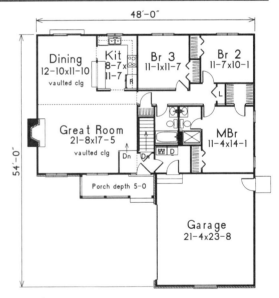

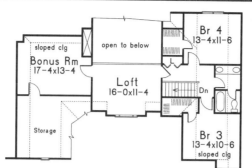

Second Floor
1,024 sq. ft.

sloped clg

Bonus Rm
17-4x13-4

open to below

Br 4
13-4x11-6

Loft
16-0x11-4

Dn

Storage

Br 3
13-4x10-6
sloped clg

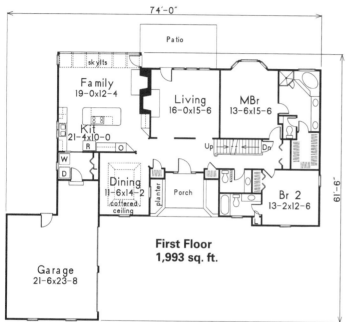

74'-0"

Patio

skylts

Family
19-0x12-4

Living
16-0x15-6

MBr
13-6x15-6

Kit
21-4x10-0

Up

Dn

R

O

W

D

Dining
11-6x14-2
coffered ceiling

planter

Porch

Br 2
13-2x12-6

61'-9"

First Floor
1,993 sq. ft.

Garage
21-6x23-8

PLAN DATA

Total Living Area: 3,017
Bedrooms: 4
Baths: 3 1/2
Garage: 2-car
Foundation Type:
Partial basement/
crawl space
Features:
2" x 6" exterior walls

First Floor
1,774 sq. ft.

69'-8"

46'-0"

MBr
17-0x17-8

vaulted

plant shelf

Great Rm
20-6x15-10

Brk
14-10x10-0

Kitchen
14-10x
10-6

R
P

Dn

Up

Dining
14-10x12-4

Foyer

Garage
21-4x20-4

L

W
P

Second Floor
850 sq. ft.

Br 4
12-6x12-0

open to below

Br 2
11-8x10-4

Dn

open to below

Br 3
12-6x12-0

Interior View - Master Bath

PLAN DATA

Total Living Area: 2,624
Bedrooms: 4
Baths: 2 1/2
Garage: 2-car
Foundation Type:
  Basement
Features:
  18' ceiling in great
  room

PLAN #565-0528

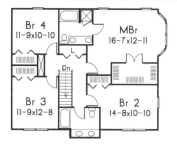

Second Floor
1,174 sq. ft.

Br 4
11-9x10-10

MBr
16-7x12-11

Br 3
11-9x12-8

Br 2
14-8x10-10

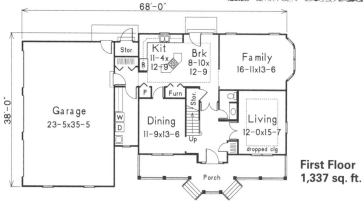

68'-0"

38'-0"

Garage
23-5x35-5

Stor.

Kit
11-4x
12-9

Brk
8-10x
12-9

Family
16-11x13-6

Dining
11-9x13-6

Furn
Stor.

Living
12-0x15-7
dropped clg

W
D

P

Up

Porch

First Floor
1,337 sq. ft.

PLAN DATA

Total Living Area:	2,511
Bedrooms:	4
Baths:	2 1/2
Garage:	3-car

Foundation Types:
Basement standard
Crawl space
Slab

PLAN #565-JA-54294

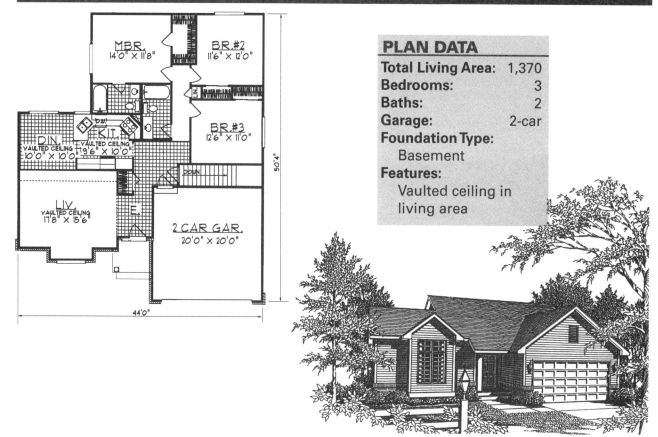

MBR
14'0" X 11'8"

BR.#2
11'6" X 12'0"

DIN.
VAULTED CEILING
10'0" X 10'0"

KIT.
VAULTED CEILING
9'6" X 10'0"

LIN.

BR.#3
12'6" X 11'0"

LIV.
VAULTED CEILING
17'8" X 15'6"

DOWN

2 CAR GAR.
20'0" X 20'0"

50'4"

44'0"

PLAN DATA

Total Living Area:	1,370
Bedrooms:	3
Baths:	2
Garage:	2-car

Foundation Type:
Basement
Features:
Vaulted ceiling in
living area

Second Floor
624 sq. ft.

PLAN DATA

Total Living Area: 2,993
Bedrooms: 4
Baths: 3
Garage: 2-car
Foundation Types:
  Slab standard
  Crawl space
Features:
  - 10' ceilings on first
    floor
  - 9' ceilings on second
    floor

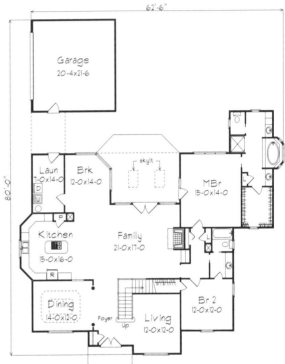

First Floor
2,369 sq. ft.

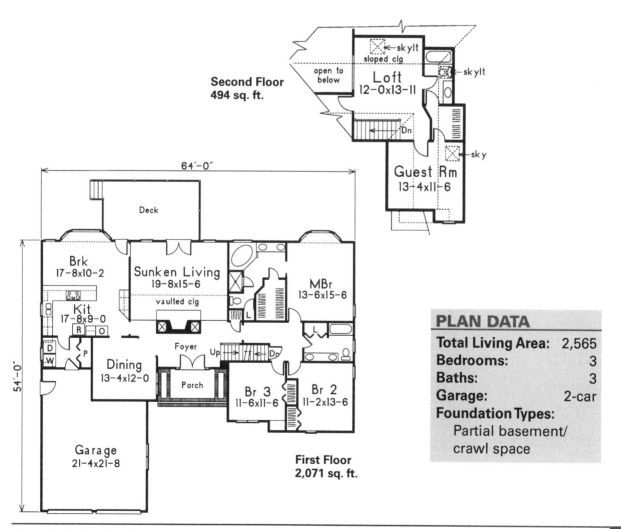

Second Floor
494 sq. ft.

skylt
sloped clg

open to below

Loft
12-0x13-11

skylt

Dn

sky

Guest Rm
13-4x11-6

64'-0"

Deck

Brk
17-8x10-2

Sunken Living
19-8x15-6

vaulted clg

MBr
13-6x15-6

Kit
17-8x9-0

R O

D
W
P

Foyer

Up

Dn

L

L

Dining
13-4x12-0

Porch

Br 3
11-6x11-6

Br 2
11-2x13-6

54'-0"

Garage
21-4x21-8

First Floor
2,071 sq. ft.

PLAN DATA

Total Living Area:	2,565
Bedrooms:	3
Baths:	3
Garage:	2-car
Foundation Types:	

Partial basement/
crawl space

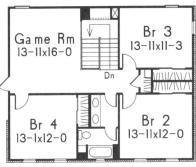

Game Rm
13-11x16-0

Br 3
13-11x11-3

Dn

Second Floor
988 sq. ft.

Br 4
13-1x12-0

Br 2
13-11x12-0

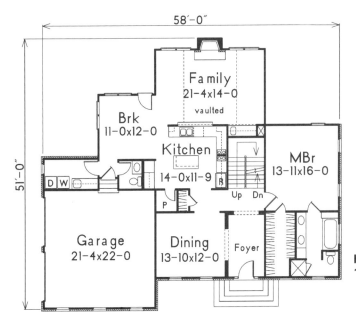

58'-0"

Family
21-4x14-0

vaulted

Brk
11-0x12-0

Kitchen
14-0x11-9

MBr
13-11x16-0

51'-0"

D W

P

Up Dn

Garage
21-4x22-0

Dining
13-10x12-0

Foyer

First Floor
1,625 sq. ft.

PLAN DATA

Total Living Area: 2,613
Bedrooms: 3
Baths: 2 1/2
Garage: 2-car
Foundation Type:
  Basement
Features:
  9' ceilings throughout
  first floor

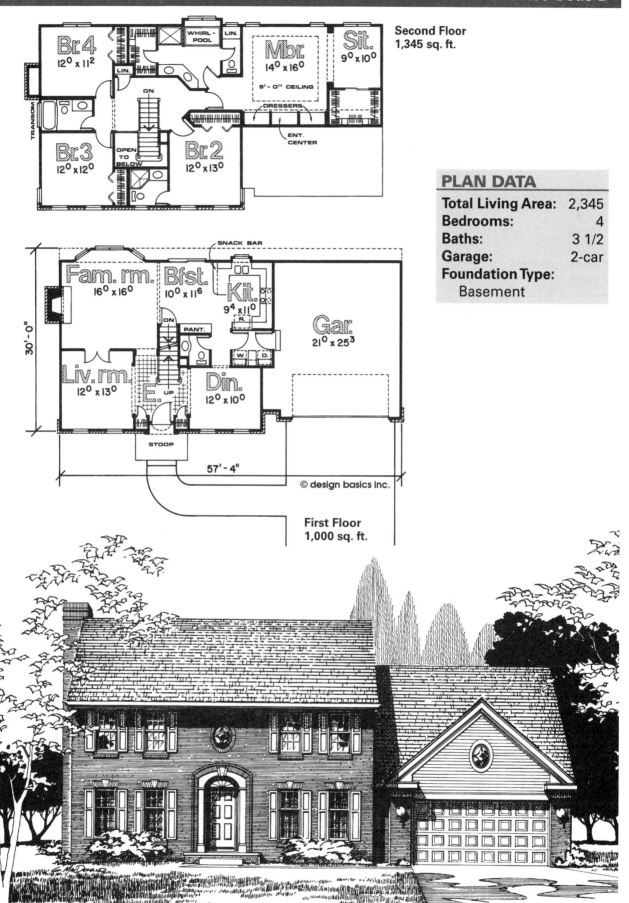

Second Floor
1,345 sq. ft.

Br. 4
$12^0 \times 11^2$

WHIRL-POOL　LIN.

LIN.

Mbr.
$14^0 \times 16^0$

9'-0" CEILING

Sit.
$9^0 \times 10^0$

DN

DRESSERS

TRANSOM

Br. 3
$12^0 \times 12^0$

OPEN TO BELOW

Br. 2
$12^0 \times 13^0$

ENT. CENTER

PLAN DATA

Total Living Area:	2,345
Bedrooms:	4
Baths:	3 1/2
Garage:	2-car
Foundation Type:	
Basement	

SNACK BAR

Fam. rm.
$16^0 \times 16^0$

Bfst.
$10^0 \times 11^6$

Kit.
$9^4 \times 11^0$

Gar.
$21^0 \times 25^3$

DN

PANT.

R.

30'-0"

Liv. rm.
$12^0 \times 13^0$

UP

Din.
$12^0 \times 10^0$

W.　D.

STOOP

57'-4"

© design basics inc.

First Floor
1,000 sq. ft.

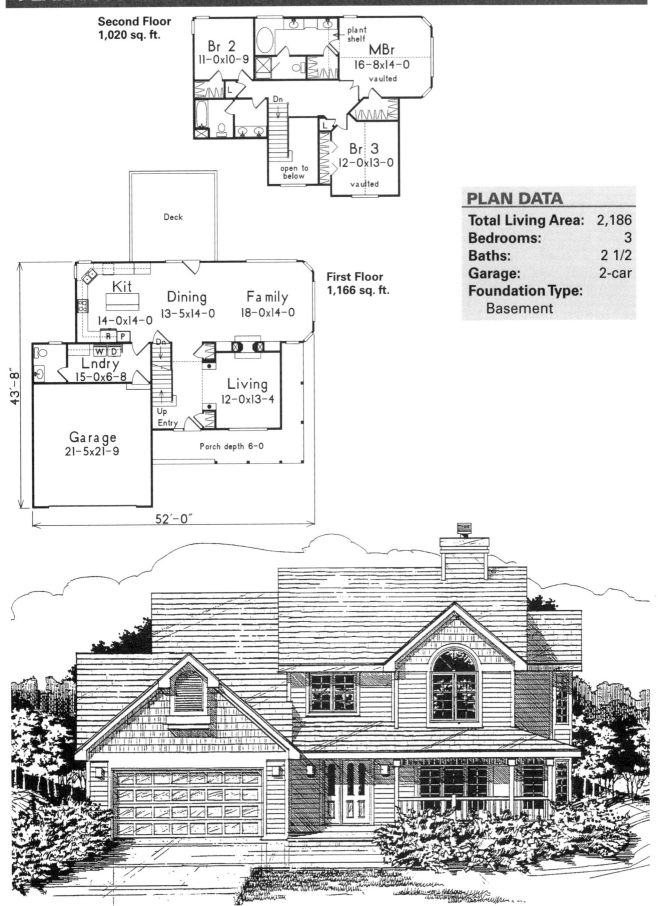

Second Floor 1,020 sq. ft.

Br 2
11-0x10-9

plant shelf

MBr
16-8x14-0
vaulted

L

Dn

open to below

L

Br 3
12-0x13-0
vaulted

Deck

Kit
14-0x14-0

Dining
13-5x14-0

Family
18-0x14-0

First Floor 1,166 sq. ft.

R P
W D

Lndry
15-0x6-8

Dn

Living
12-0x13-4

Up
Entry

43'-8"

Garage
21-5x21-9

Porch depth 6-0

52'-0"

PLAN DATA

Total Living Area:	2,186
Bedrooms:	3
Baths:	2 1/2
Garage:	2-car
Foundation Type:	
Basement	

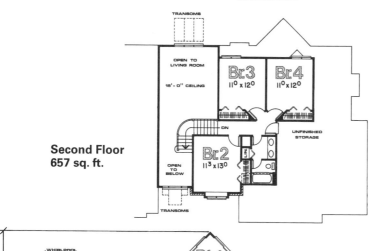

Second Floor
657 sq. ft.

Br. 3
11⁰ x 12⁰

Br. 4
11⁰ x 12⁰

OPEN TO LIVING ROOM

15'-0" CEILING

UNFINISHED STORAGE

Br. 2
11³ x 13⁰

OPEN TO BELOW

TRANSOMS

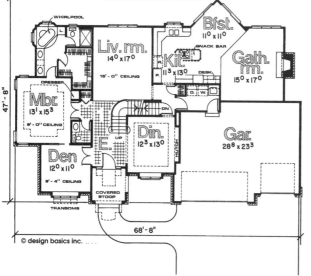

First Floor
1,829 sq. ft.

WHIRLPOOL

Liv. rm.
14⁰ x 17⁰

15'-0" CEILING

Bfst.
11⁰ x 11⁰

SNACK BAR

Kit.
11³ x 13⁰

Gath. rm.
15⁰ x 17⁰

Mbr.
13' x 15³

9'-0" CEILING

Din.
12³ x 13⁰

Gar.
28⁸ x 23³

Den
12⁰ x 11⁰

8'-4" CEILING

COVERED STOOP

TRANSOMS

47'-8"

68'-8"

© design basics inc.

PLAN DATA

Total Living Area:	2,486
Bedrooms:	4
Baths:	2 1/2
Garage:	3-car
Foundation Type:	
Basement	

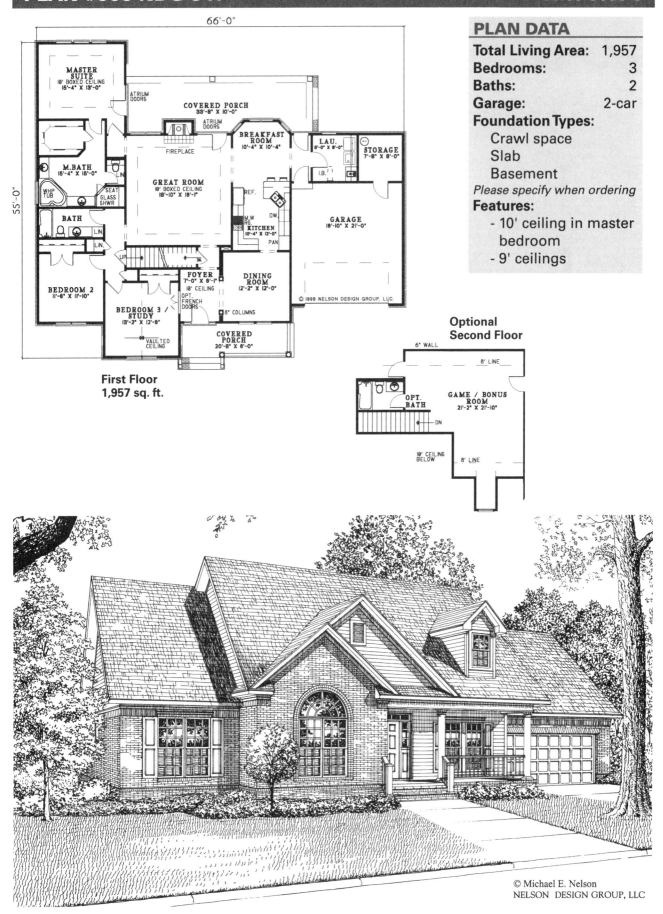

66'-0"

55'-0"

MASTER SUITE
10' BOXED CEILING
15'-4" X 13'-0"

ATRIUM DOORS

COVERED PORCH
33'-8" X 10'-0"

ATRIUM DOORS

BREAKFAST ROOM
10'-4" X 10'-4"

LAU.
8'-0" X 8'-0"

STORAGE
7'-8" X 8'-0"

FIREPLACE

M.BATH
15'-4" X 15'-0"

GREAT ROOM
10' BOXED CEILING
18'-10" X 19'-1"

REF.

I.B.

GARAGE
19'-10" X 21'-0"

WHP TUB

SEAT

GLASS SHWR

BATH

LIN.

LIN.

DW

M.W RG.

KITCHEN
10'-4" X 12'-0"

PAN

BEDROOM 2
11'-6" X 11'-10"

UP

DN

FOYER
7'-0" X 8'-1"
10' CEILING

DINING ROOM
12'-2" X 12'-0"

© 1998 NELSON DESIGN GROUP, LLC.

BEDROOM 3 / STUDY
13'-2" X 12'-0"

OPT. FRENCH DOORS

8' COLUMNS

VAULTED CEILING

COVERED PORCH
20'-8" X 8'-0"

**First Floor
1,957 sq. ft.**

Optional Second Floor

6" WALL

8' LINE

OPT. BATH

GAME / BONUS ROOM
21'-2" X 21'-10"

DN

10' CEILING BELOW

8' LINE

PLAN DATA

Total Living Area: 1,957
Bedrooms: 3
Baths: 2
Garage: 2-car
Foundation Types:
Crawl space
Slab
Basement
Please specify when ordering
Features:
- 10' ceiling in master bedroom
- 9' ceilings

© Michael E. Nelson
NELSON DESIGN GROUP, LLC

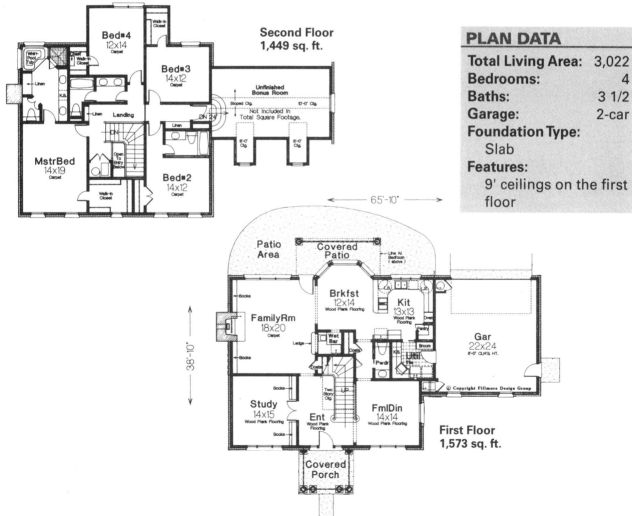

Second Floor
1,449 sq. ft.

Bed#4
12x14
Carpet

Walk-in Closet

Bed#3
14x12
Carpet

Unfinished Bonus Room
Sloped Clg.   10'-0" Clg.
Not Included in
Total Square Footage.

Whirl-Pool Tub

Linen

Landing

DN 24

Linen

MstrBed
14x19
Carpet

Open To Below

DN

Linen

Bed#2
14x12
Carpet

Walk-in Closet

8'-0" Clg.   8'-0" Clg.

PLAN DATA

Total Living Area:	3,022
Bedrooms:	4
Baths:	3 1/2
Garage:	2-car
Foundation Type:	
Slab	
Features:	
9' ceilings on the first floor	

← 65'-10" →

Patio Area

Covered Patio

Line At Bedroom (above)

Brkfst
12x14
Wood Plank Flooring

Kit
13x13
Wood Plank Flooring

FamilyRm
18x20
Carpet

38'-10"

Books

Ledge

Wet Bar

Pwdr

Gar
22x24
8'-0" CLNG. HT.

© Copyright Fillmore Design Group

Study
14x15
Wood Plank Flooring

Two Story Clg.

UP

Ent
Wood Plank Flooring

FmlDin
14x14
Wood Plank Flooring

First Floor
1,573 sq. ft.

Covered Porch

PLAN DATA

Total Living Area: 1,856
Bedrooms: 3
Baths: 2
Garage: 2-car
Foundation Types:
  Slab standard
  Crawl space
Features:
  - 12' ceiling in living room
  - 2" x 6" exterior walls
  - Extra storage in garage

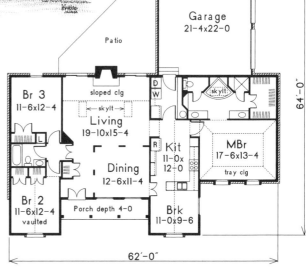

PLAN #565-DBI-1748-19

Price Code C

PLAN DATA

Total Living Area: 1,911
Bedrooms: 3
Baths: 2
Garage: 2-car
Foundation Type:
  Basement

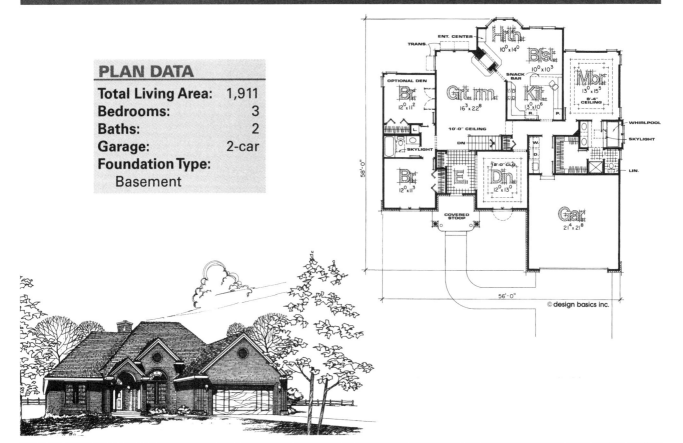

© design basics inc.

PLAN DATA

Total Living Area: 1,340
Bedrooms: 3
Baths: 2
Garage: 2-car
Foundation Type:
  Basement
Features:
  - Basement has space for a bedroom/bath expansion
  - Extra storage in garage
  - Drive-under garage

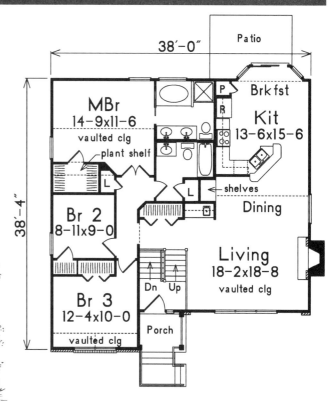

Patio

38'-0"

38'-4"

MBr
14-9x11-6
vaulted clg

plant shelf

L

Br 2
8-11x9-0

Br 3
12-4x10-0
vaulted clg

P
R

Brk fst

Kit
13-6x15-6

shelves

Dining

L

Dn Up

Living
18-2x18-8
vaulted clg

Porch

BEDROOM 2
12'-2" X 13'-0"

BRKFAST ROOM
12'-6" X 9'-6"

SCREENED PORCH
16'-2" X 11'-8"

MASTER SUITE
14'-11" X 15'-6"
10' BOXED CEILING

61' 4"

LIN

BATH

KITCHEN
12'-6" X 12'-0"

GREAT ROOM
16'-2" X 16'-8"
10' BOXED CEILING

DW

REF

PAN

M.BATH
10'-6" X 16'-4"

FRENCH DOORS

WHP TUB

GLASS SHWR

68' 4"

BEDROOM 3
10'-2" X 14'-5"

UP

LAU.
6'-8" X 6'-8"

DN

BENCH W/ STRG

FOYER
8'-6" X 8'-8"
10' CEILING

W.I.C.

DINING ROOM
11'-2" X 11'-8"
10' CEILING

FRENCH DOORS

STUDY / DEN
10'-10" X 11'-8"
10' CEILING

COVERED PORCH
30'-8" X 7'-8"

GARAGE
21'-0" X 21'-8"

First Floor
2,100 sq. ft.

OPTIONAL BONUS AREA
11'-8" X 20'-2"

SLOPED CEILING

8' LINE

4' WALL

4' WALL

Optional
Second Floor

PLAN DATA

Total Living Area: 2,100
Bedrooms: 3
Baths: 2
Garage: 2-car
Foundation Types:
  Crawl space
  Slab
  Basement
Please specify when ordering

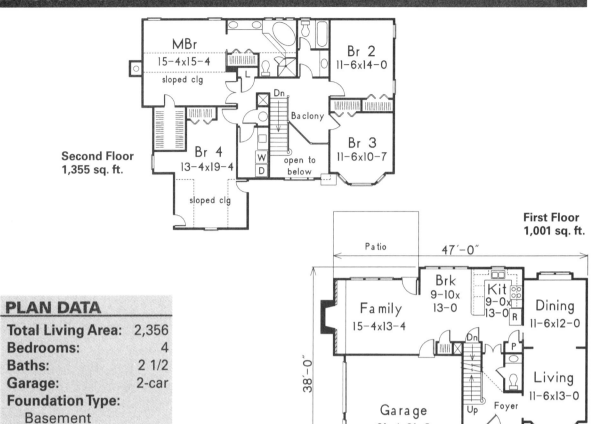

Second Floor
1,355 sq. ft.

MBr
15-4x15-4
sloped clg

Br 2
11-6x14-0

Dn

Baclony

Br 4
13-4x19-4

open to below

Br 3
11-6x10-7

W
D

sloped clg

First Floor
1,001 sq. ft.

Patio

47'-0"

Family
15-4x13-4

Brk
9-10x
13-0

Kit
9-0x
13-0

Dining
11-6x12-0

Dn

38'-0"

Garage
21-4x21-8

Up

P

Living
11-6x13-0

Foyer

Porch

PLAN DATA

Total Living Area:	2,356
Bedrooms:	4
Baths:	2 1/2
Garage:	2-car
Foundation Type:	
Basement	

Second Floor - Four bedroom
970 sq. ft.

MASTER BEDROOM 12'x16'-8"
M. BATH
BATH
BEDROOM 4 13'-4"x10'-10"
dn
BEDROOM 2 15'-5"x10'
BEDROOM 3 12'-2"x10'

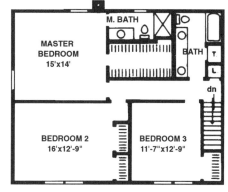

Second Floor - Three bedroom
970 sq. ft.

MASTER BEDROOM 15'x14'
M. BATH
BATH
dn
BEDROOM 2 16'x12'-9"
BEDROOM 3 11'-7"x12'-9"

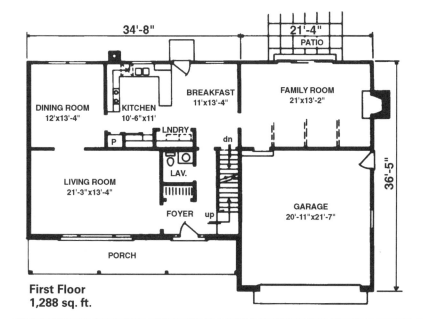

First Floor
1,288 sq. ft.

34'-8"
21'-4"
PATIO
DINING ROOM 12'x13'-4"
KITCHEN 10'-6"x11'
BREAKFAST 11'x13'-4"
FAMILY ROOM 21'x13'-2"
LNDRY
P
dn
36'-5"
LIVING ROOM 21'-3"x13'-4"
LAV.
FOYER
up
GARAGE 20'-11"x21'-7"
PORCH

PLAN DATA

Total Living Area: 2,258
Bedrooms: 3
Baths: 2 1/2
Garage: 2-car
Foundation Types:
  Plan #565-T-143-1
  Basement
  Plan #565-T-143-2
  Crawl space & slab
Features:
  Optional 4-bedroom
  plan

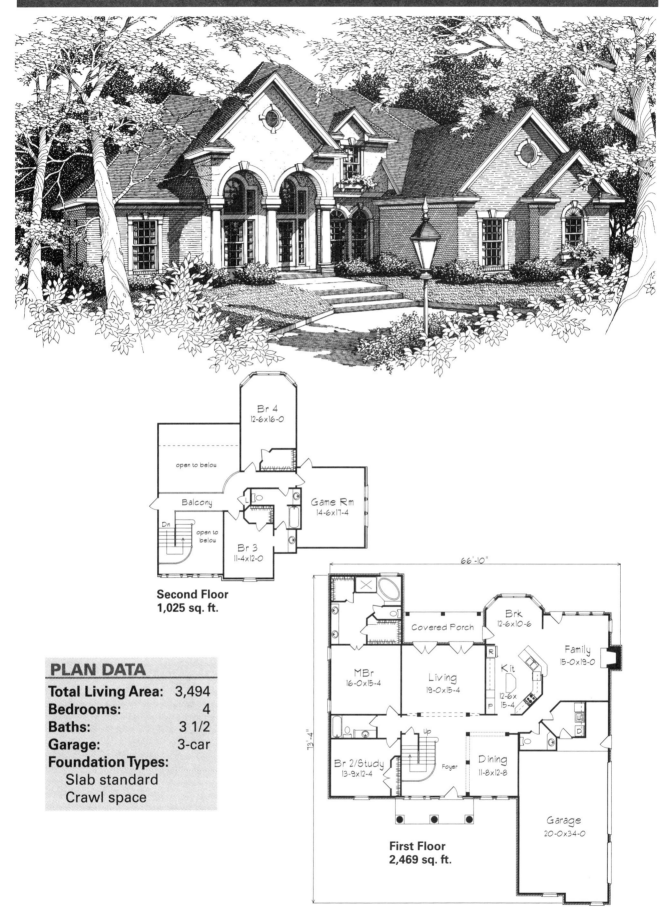

Second Floor
1,025 sq. ft.

Br 4
12-6x16-0

open to below

Balcony

Dn

open to below

Game Rm
14-6x17-4

Br 3
11-4x12-0

PLAN DATA

Total Living Area: 3,494
Bedrooms: 4
Baths: 3 1/2
Garage: 3-car
Foundation Types:
  Slab standard
  Crawl space

66'-10"

73'-4"

Covered Porch

Brk
12-6x10-6

MBr
16-0x15-4

Living
19-0x15-4

Kit
12-6x
15-4

Family
15-0x19-0

Br 2/Study
13-9x12-4

Up

Foyer

Dining
11-8x12-8

Garage
20-0x34-0

First Floor
2,469 sq. ft.

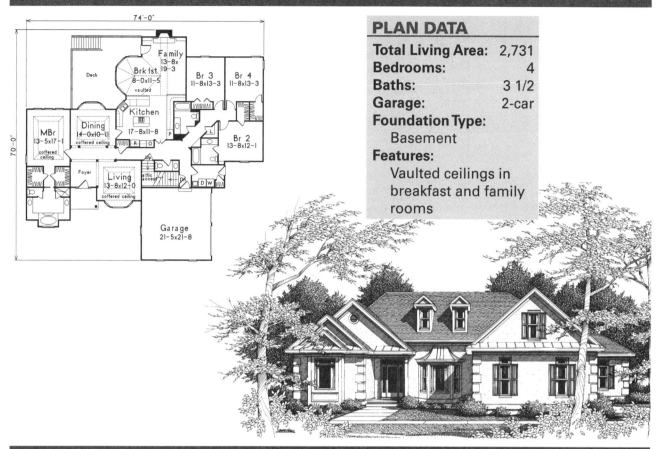

PLAN DATA

Total Living Area: 2,731
Bedrooms: 4
Baths: 3 1/2
Garage: 2-car
Foundation Type:
Basement
Features:
Vaulted ceilings in breakfast and family rooms

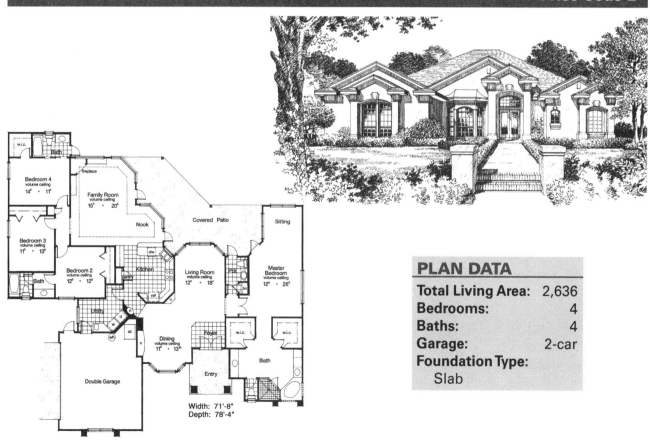

PLAN DATA

Total Living Area: 2,636
Bedrooms: 4
Baths: 4
Garage: 2-car
Foundation Type:
Slab

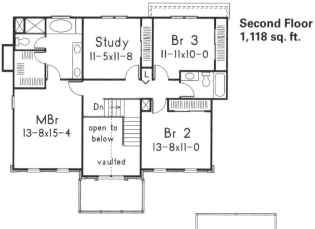

Second Floor
1,118 sq. ft.

Study
11-5x11-8

Br 3
11-11x10-0

MBr
13-8x15-4

Dn

open to
below

vaulted

Br 2
13-8x11-0

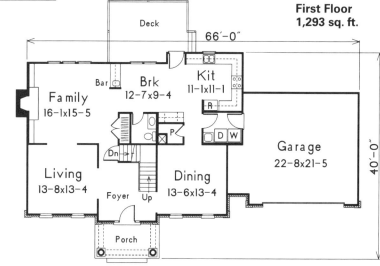

First Floor
1,293 sq. ft.

Deck

66'-0"

Bar

Family
16-1x15-5

Brk
12-7x9-4

Kit
11-1x11-1

R

Garage
22-8x21-5

40'-0"

Living
13-8x13-4

Dn

P

D W

Dining
13-6x13-4

Foyer

Up

Porch

PLAN DATA

Total Living Area: 2,411
Bedrooms: 3
Baths: 2 1/2
Garage: 2-car
Foundation Types:
   Basement standard
   Slab
   Crawl space

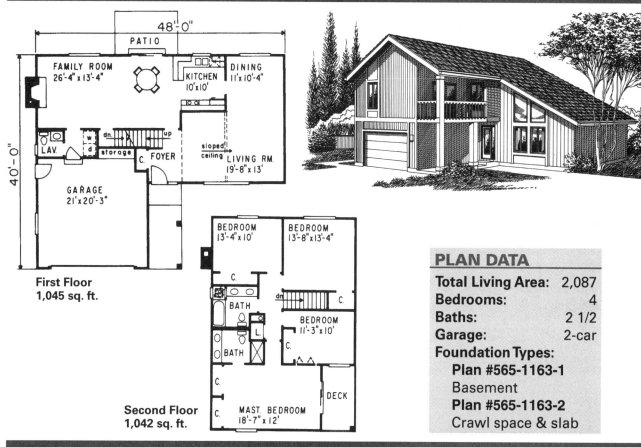

48'-0"

PATIO

FAMILY ROOM
26'-4" x 13'-4"

KITCHEN
10' x 10'

DINING
11' x 10'-4"

40'-0"

LAV.

w/d

dn. storage up

C. FOYER

sloped ceiling

LIVING RM.
19'-8" x 13'

GARAGE
21' x 20'-3"

First Floor
1,045 sq. ft.

BEDROOM
13'-4" x 10'

BEDROOM
13'-8" x 13'-4"

C.

BATH

dn

C.

BEDROOM
11'-3" x 10'

BATH

C.

C.

C.

DECK

Second Floor
1,042 sq. ft.

MAST. BEDROOM
18'-7" x 12'

PLAN DATA

Total Living Area:	2,087
Bedrooms:	4
Baths:	2 1/2
Garage:	2-car

Foundation Types:
  Plan #565-1163-1
  Basement
  Plan #565-1163-2
  Crawl space & slab

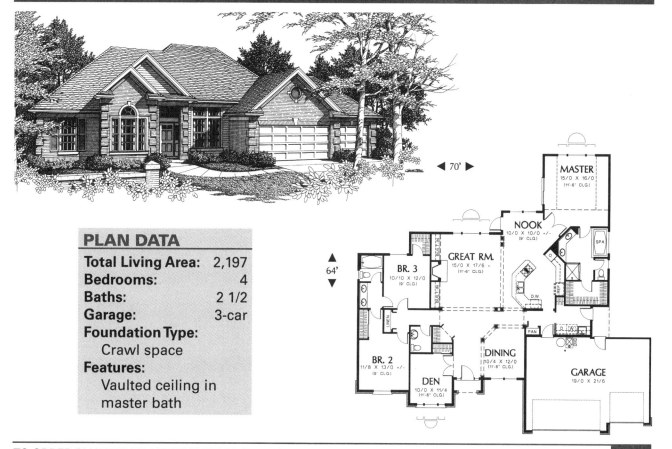

◄ 70' ►

64'

MASTER
15/0 X 16/0
(11'-6" CLG.)

NOOK
10/0 X 10/0 +/-
(9' CLG.)

SPA

BR. 3
10/10 X 12/0
(9' CLG.)

GREAT RM.
15/0 X 17/6 +
(11'-6" CLG.)

REF.

D.W.

LINEN

BR. 2
11/8 X 13/0 +/-
(9' CLG.)

DEN
10/0 X 11/4
(11'-6" CLG.)

DINING
10/4 X 12/0
(11'-6" CLG.)

PAN.

GARAGE
19/0 X 21/6

PLAN DATA

Total Living Area:	2,197
Bedrooms:	4
Baths:	2 1/2
Garage:	3-car

Foundation Type:
  Crawl space
Features:
  Vaulted ceiling in
  master bath

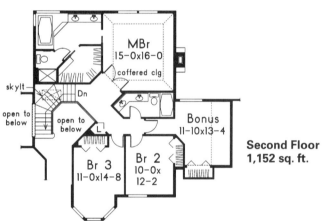

MBr
15-0x16-0

coffered clg

skylt

open to below

Dn

open to below

L

Bonus
11-10x13-4

Br 3
11-0x14-8

Br 2
10-0x
12-2

**Second Floor
1,152 sq. ft.**

PLAN DATA

Total Living Area:	2,744
Bedrooms:	3
Baths:	2 1/2
Garage:	3-car
Foundation Type:	
Crawl space	

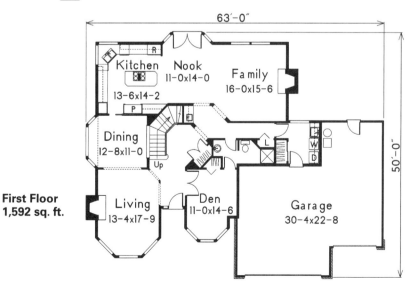

63'-0"

R

Kitchen
13-6x14-2

Nook
11-0x14-0

Family
16-0x15-6

P

Dining
12-8x11-0

Up

L

W
D

50'-0"

**First Floor
1,592 sq. ft.**

Living
13-4x17-9

Den
11-0x14-6

Garage
30-4x22-8

PLAN #565-0485

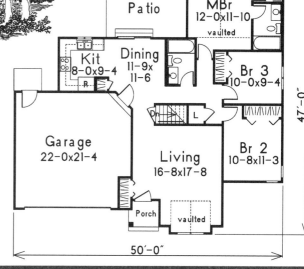

PLAN DATA

Total Living Area: 1,195
Bedrooms: 3
Baths: 2
Garage: 2-car
Foundation Type:
  Basement

PLAN #565-BF-1416

Price Code A

PLAN DATA

Total Living Area: 1,434
Bedrooms: 3
Baths: 2
Garage: 2-car
Foundation Types:
  Slab
  Crawl space
Please specify when ordering
Features:
  Extra storage in
  garage

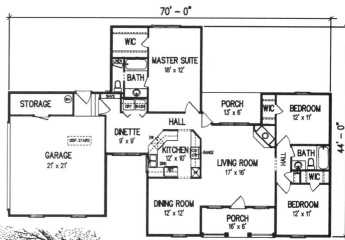

← 68'-0" →

70'-8"

MSTR. BDRM. 17X14 VAULTED CLG. 9" TO 10"	PATIO AREA		BDRM#2 11X11 VAULTED CLG. 9" TO 10"	B
COVERED AREA	BRKFT 12X11		BDRM#3 12X12 8" CLG.
MSTR BATH	GREAT ROOM 22X16	KITCN 14X12	
W-I-CLOS	CATHEDRAL CLG.	ENTERTAINMT CENTER	BDRM#4 12X11 8" CLG.
ENTRY	GALLERY	
LIVING ROOM 14X15	FORMAL DINING 11X12	THREE CAR GARAGE

PLAN DATA

Total Living Area: 2,578
Bedrooms: 4
Baths: 3 1/2
Garage: 3-car
Foundation Type:
  Slab
Features:
  2" x 6" exterior walls

PLAN DATA

Total Living Area: 1,467
Bedrooms: 3
Baths: 2
Garage: 2-car
Foundation Type:
  Crawl space

◄49'►

43'

VAULTED DINING 11/0 X 14/0	VAULTED LIVING 15/8 X 14/0	VAULTED MASTER 13/0 X 11/8
8/0 X 12/8		
PANTRY DESK	PLANT SHELF OVER AT 9'	
GARAGE 19/4 X 19/8		LINEN
	BR. 3 10/8 X 10/4	BR. 2 12/0 X 10/0

©Alan Mascord Design Associates, Inc.

PLAN #565-0224

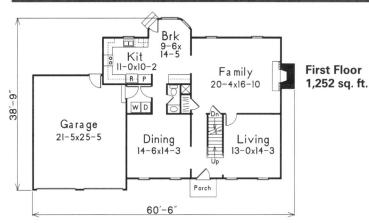

**First Floor
1,252 sq. ft.**

- Brk 9-6x14-5
- Kit 11-0x10-2
- Family 20-4x16-10
- Garage 21-5x25-5
- Dining 14-6x14-3
- Living 13-0x14-3
- Porch
- 38'-9"
- 60'-6"

PLAN DATA

Total Living Area:	2,461
Bedrooms:	4
Baths:	2 1/2
Garage:	2-car

Foundation Types:
- Basement standard
- Crawl space
- Slab

**Second Floor
1,209 sq. ft.**

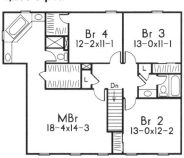

- Br 4 12-2x11-1
- Br 3 13-0x11-1
- MBr 18-4x14-3
- Br 2 13-0x12-2

PLAN #565-0739

- 55'-8"
- 46'-4"
- Balcony
- MBr 18-4x13-0
- Kit 10-2x11-9
- Dining
- Great Rm 16-0x21-4 vaulted
- Entry
- Br 2 12-8x14-0
- Br 3 11-4x12-6
- Porch depth 6-0

**First Floor
1,004 sq. ft.**

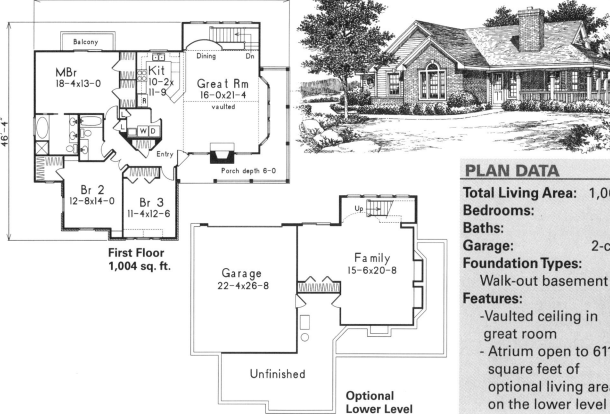

- Garage 22-4x26-8
- Family 15-6x20-8
- Unfinished
- **Optional Lower Level**

PLAN DATA

Total Living Area:	1,004
Bedrooms:	3
Baths:	2
Garage:	2-car

Foundation Types:
- Walk-out basement

Features:
- Vaulted ceiling in great room
- Atrium open to 611 square feet of optional living area on the lower level

Second Floor
573 sq. ft.

Br 2
17-8x12-0

L

Dn

Br 3
10-6x13-0

open to
below

First Floor
951 sq. ft.

38'-0"

Patio

Living
17-8x12-0

MBr
12-4x15-4

39'-4"

P

Kit
10-6x
10-6

Dn

Dining
10-6x9-10

Up

Garage
19-4x20-4

Porch

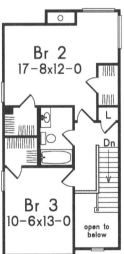

PLAN DATA

Total Living Area:	1,524
Bedrooms:	3
Baths:	2 1/2
Garage:	2-car
Foundation Type:	
Basement	

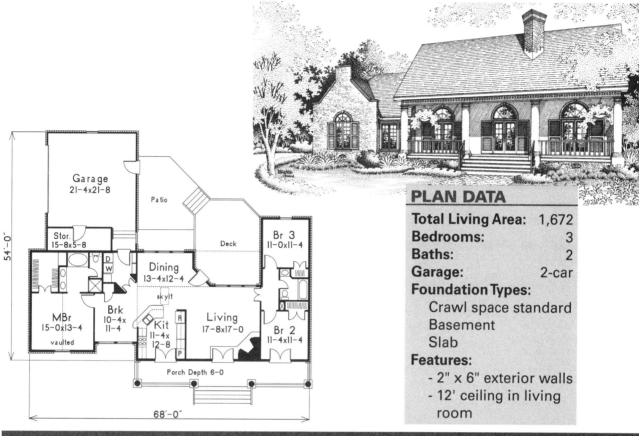

PLAN DATA

Total Living Area:	1,672
Bedrooms:	3
Baths:	2
Garage:	2-car

Foundation Types:
Crawl space standard
Basement
Slab

Features:
- 2" x 6" exterior walls
- 12' ceiling in living room

PLAN DATA

Total Living Area:	1,373
Bedrooms:	3
Baths:	2
Garage:	2-car

Foundation Types:
Slab
Crawl space
Walk-out basement
Please specify when ordering

Features:
9' ceilings

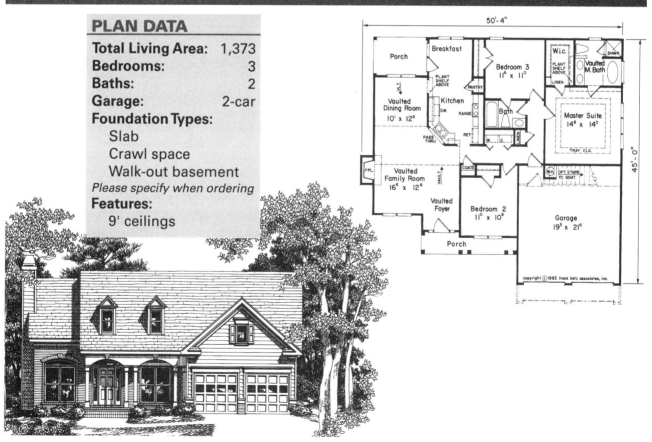

PLAN DATA

Total Living Area: 2,358
Bedrooms: 4
Baths: 2 1/2
Garage: 2-car
Foundation Types:
  Basement standard
  Crawl space
  Slab

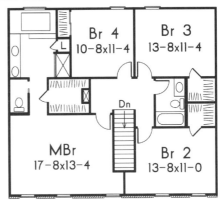

Br 4
10-8x11-4

Br 3
13-8x11-4

L

Dn

MBr
17-8x13-4

Br 2
13-8x11-0

**Second Floor
1,140 sq. ft.**

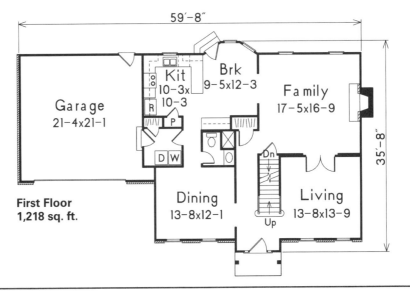

59'-8"

Garage
21-4x21-1

Kit
10-3x
10-3

R

P

Brk
9-5x12-3

Family
17-5x16-9

35'-8"

D W

Dn

Dining
13-8x12-1

Living
13-8x13-9

Up

**First Floor
1,218 sq. ft.**

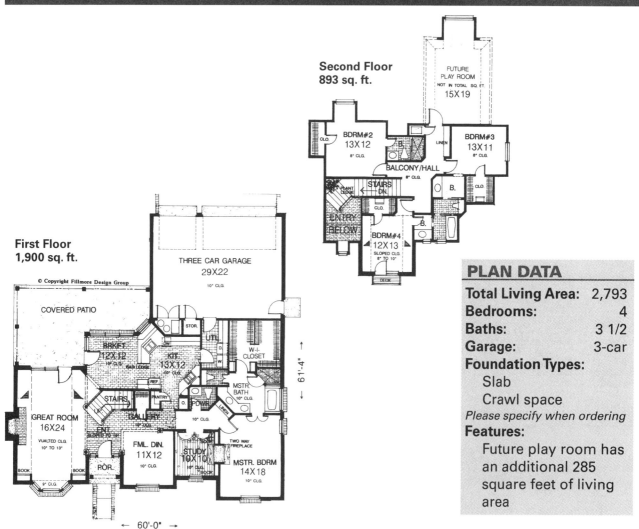

Second Floor
893 sq. ft.

FUTURE PLAY ROOM
NOT IN TOTAL SQ. FT.
15X19

BDRM#2
13X12
8" CLG.

BDRM#3
13X11
8" CLG.

CLO.

LINEN

B.

BALCONY/HALL
8" CLG.

STAIRS DN.

CLO.

PLANT LEDGE

ENTRY BELOW

CLO.

B.

BDRM#4
12X13
SLOPED CLG.
8" TO 10"

B.

DECK

First Floor
1,900 sq. ft.

THREE CAR GARAGE
29X22
10" CLG.

© Copyright Fillmore Design Group

COVERED PATIO

STOR.

UTL.

DW

BRKFT.
12X12
10" CLG.

KIT
13X12
10" CLG.

W-I-CLOSET

D

W

REF.

MSTR. BATH
10" CLG.

STAIRS
UP

PANTRY

O.

GREAT ROOM
16X24

GALLERY
10" CLG.

VUALTED CLG.
10" TO 13"

ENT.

POWDER

LINEN

10" CLG.

BOOK

BOOK

POR.

FML. DIN.
11X12
10" CLG.

STUDY
10X10
10" CLG.

TWO WAY FIREPLACE

MSTR. BDRM
14X18
10" CLG.

9" CLG.

61'-4"

← 60'-0" →

PLAN DATA

Total Living Area: 2,793
Bedrooms: 4
Baths: 3 1/2
Garage: 3-car
Foundation Types:
  Slab
  Crawl space
Please specify when ordering
Features:
  Future play room has
  an additional 285
  square feet of living
  area

PLAN DATA

Total Living Area: 2,128
Bedrooms: 3
Baths: 2 1/2
Garage: 2-car
Foundation Type:
  Basement

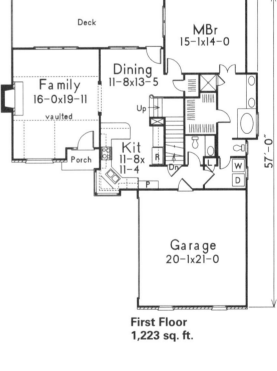

46'-0"

Deck

MBr
15-1x14-0

Family
16-0x19-11
vaulted

Dining
11-8x13-5

Kit
11-8x
11-4

Up

Porch

P

W
D

Dn

R

L

57'-0"

Garage
20-1x21-0

First Floor
1,223 sq. ft.

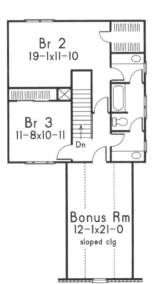

Br 2
19-1x11-10

Br 3
11-8x10-11

Dn

Bonus Rm
12-1x21-0
sloped clg

Second Floor
905 sq. ft.

PLAN #565-NDG-514

PLAN DATA

Total Living Area: 2,394
Bedrooms: 4
Baths: 2
Garage: 2-car
Foundation Types:
  Crawl space
  Slab
Please specify when ordering
Features:
  Optional three-car garage

First Floor
2,394 sq. ft.

Optional Second Floor

PLAN #565-GSD-1123

PLAN DATA

Total Living Area: 1,734
Bedrooms: 3
Baths: 2
Garage: 2-car
Foundation Type:
  Crawl space
Features:
  - 10' ceiling in great room
  - 9' ceiling in master bedroom

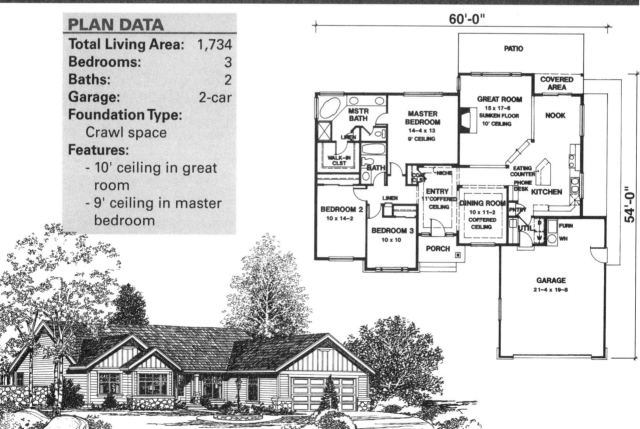

Second Floor
1,242 sq. ft.

First Floor
1,257 sq. ft.

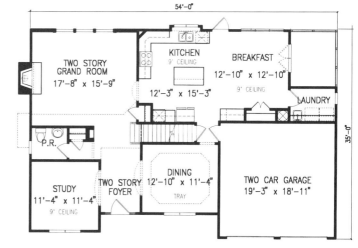

PLAN DATA

Total Living Area:	2,499
Bedrooms:	4
Baths:	2 1/2
Garage:	2-car
Foundation Type:	
Basement	

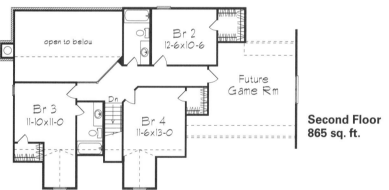

open to below

Br 2
12-6x10-6

Future
Game Rm

Br 3
11-10x11-0

Dn

Br 4
11-6x13-0

**Second Floor
865 sq. ft.**

PLAN DATA

Total Living Area: 2,357
Bedrooms: 4
Baths: 3 1/2
Garage: 2-car
Foundation Types:
 Slab standard
 Crawl space
Features:
 2" x 6" exterior walls

66'-0"

Covered
Porch

Living
21-0x15-6

Brk
10-0x9-6

Storage

Kit
12-0x13-0

raised ceiling

Garage
20-7x21-6

34'-3"

MBr
13-0x17-8

Dining
12-0x12-8

Up

Porch Depth 5-0

**First Floor
1,492 sq. ft.**

**Second Floor
1,060 sq. ft.**

Deck

Br 2
14-0x13-0

open to below

Deck

Game Rm
17-0x15-0

Balcony

Dn

open to below

Br 3
15-0x12-6

61'-0"

69'-0"

Patio

Family
16-0x19-0

Patio

MBr
14-0x17-0

Dining
11-0x13-0

Brk
11-0x13-0

Up

Kit
13-0x12-0

Bar

R

P

Br 4
11-0x13-0

Porch

sloped clg

**First Floor
2,109 sq. ft.**

Garage
20-4x19-4

PLAN DATA

Total Living Area:	3,169
Bedrooms:	4
Baths:	4
Garage:	2-car

Foundation Types:
Slab standard
Crawl space

Features:
9' ceilings on first
floor

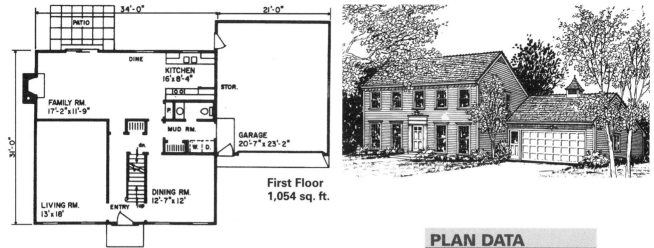

34'-0" 21'-0"

PATIO

DINE

KITCHEN
16'x8'-4"

STOR.

FAMILY RM.
17'-2"x11'-9"

MUD RM.

GARAGE
20'-7" x 23'-2"

W. D.

dn.

31'-0"

LIVING RM.
13'x18'

ENTRY up

DINING RM.
12'-7"x12'

First Floor
1,054 sq. ft.

BED RM.
12'-4"x10'-9"

BED RM.
12'x10'-9"

L

WALK
IN
CLO.

BATH

dn.

Second Floor
953 sq. ft.

MASTER
BED RM.
12'x18'

BATH

BED RM.
12'-7"x10'

PLAN DATA

Total Living Area:	2,007
Bedrooms:	4
Baths:	2 1/2
Garage:	2-car
Foundation Type:	
Basement	

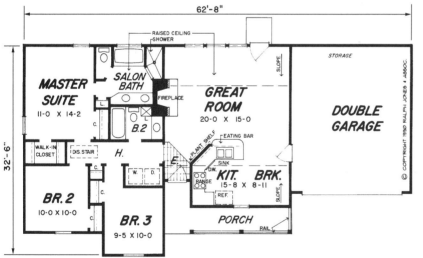

62'-8"

RAISED CEILING
SHOWER

SLOPE

STORAGE

MASTER
SUITE
11-0 X 14-2

SALON
BATH

FIREPLACE

GREAT
ROOM
20-0 X 15-0

DOUBLE
GARAGE

B.2

32'-6"

WALK-IN
CLOSET

DIS.STAIR

H.

W. D.

PLANT SHELF

EATING BAR

SINK

KIT.
15-8 X 8-11

BRK.

SLOPE

© COPYRIGHT 1990 RALPH JONES 4 ASSOC.

BR. 2
10-0 X 10-0

DW.

RANGE

REF.

BR. 3
9-5 X 10-0

PORCH

RAIL.

PLAN DATA

Total Living Area:	1,192
Bedrooms:	3
Baths:	2
Garage:	2-car

Foundation Types:
Slab
Crawl space
Please specify when ordering
Features:
Extra storage in
garage

Second Floor
988 sq. ft.

Br 3
11-0x11-4

Br 4
8-6x11-0

Br 2
10-10x11-2

MBr
13-0x16-10

open to below

Dn

L

PLAN DATA

Total Living Area: 2,013
Bedrooms: 4
Baths: 2 1/2
Garage: 2-car
Foundation Type:
   Basement

56'-0"

30'-0"

Garage
19-4x21-4

Kit
9-4x11-6

Dinette
10-4x11-4

Family
13-0x15-4

Dining
11-2x11-4

Foyer

Living
11-4x13-0

Dn

up

Porch

First Floor
1,025 sq. ft.

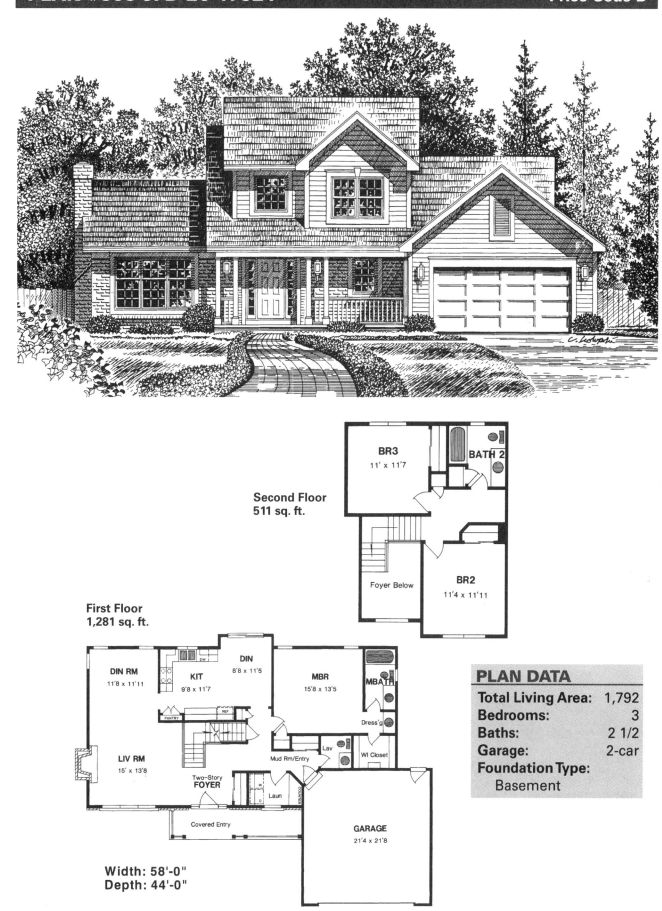

**Second Floor
511 sq. ft.**

BR3
11' x 11'7

BATH 2

Foyer Below

BR2
11'4 x 11'11

**First Floor
1,281 sq. ft.**

DIN RM
11'8 x 11'11

KIT
9'8 x 11'7

DIN
8'8 x 11'5

MBR
15'8 x 13'5

MBATH

PANTRY

REF

Dress'g

LIV RM
15' x 13'8

Lav

WI Closet

Mud Rm/Entry

Two-Story
FOYER

W

Laun

COUNTER

Covered Entry

GARAGE
21'4 x 21'8

**Width: 58'-0"
Depth: 44'-0"**

PLAN DATA

Total Living Area:	1,792
Bedrooms:	3
Baths:	2 1/2
Garage:	2-car
Foundation Type:	
Basement	

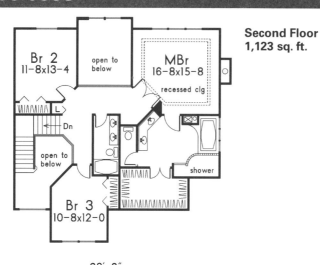

Second Floor
1,123 sq. ft.

Br 2
11–8x13–4

open to below

MBr
16–8x15–8
recessed clg

Dn

open to below

shower

Br 3
10–8x12–0

PLAN DATA

Total Living Area: 2,723
Bedrooms: 3
Baths: 2 1/2
Garage: 3-car
Foundation Type:
  Crawl space

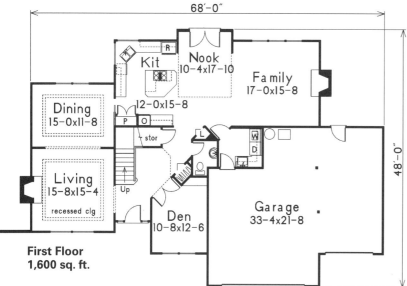

68'–0"

Kit
12–0x15–8

Nook
10–4x17–10

Family
17–0x15–8

Dining
15–0x11–8

stor

48'–0"

Living
15–8x15–4
recessed clg

Up

Den
10–8x12–6

Garage
33–4x21–8

First Floor
1,600 sq. ft.

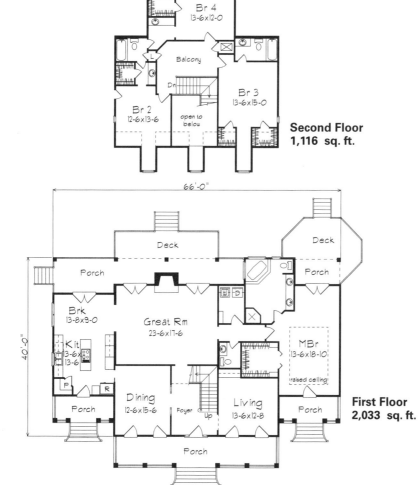

Second Floor
1,116 sq. ft.

Br 4
13-6x12-0

Balcony

Dn

Br 3
13-6x15-0

Br 2
12-6x13-6

open to below

66'-0"

40'-0"

Deck

Deck

Porch

Porch

Brk
13-8x9-0

Great Rm
23-6x17-6

MBr
13-6x18-10

Kit
13-6x13-6

raised ceiling

P

R

Dining
12-6x15-6

Foyer

Up

Living
13-6x12-8

Porch

Porch

Porch

Porch

First Floor
2,033 sq. ft.

PLAN DATA

Total Living Area: 3,149
Bedrooms: 4
Baths: 3 1/2
Garage: detached 2-car
Foundation Types:
   Slab standard
   Crawl space
Features:
- 10' ceilings on first floor
- 9' ceilings on second floor

Second Floor
829 sq. ft.

Br 2
11-4x13-0

skylt

open to below

Balcony

Dn

open to below

Br 3
10-8x11-2
raised ceiling

Bonus
12-0x20-9

raised ceiling

Porch

Brk
11-4x10-0

skylt

Family
18-0x14-0

Kitchen
11-4x9-4

Stor.

MBr
13-4x15-8
raised ceiling

Dn Up Foyer

Dining
11-0x12-0

Garage
21-0x21-0

Porch

41'-4"

59'-0"

First Floor
1,299 sq. ft.

PLAN DATA

Total Living Area:	2,128
Bedrooms:	3
Baths:	2 1/2
Garage:	2-car
Foundation Type:	
Basement	
Features:	
Raised ceiling in master bath	

5,40 X 4,30
18'-0" X 14'-4"

4,50 X 4,50
15'-0" X 15'-0"

3,80 X 4,80
12'-8" X 16'-0"

3,00 X 4,20
10'-0" X 14'-0"

3,00 X 3,60
10'-0" X 12'-0"

**Second Floor
1,233 sq. ft.**

PLAN DATA

Total Living Area:	2,300
Bedrooms:	3
Baths:	2 1/2
Garage:	2-car

Foundation Type:
  Basement

Features:
- 9' ceilings on first floor
- 2" x 6" exterior walls

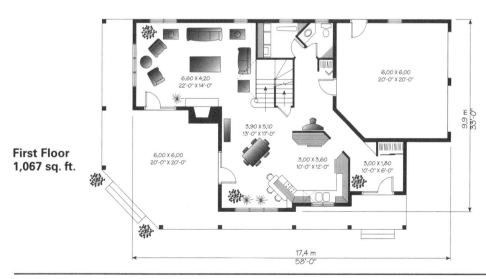

6,80 X 4,20
22'-0" X 14'-0"

6,00 X 6,00
20'-0" X 20'-0"

3,90 X 5,10
13'-0" X 17'-0"

6,00 X 6,00
20'-0" X 20'-0"

3,00 X 3,60
10'-0" X 12'-0"

3,00 X 1,80
10'-0" X 6'-0"

9,9 m
33'-0"

**First Floor
1,067 sq. ft.**

17,4 m
58'-0"

Second Floor
1,218 sq. ft.

open to below

Br 2
13-6x14-9

Br 4
14-9x11-8

Furn Room

L

L

Dn →

L

storage

open to below

Br 3
13-2x14-6

PLAN DATA

Total Living Area: 3,368
Bedrooms: 4
Baths: 3 full, 2 half
Garage: 2-car
Foundation Type:
  Basement
Features:
  Cathedral ceiling in great room

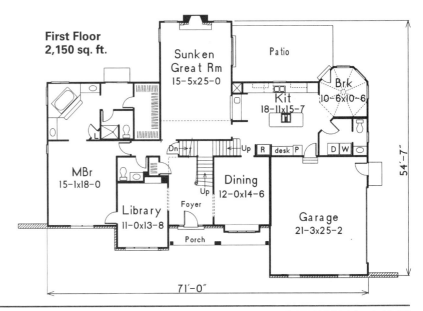

First Floor
2,150 sq. ft.

Sunken Great Rm
15-5x25-0

Patio

Brk
10-6x10-6

Kit
18-11x15-7

R desk P

D W

Dn →   Up

MBr
15-1x18-0

Up

Dining
12-0x14-6

Library
11-0x13-8

Foyer

Garage
21-3x25-2

Porch

54'-7"

71'-0"

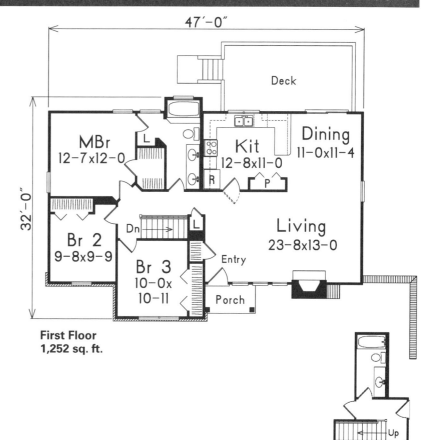

47'-0"

32'-0"

Deck

MBr
12-7x12-0

L

Kit
12-8x11-0

Dining
11-0x11-4

R

P

Br 2
9-8x9-9

Dn

L

Living
23-8x13-0

Br 3
10-0x
10-11

Entry

Porch

First Floor
1,252 sq. ft.

Up

L

Lower Level
151 sq. ft.

PLAN DATA

Total Living Area: 1,403
Bedrooms: 3
Baths: 2
Garage: 2-car
Foundation Type:
  Basement
Features:
  Drive-under garage

J.N. HANSEN D.G.

Second Floor
1,832 sq. ft.

Br 2
12-0x13-2

MBr
17-8x15-6
raised ceiling

Dn   Up

skylt

Br 4
13-4x15-0

open to
below

Br 3
10-8x
13-0

Bonus
19-4x13-4
vaulted

63'-0"

51'-0"

Nook
9-4x
11-4

Din
11-0x
13-6
raised ceiling

Kit
10-8x13-6

Family
17-8x15-6

Living
13-4x
16-6
raised ceiling

Stor.

W D

Up

Up   Foyer

Den
10-8x
12-0

Dn

Porch

Garage
27-4x23-10

First Floor
1,484 sq. ft.

PLAN DATA

Total Living Area: 3,316
Bedrooms: 4
Baths: 2 1/2
Garage: 3-car
Foundation Type:
   Crawl space
Features:
   - 9' ceilings
   - 2" x 6" exterior walls

PLAN DATA

Total Living Area:	1,993
Bedrooms:	3
Baths:	2
Garage:	2-car
Foundation Type:	
Slab	

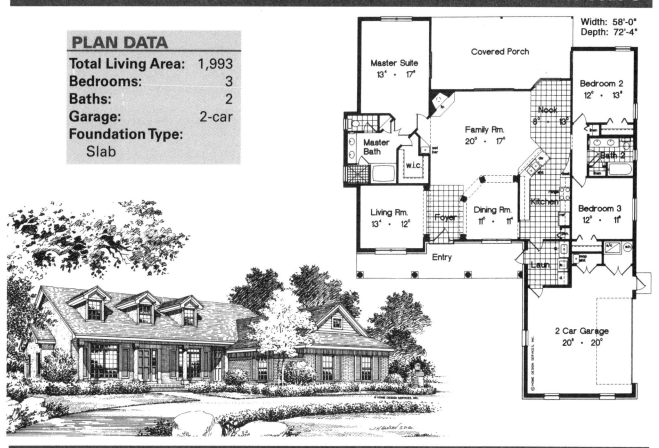

Width: 58'-0"
Depth: 72'-4"

Covered Porch

Master Suite 13⁴ · 17⁸

Bedroom 2 12⁰ · 13⁸

Master Bath

w.i.c.

Family Rm. 20⁰ · 17⁰

Nook 8⁰ · 13⁸

Bath 2

Living Rm. 13⁴ · 12⁰

Foyer

Dining Rm. 11⁰ · 11⁴

Kitchen

Bedroom 3 12⁰ · 11⁸

Entry

Laun.

2 Car Garage 20⁸ · 20⁸

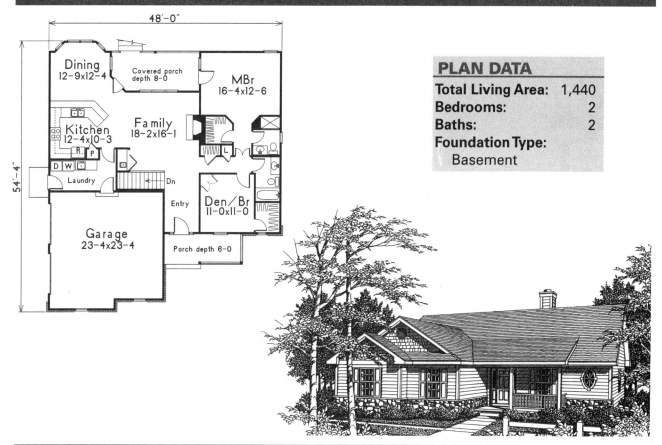

48'-0"

54'-4"

Dining 12-9x12-4

Covered porch depth 8-0

MBr 16-4x12-6

Kitchen 12-4x10-3

Family 18-2x16-1

R P

D W

Laundry

Dn

Entry

Den/Br 11-0x11-0

Garage 23-4x23-4

Porch depth 6-0

PLAN DATA

Total Living Area:	1,440
Bedrooms:	2
Baths:	2
Foundation Type:	
Basement	

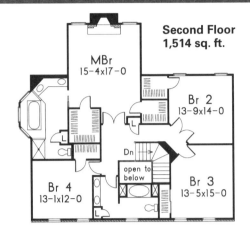

Second Floor
1,514 sq. ft.

MBr
15-4x17-0

Br 2
13-9x14-0

Br 4
13-1x12-0

Dn

open to
below

Br 3
13-5x15-0

PLAN DATA

Total Living Area:	3,200
Bedrooms:	4
Baths:	2 1/2
Garage:	2-car
Foundation Type:	
Basement	

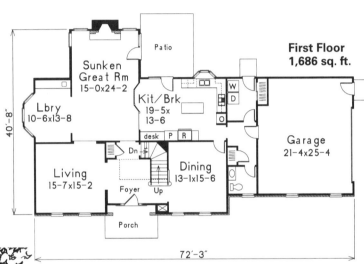

First Floor
1,686 sq. ft.

Patio

Sunken
Great Rm
15-0x24-2

Lbry
10-6x13-8

Kit/Brk
19-5x
13-6

W
D

Garage
21-4x25-4

desk | P | R

Dn

Living
15-7x15-2

Dining
13-1x15-6

Foyer

Up

Porch

40'-8"

72'-3"

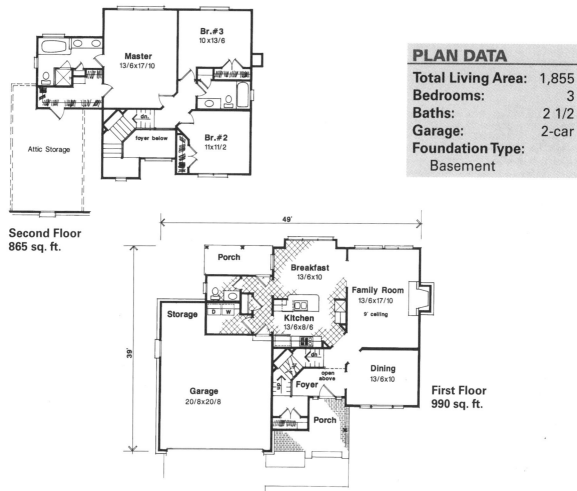

Master
13/6 x 17/10

Br.#3
10 x 13/6

Br.#2
11 x 11/2

dn.

foyer below

Attic Storage

Second Floor
865 sq. ft.

PLAN DATA

Total Living Area:	1,855
Bedrooms:	3
Baths:	2 1/2
Garage:	2-car
Foundation Type:	
Basement	

49'

39'

Porch

Breakfast
13/6 x 10

Family Room
13/6 x 17/10
9' ceiling

Storage

D W

Kitchen
13/6 x 8/6

dn.

Dining
13/6 x 10

open above

Foyer

up

Garage
20/8 x 20/8

Porch

First Floor
990 sq. ft.

Second Floor
792 sq. ft.

Br 3
12-4x12-5

Balcony

Game Rm
17-4x13-8

open to below

Dn

plant shelf

Loft

Br 4
12-0x12-4

PLAN DATA

Total Living Area:	2,696
Bedrooms:	4
Baths:	3
Garage:	2-car
Foundation Types:	
Slab standard	
Crawl space	

Garage
21-0x21-0

Kit
12-4x13-2

Great Rm
17-4x17-4
12-0 ceiling

Covered Porch

MBr
16-8x14-8

Brk
12-4x12-6

Dining
15-4x11-4

Foyer

Up

Porch

Br 2
11-4x11-8

64'-0"

66'-10"

First Floor
1,904 sq. ft.

PLAN DATA

Total Living Area: 2,261
Bedrooms: 4
Baths: 3 1/2
Garage: 2-car
Foundation Types:
  Slab
  Crawl space
Please specify when ordering

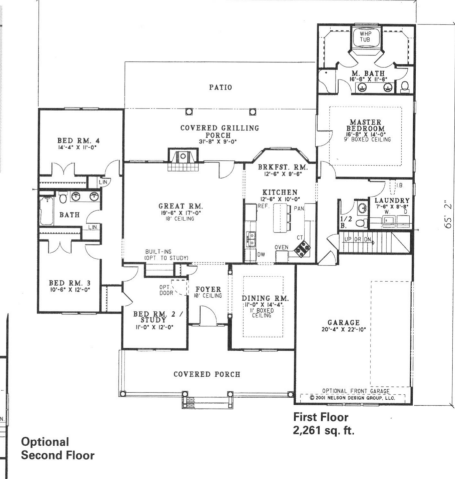

66' 0"

65' 2"

WHP TUB

M. BATH
16'-8" X 11'-6"

PATIO

COVERED GRILLING PORCH
31'-8" X 9'-0"

MASTER BEDROOM
16'-8" X 14'-0"
9' BOXED CEILING

BED RM. 4
14'-4" X 11'-0"

BRKFST. RM.
12'-6" X 9'-6"

KITCHEN
12'-6" X 10'-0"

LAUNDRY
7'-6" X 8'-8"

GREAT RM.
19'-6" X 17'-0"
10' CEILING

REF. PAN

1/2 B.

BATH

OVEN

DW CT

UP OR DN

BUILT-INS
(OPT TO STUDY)

BED RM. 3
10'-6" X 12'-0"

OPT DOOR

FOYER
10' CEILING

DINING RM.
11'-0" X 14'-4"
11' BOXED CEILING

GARAGE
20'-4" X 22'-10"

BED RM. 2 /
STUDY
11'-0" X 12'-0"

COVERED PORCH

OPTIONAL FRONT GARAGE
© 2001 Nelson Design Group, LLC.

**First Floor
2,261 sq. ft.**

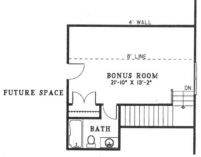

4' WALL

8' LINE

BONUS ROOM
21'-10" X 13'-2"

DN.

FUTURE SPACE

BATH

ATTIC STORAGE

**Optional
Second Floor**

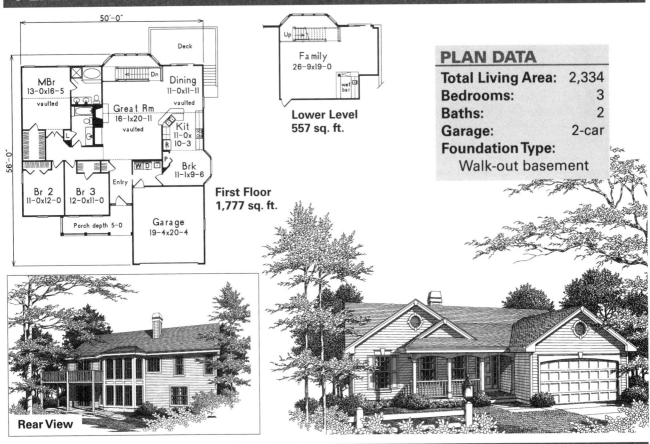

PLAN #565-0710

Price Code D

50'-0"

Deck

MBr
13-0x16-5
vaulted

Dining
11-0x11-11
vaulted

Great Rm
16-1x20-11
vaulted

Kit
11-0x
10-3

56'-0"

Br 2
11-0x12-0

Br 3
12-0x11-0

Entry

Brk
11-1x9-6

WD

Porch depth 5-0

Garage
19-4x20-4

**First Floor
1,777 sq. ft.**

Up

Family
26-9x19-0

wet
bar

**Lower Level
557 sq. ft.**

PLAN DATA

Total Living Area: 2,334
Bedrooms: 3
Baths: 2
Garage: 2-car
Foundation Type:
Walk-out basement

Rear View

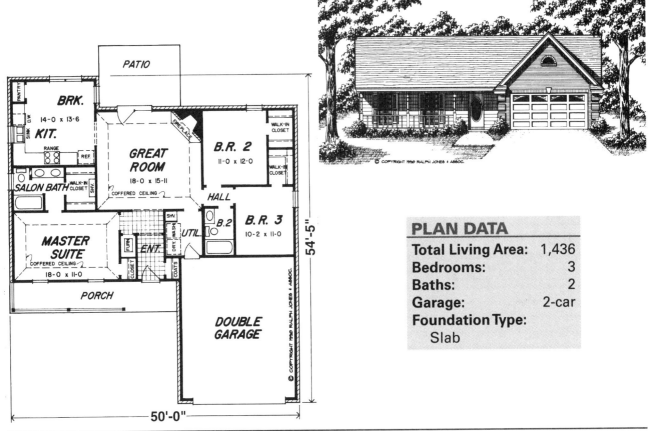

PLAN #565-RJ-A1485

Price Code A

PATIO

PANTRY

BRK.
14-0 x 13-6

KIT.

SINK DW

RANGE

REF.

SALON BATH

WALK-IN
CLOSET

SHV

GREAT
ROOM
18-0 x 15-11
COFFERED CEILING

FIRE PLACE

B.R. 2
11-0 x 12-0

WALK-IN
CLOSET

WALK-IN
CLOSET

HALL

MASTER
SUITE
COFFERED CEILING
18-0 x 11-0

ENT

FURN

DRY WASH

UTIL

SHV

B.2

B.R. 3
10-2 x 11-0

CLOSET

COATS

PORCH

DOUBLE
GARAGE

54'-5"

50'-0"

PLAN DATA

Total Living Area: 1,436
Bedrooms: 3
Baths: 2
Garage: 2-car
Foundation Type:
Slab

© COPYRIGHT 1990 RALPH JONES & ASSOC.

PLAN #565-0400

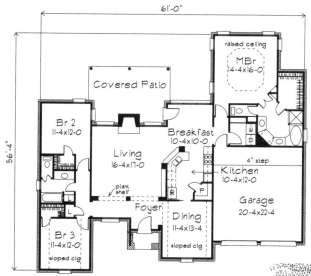

61'-0"

56'-4"

raised ceiling

MBr
14-4x16-0

Covered Patio

Br 2
11-4x12-0

Breakfast
10-4x10-0

Living
16-4x17-0

4" step

Kitchen
10-4x12-0

plant shelf

Foyer

Dining
11-4x13-4

Garage
20-4x22-4

Br 3
11-4x12-0
sloped clg

sloped clg

PLAN DATA

Total Living Area: 1,923
Bedrooms: 3
Baths: 2
Garage: 2-car
Foundation Type:
  Slab

Rear View

PLAN #565-1276-1 & 2

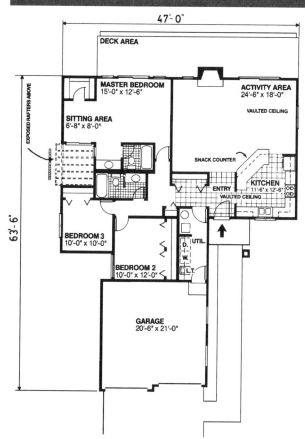

47'-0"

DECK AREA

63'-6"

EXPOSED RAFTERS ABOVE

MASTER BEDROOM
15'-0" x 12'-6"

ACTIVITY AREA
24'-6" x 18'-0"

VAULTED CEILING

SITTING AREA
6'-8" x 8'-0"

SNACK COUNTER

KITCHEN
11'-6" x 12'-6"

ENTRY

VAULTED CEILING

BEDROOM 3
10'-0" x 10'-0"

UTIL.
D.
W.
L.T.

BEDROOM 2
10'-0" x 12'-0"

GARAGE
20'-6" x 21'-0"

PLAN DATA

Total Living Area: 1,533
Bedrooms: 3
Baths: 2
Garage: 2-car
Foundation Types:
  Plan #565-1276-1
  Partial basement &
  crawl space
  Plan #565-1276-2
  Slab

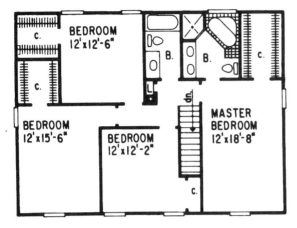

**Second Floor
1,160 sq. ft.**

PLAN DATA

Total Living Area:	2,372
Bedrooms:	4
Baths:	2 1/2
Garage:	2-car

Foundation Types:
  Plan #565-1217-1
  Basement
  Plan #565-1217-2
  Crawl space & slab

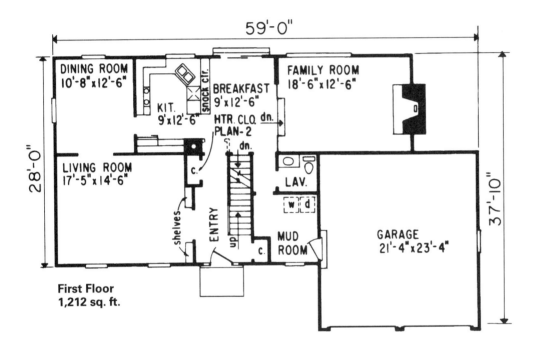

**First Floor
1,212 sq. ft.**

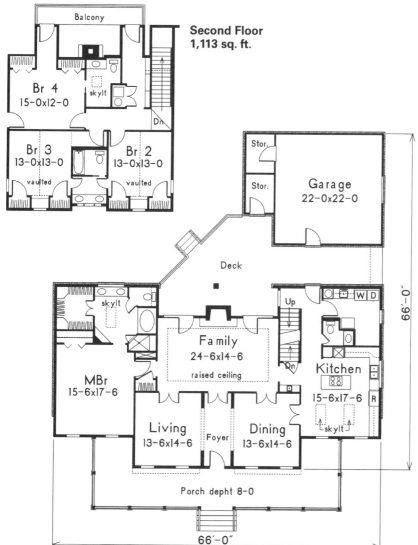

Second Floor
1,113 sq. ft.

Balcony

Br 4
15-0x12-0

skylt

Dn

Br 3
13-0x13-0
vaulted

Br 2
13-0x13-0
vaulted

Stor.

Stor.

Garage
22-0x22-0

Deck

Family
24-6x14-6
raised ceiling

Up

Dn

W D

Kitchen
15-6x17-6

R

MBr
15-6x17-6

skylt

skylt

Living
13-6x14-6

Foyer

Dining
13-6x14-6

66'-0"

Porch depht 8-0

66'-0"

First Floor
2,040 sq. ft.

PLAN DATA

Total Living Area: 3,153
Bedrooms: 4
Baths: 3 1/2
Garage: 2-car
Foundation Types:
   Basement standard
   Crawl space
   Slab
Features:
   - 2" x 6" exterior walls
   - Extra storage in
     garage
   - Drive-under garage

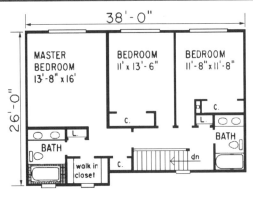

38'-0"

26'-0"

MASTER BEDROOM
13'-8" x 16'

BEDROOM
11' x 13'-6"

BEDROOM
11'-8" x 11'-8"

c.

c.

L.

BATH

L.

BATH

walk in closet

c.

dn

Second Floor
940 sq. ft.

PLAN DATA

Total Living Area: 1,852
Bedrooms: 3
Baths: 2 1/2
Garage: 2-car
Foundation Types:
 Plan #565-1214-1
 Basement
 Plan #565-1214-2
 Crawl space & slab

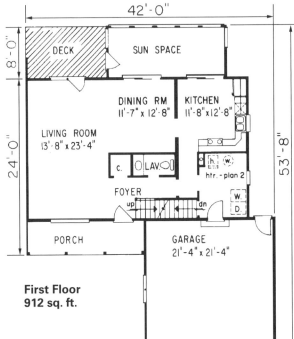

42'-0"

8'-0"

24'-0"

53'-8"

DECK

SUN SPACE

DINING RM
11'-7" x 12'-8"

KITCHEN
11'-8" x 12'-8"

LIVING ROOM
13'-8" x 23'-4"

c.

LAV

h w.

htr. - plan 2

FOYER

up

dn

W.
D.

PORCH

GARAGE
21'-4" x 21'-4"

First Floor
912 sq. ft.

maLou

First Floor
1,904 sq. ft.

Second Floor
922 sq. ft.

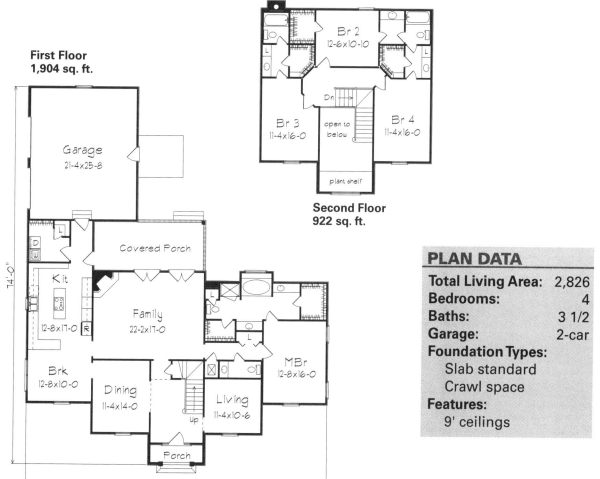

Garage
21-4x25-8

Covered Porch

Kit

Family
22-2x17-0

Brk
12-8x10-0

Dining
11-4x14-0

Living
11-4x10-6

MBr
12-8x16-0

Porch

up

12-8x17-0

74'-0"

60'-6"

Br 2
12-6x10-10

Dn

Br 3
11-4x16-0

open to
below

Br 4
11-4x16-0

plant shelf

PLAN DATA

Total Living Area: 2,826
Bedrooms: 4
Baths: 3 1/2
Garage: 2-car
Foundation Types:
  Slab standard
  Crawl space
Features:
  9' ceilings

Second Floor - Three bedroom option
952 sq. ft.

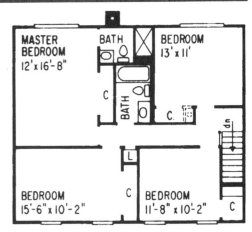

Second Floor - Four bedroom option
952 sq. ft.

PLAN DATA

Total Living Area: 2,212
Bedrooms: 3
Baths: 2 1/2
Garage: 2-car
Foundation Types:
Plan #565-1134-1
Partial basement/
crawl space
Plan #565-1134-2
Crawl space
Features:
Optional 4-bedroom
plan

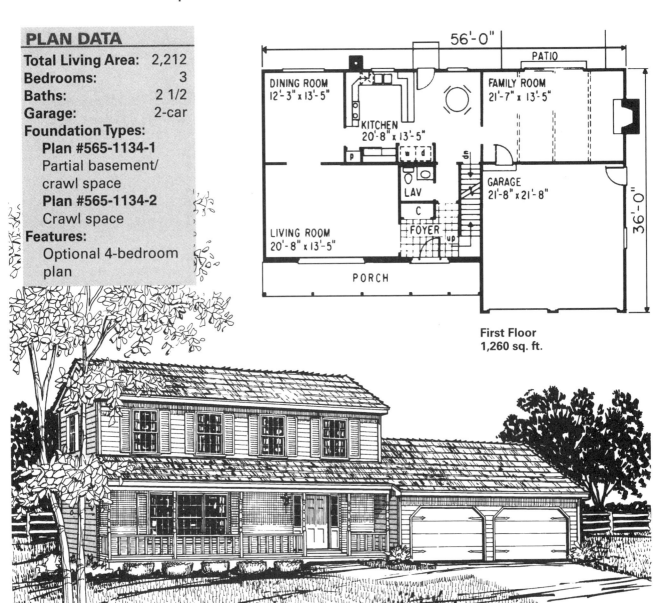

First Floor
1,260 sq. ft.

Second Floor
1,140 sq. ft.

Br 3
13-1x12-5

Br 4
10-8x11-2

Br 2
13-1x10-8

Dn

MBr
18-3x13-0

L

L

First Floor
1,188 sq. ft.

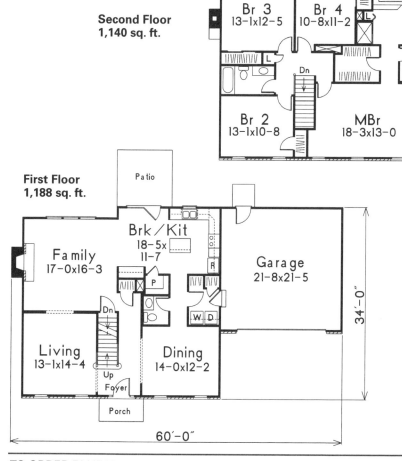

Patio

Brk/Kit
18-5x
11-7

R

Garage
21-8x21-5

Family
17-0x16-3

P

W D

Dn

Living
13-1x14-4

Dining
14-0x12-2

Up

Foyer

Porch

34'-0"

60'-0"

PLAN DATA

Total Living Area: 2,328
Bedrooms: 4
Baths: 2 1/2
Garage: 2-car
Foundation Types:
  Basement standard
  Slab
  Crawl space

PLAN DATA

Total Living Area:	2,224
Bedrooms:	4
Baths:	3
Garage:	2-car
Foundation Type:	
Slab	

Width: 58'-6"
Depth: 72'-0"

PLAN #565-CHP-2443-A-67

Price Code D

PLAN DATA

Total Living Area:	2,450
Bedrooms:	4
Baths:	2 1/2
Garage:	2-car
Foundation Type:	
Basement	

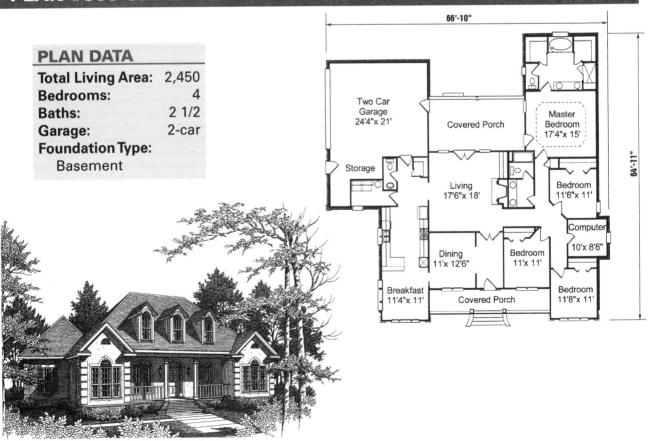

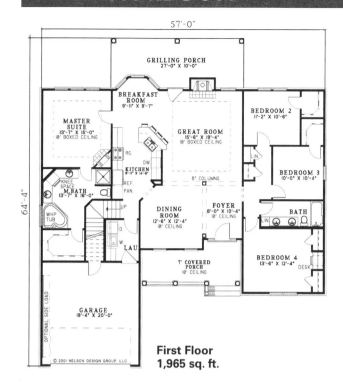

57'-0"

64'-4"

GRILLING PORCH
27'-0" X 10'-0"

BREAKFAST ROOM
9'-11" X 9'-7"

MASTER SUITE
13'-7" X 16'-0"
10' BOXED CEILING

GREAT ROOM
15'-6" X 19'-4"
10' BOXED CEILING

BEDROOM 2
11'-2" X 10'-6"

KITCHEN
8'-11" X 14'-6"

M.BATH
13'-7" X 18'-0"

KNEE SPACE

WHP TUB

8" COLUMNS

BEDROOM 3
10'-0" X 10'-4"

DINING ROOM
12'-6" X 12'-4"
10' CEILING

FOYER
8'-0" X 10'-4"
10' CEILING

BATH

7' COVERED PORCH
10' CEILING

BEDROOM 4
13'-6" X 12'-4"

DESK

OPTIONAL SIDE LOAD

GARAGE
19'-4" X 20'-0"

© 2001 NELSON DESIGN GROUP, LLC.

**First Floor
1,965 sq. ft.**

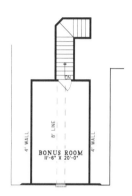

4' WALL

8' LINE

4' WALL

DN

BONUS ROOM
11'-6" X 20'-0"

**Optional
Second Floor**

PLAN DATA

Total Living Area:	1,965
Bedrooms:	4
Baths:	2
Garage:	2-car

Foundation Types:
Slab
Crawl space
Please specify when ordering

© Michael E. Nelson
NELSON DESIGN GROUP, LLC

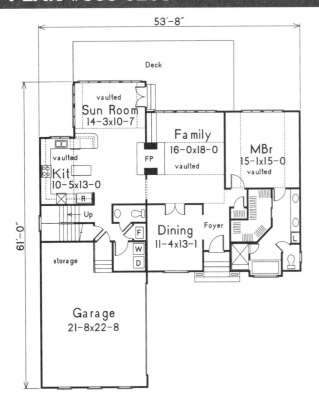

53'-8"

Deck

vaulted
Sun Room
14-3x10-7

Family
16-0x18-0

MBr
15-1x15-0
vaulted

FP

vaulted
Kit
10-5x13-0

vaulted

R

Up

Dining
11-4x13-1

Foyer

F
W
D

storage

L

Garage
21-8x22-8

61'-0"

First Floor
1,670 sq. ft.

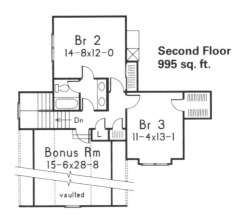

Br 2
14-8x12-0

Second Floor
995 sq. ft.

Br 3
11-4x13-1

Dn

L

Bonus Rm
15-6x28-8

vaulted

PLAN DATA

Total Living Area:	2,665
Bedrooms:	3
Baths:	2 1/2
Garage:	2-car
Foundation Type:	
Crawl space	

PLAN DATA

Total Living Area:	1,671
Bedrooms:	3
Baths:	2 1/2
Garage:	2-car

Foundation Types:
  Walk-out basement
  Crawl space
Please specify when ordering

Features:
  9' ceilings on first
  floor

Second Floor
784 sq. ft.

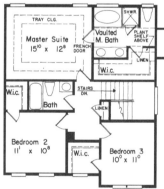

First Floor
887 sq. ft.

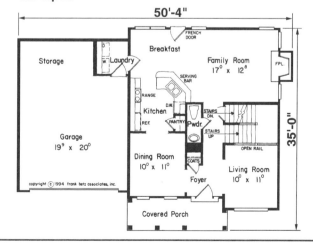

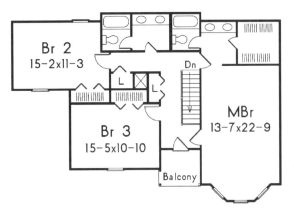

Second Floor
1,135 sq. ft.

- Br 2 15-2x11-3
- Dn
- Br 3 15-5x10-10
- MBr 13-7x22-9
- Balcony

PLAN DATA

Total Living Area:	2,262
Bedrooms:	3
Baths:	2 1/2
Garage:	2-car
Foundation Types:	
Crawl space standard	
Basement	
Slab	

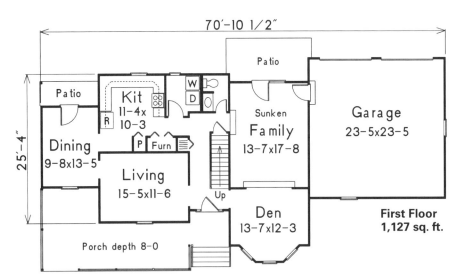

70'-10 1/2"

25'-4"

- Patio
- Kit 11-4x 10-3
- R
- W D
- Patio
- Sunken Family 13-7x17-8
- Garage 23-5x23-5
- Dining 9-8x13-5
- P Furn
- Living 15-5x11-6
- Up
- Den 13-7x12-3
- Porch depth 8-0

First Floor
1,127 sq. ft.

Second Floor
895 sq. ft.

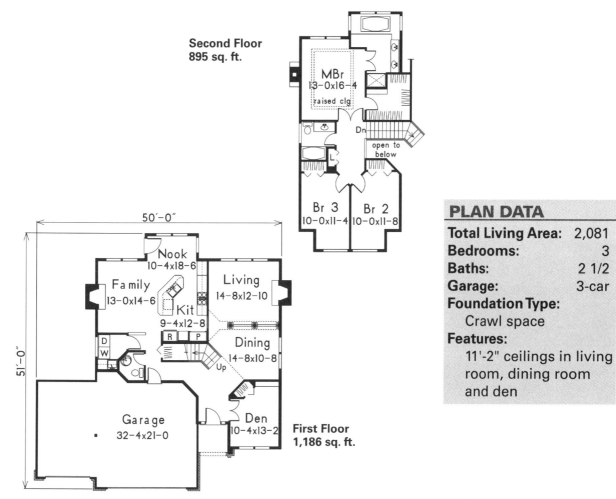

MBr
13-0x16-4
raised clg

Dn

open to
below

Br 3
10-0x11-4

Br 2
10-0x11-8

50'-0"

Nook
10-4x18-6

Family
13-0x14-6

Living
14-8x12-10

Kit
9-4x12-8

51'-0"

R   P

Dining
14-8x10-8

D
W

Up

Garage
32-4x21-0

Den
10-4x13-2

First Floor
1,186 sq. ft.

PLAN DATA

Total Living Area: 2,081
Bedrooms: 3
Baths: 2 1/2
Garage: 3-car
Foundation Type:
  Crawl space
Features:
  11'-2" ceilings in living
  room, dining room
  and den

PLAN DATA

Total Living Area: 2,962
Bedrooms: 4
Baths: 3
Garage: 3-car
Foundation Type:
Slab
Features:
Vaulted ceiling in
breakfast nook

Width: 66'-8"
Depth: 76'-8"

PLAN #565-AX-93308

Price Code B

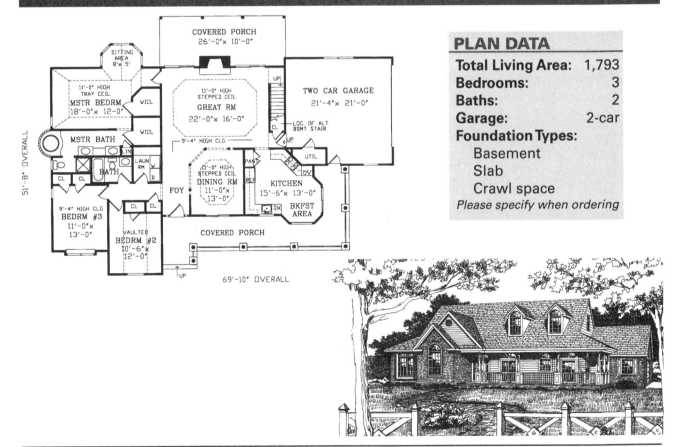

PLAN DATA

Total Living Area: 1,793
Bedrooms: 3
Baths: 2
Garage: 2-car
Foundation Types:
Basement
Slab
Crawl space
Please specify when ordering

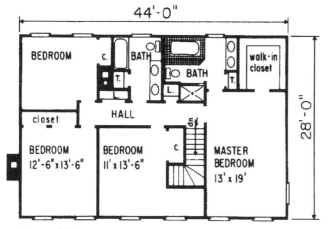

44'-0"

28'-0"

BEDROOM

c. BATH

BATH

walk-in closet

closet

HALL

BEDROOM
12'-6"x13'-6"

BEDROOM
11'x13'-6"

c.

MASTER BEDROOM
13' x 19'

Second Floor
1,232 sq. ft.

PLAN DATA
Total Living Area: 2,763
Bedrooms: 4
Baths: 2 1/2
Garage: 3-car
Foundation Types:
  Plan #565-1208-1
  Basement
  Plan #565-1208-2
  Crawl space & slab

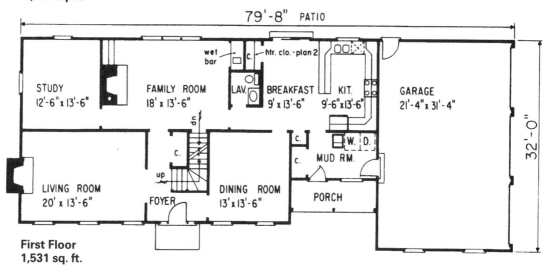

79'-8" PATIO

32'-0"

STUDY
12'-6"x13'-6"

FAMILY ROOM
18' x 13'-6"

wet bar

c.

htr. clo. - plan 2

LAV.

BREAKFAST
9' x 13'-6"

KIT.
9'-6"x13'-6"

GARAGE
21'-4"x 31'-4"

up

c.

c.

W. D.

LIVING ROOM
20' x 13'-6"

FOYER

DINING ROOM
13'x 13'-6"

c.

MUD RM.

PORCH

First Floor
1,531 sq. ft.

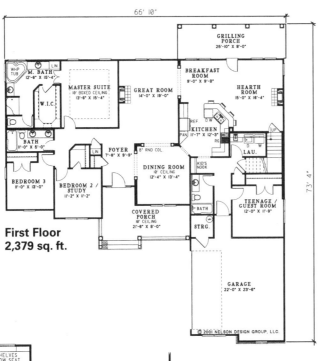

First Floor
2,379 sq. ft.

66' 10"

73' 4"

GRILLING PORCH
26'-10" X 8'-0"

M. BATH
12'-6" X 15'-4"

WHP TUB

LIN

W.I.C.

MASTER SUITE
10' BOXED CEILING
13'-6" X 15'-4"

GREAT ROOM
14'-0" X 19'-0"

BREAKFAST ROOM
9'-0" X 9'-8"

HEARTH ROOM
15'-0" X 16'-4"

BATH
11'-0" X 6'-0"

KITCHEN
11'-7" X 12'-3"

REF.
PAN.
DW

LAU.
D W

BEDROOM 3
11'-0" X 13'-0"

BEDROOM 2 / STUDY
11'-2" X 11'-2"

FOYER
7'-8" X 9'-9"

LIN

8" RND COL.

DINING ROOM
10' CEILING
12'-4" X 13'-4"

KID'S NOOK

BATH

STRG.

TEENAGE / GUEST ROOM
12'-0" X 11'-9"

COVERED PORCH
10' CEILING
21'-6" X 8'-0"

GARAGE
22'-0" X 23'-6"

© 2001 NELSON DESIGN GROUP, LLC.

Optional Second Floor

BOOK SHELVES W/ WINDOW SEAT

GUEST ROOM
12'-0" X 13'-0"

7' WALL

OPTIONAL FIRE PLACE

ATTIC STORAGE
15'-0" X 16'-4"

GAME ROOM / MEDIA ROOM
24'-8" X 16'-0"

LIN

DN

ATTIC STORAGE
8' LINE

PLAN DATA

Total Living Area:	2,379
Bedrooms:	5
Baths:	4
Garage:	2-car
Foundation Types:	
Slab	
Crawl space	

Please specify when ordering